Facility Siting
and
Public Opposition

Facility Siting
and
Public Opposition

Michael O'Hare
Lawrence Bacow
Debra Sanderson

VNR VAN NOSTRAND REINHOLD COMPANY
NEW YORK CINCINNATI TORONTO LONDON MELBOURNE

Copyright © 1983 by Michael O'Hare, Lawrence Bacow, and Debra Sanderson

Library of Congress Catalog Card Number: 83-1375
ISBN: 0-442-26287-6

Manufactured in the United States of America

Published by Van Nostrand Reinhold Company Inc.
135 West 50th Street, New York, N.Y. 10020

Van Nostrand Reinhold
480 Latrobe Street
Melbourne, Victoria 3000, Australia

Van Nostrand Reinhold Company Limited
Molly Millars Lane
Wokingham, Berkshire, England

15 14 13 12 11 10 9 8 7 6 5 4 3 2 1

Library of Congress Cataloging in Publication Data

O'Hare, Michael, 1943-
  Facility siting and public opposition.

  Includes index.
  1. Industries, Location of—Public opinion.
2. Industries, Location of—Massachusetts—Public
opinion—Case studies. 3. Public opinion—Massachusetts
I. Bacow, Lawrence S. II. Sanderson, Debra.
III. Title.
HC79.D5037   1983   338.6'042   83-1375
ISBN 0-442-26287-6

To Our Parents

Preface

Why are American society's major capital investments so difficult to site? Power plants, waste processing plants, airports, prisons—proposals for these and many other kinds of projects seem to fail again and again despite extensive siting and environmental research, dying (before a shovelful of earth is turned) in a welter of lawsuits, local conflict, political challenges, and bad feeling.

We believe that these failures are due in large part to a conventional facility siting process that solves the wrong political problems and often frustrates the right ones. In this book, *Facility Siting and Public Opposition,* we propose a fundamentally new approach to facility siting—based on negotiated compensation for local disamenity—and, in support of our suggestions, we provide theoretical analysis of the use of information and compensation in major public decisions. Our focus is on the relationship between facility developers (private or public) and the near neighbors of new facilities; we pay relatively little attention to the environmental regulations that protect more distant parties from air or water pollution. While we consider existing environmental legislation far from perfect, we don't think it or its defects are at the heart of the "siting problem" that has so impeded both wise and foolish capital investment in recent years.

Our proposals are grounded in research that is both abstract and general, but they are also tested against several case studies for different kinds of facilities. Moreover, we are fortunate enough to have seen the essentials of our proposals enacted in Massachusetts. We are therefore able to present and analyze legislation currently in force that is consistent with most of our recommendations.

This book originated at M.I.T. in research begun in 1976 under a U.S. Department of Energy contract.[1] Two of us—O'Hare as Associate Professor, and Sanderson as a graduate student in the Department of Urban Studies and Planning—were engaged in analyzing the socio-economic impacts of energy developments on Western boom towns, and suggesting methods for resolving the problems. In doing that study, we found it important not only to reduce the social costs that a facility imposes once it is built, but also to site facilities in the first place so as to minimize such costs. The following year, Bacow joined the M.I.T. faculty as Assistant Professor, and Sanderson became the project Research Director. With continued DOE support,[2] we began developing concepts of negotiation and compensation as elements of a siting process that is designed to reveal social costs and to constructively resolve public opposition. Through that contract, we conducted case studies of energy facility siting efforts in New England, studied decision-making by special interest groups, developed theories about compensation, negotiation, and information use, prepared model facility siting legislation, analyzed the legal constraints on the formation of binding agreements between communities and corporations, and developed a practitioner's guide to the use of compensation and negotiation in facility siting. Much of that theoretical work, published earlier, has been drawn on for Chapters 5, 7, and 9.[3] The case studies, some of which are condensed here, are published by the M.I.T. Laboratory of Architecture and Planning,[4] and the practitioner's guide by the M.I.T. Center for Energy Policy Research.[5]

The Center provided invaluable financial support during a critical final year when DOE funding was no longer available. More recently, O'Hare's work at Harvard during preparation of the book was supported partly by the Alfred P. Sloan Foundation. Without the financial and administrative support of DOE, the Center, the Department, the Foundation, and the Laboratory of Architecture and Planning, the present work would have never been done. Our opinions and positions, of course, are not necessarily those of the U.S. Government, M.I.T., Harvard, or the above-mentioned organizations.

Our research was greatly advanced by the comments, criticisms, and participation of several colleagues. Foremost among all those on whom we have relied is Lawrence Susskind. Larry was the principal investigator for the first year of the DOE project and its primary organizer and entrepreneur. Despite the distractions of his department chairmanship, he worked with us throughout our research; he constantly challenged us with reality and experience, sharpened and extended our ideas, and provided both intellectual and administrative management. He graciously combined the roles of internal critic and external advocate; as children have godparents, books have god-authors and Larry is such to this one.

David Kretzmer, visiting from the Hebrew University in 1977–78, guided us through legal thickets of local government's authority to contract. Joseph Ferreira, Jr. worked with us on risk assessment and liability issues. We were also fortunate to have the help of more than a dozen thoughtful and inquisitive graduate student research assistants; in addition to those cited in connection with case studies, they are Stephen Casella, Howard Davis, Benjamin Friedman, Gail Kendall, Deborah McKechnie, James Milkey, Karen Pierson, Judah Rose, Deborah Shmueli, and Alvin Streeter.

Despite lack of any formal connection to the project, other colleagues gave freely of their time and assistance. Some of this help was unwitting: without Mancur Olson's pathbreaking book,[6] we would not have recognized the importance of local compensation, and the first explicit suggestion of compensation for neighbors of waste facilities that we know of was David Gordon Wilson's, in a paper from 1972.[7] Eugene Bardach, Timothy J. Sullivan, Edith Stokey, and Richard Zeckhauser read all or part of the original pages of the manuscript, and it is much better for their suggestions.

While the present book is about the facility siting process and not a study of the Massachusetts Hazardous Waste Facility Siting Act, our experience in helping to develop that legislation and in observing its early stages of implementation has greatly increased our understanding of the practical and administrative implications of our suggestions. Two of us, O'Hare and Sanderson, worked for the Commonwealth of Massachusetts while the legislation was being developed; Sanderson has remained in state service, and Bacow is a member of the siting council it created. More specifically, John Bewick, the new Secretary of Environmental Affairs in Massachusetts, had the risky idea of hiring O'Hare, a professor with no government experience, as Assistant Secretary for Policy in 1979. A year later, the chairmen of the Massachusetts Special Commission on Hazardous Waste, Senator Robert Wetmore and Representative Richard Dwinell, engaged Sanderson as staff director. We thus had the pleasure of seeing many of our ideas on facility siting tested, debated, and ultimately enacted. We are extremely grateful to the foregoing for the opportunities and for their support. Richard Nylen, then counsel and legislative liaison for Secretary Bewick, increased our understanding of the siting process as he provided extensive technical and substantive input to the bill.

We wish that we could identify the other people in government who contributed specially to our thinking, as we have tried to do for our academic colleagues. However, one of the things that we have learned by working with them is that the process of government is so collaborative and interactive that credit for accomplishments must be spread extremely widely if it is to be apportioned justly; we have had to conclude that the academic model for acknowledgments simply doesn't apply. We hope our friends in public service will accept our general thanks, and will recognize their many hands in the practical parts of the chapters below.

Finally, we are grateful to each other for our enthusiasm and forbearance. Each of us has agreed that all remaining errors that escaped the attention of the people cited above are his or her own.

Michael O'Hare
Lawrence Bacow
Debra Sanderson

Notes

1. No. E (49–18)–2295.
2. Contract No. EA–76–A–001–2295 #35.
3. M. O'Hare, "Not On My Block, You Don't: Facility Siting and the Strategic Importance of Compensation," *Public Policy* Vol. 25, No. 2 (1977), © John Wiley & Sons; "Information Management and Public Choice," in J. P. Crecine, ed., *Research in Public Policy Land Management,* © JAI Press, Greenwich, Conn., 1979; "Improving the Use of Environmental Decisionmaking," *Environmental Impact Assessment Review,* Vol. 1, No. 3 (1980), © Plenum Publishing Corp; L. Bacow, "The Technical and Judgmental Dimensions of Impact Assessment," *Environmental Impact Assessment Review,* Vol. 1, No. 2 (1980), © Plenum Publishing Corp; L. Bacow and J. Milkey, "Overcoming Local Opposition to Hazardous Waste Facilities: The Massachusetts Approach," *Harvard Environmental Law Review* (Spring 1982) © L. Bacow; L. Bacow and D. Sanderson, *Facility Siting and Compensation: A Handbook for Communities and Developers,* Center for Energy Policy Research, M.I.T. (1980).

   Parts of the above-mentioned articles are included here (cited in particular chapters) with permission of, or by prepublication arrangement with, the publishers.
4. Publication list available from the laboratory, Rm. 4–209 M.I.T., Cambridge, MA 02139.
5. Rm. E40–311, M.I.T., Cambridge, MA 02139
6. *The Logic of Collective Action,* Harvard University Press, Cambridge, 1965.
7. "Pollution and Solid Waste Disposal," Boston Development Strategy Project, M.I.T. Department of Urban Studies and Planning, 1972.

Contents

Facility Siting
and
Public Opposition

1
The "Siting Problem"

Some things are always in the wrong place: litter and weeds have this property by definition. More interesting are the things that seem to have no right place, despite the fact that everyone thinks we ought to have them: airports, prisons, landfills, power plants, and even low-income housing. All are generally thought essential to society—and yet widely opposed wherever they threaten to alight. This book is about facilities that have this property.

The problem of locally undesirable, though generally beneficial, facilities has become more than a nuisance or a paradox of planning theory. Some of these facilities threaten to be impossible to provide at all if the means can't be found for reducing or overcoming local opposition to their presence. Furthermore, the situation seems to be getting worse; when the cost to society of failing to site new facilities resulting in making do with a barely adequate existing facilities (electric generating stations) or with some overcrowding (airports and prisons), the failure of a new proposal was costly but not critical. But a newer generation of siting problems arose with such prickly issues as low-level nuclear waste disposal location and with hazardous waste processing and landfill facilities; in many regions of the country none of these exists and the failure to provide them will result in large and certain damage to public economic and physical health.

But we are not concerned solely with getting things built. It is costly to build an unnecessary or superfluous facility or even a needed facility in the wrong place. A well-conceived siting process will not only facilitate the construction of what we really want, but will also discourage the construction of the "wrong" projects in the "wrong" place. Such mistakes are not a purely academic concern: intensive construction in fragile coastal areas, the location of pollution sources upwind of populated areas, or building landfills in wetlands or above

1

aquifers are all at least suggestive, and often conclusive, evidence that our current siting processes are capable of improvement.

The lack of a needed facility cannot be attributed to a single incident. No single one of the thirteen failures to build a refinery in New England within the last ten years is "the reason" for New England's lack of significant oil refinery capacity; the general failure is, irreducibly, the result of a series of small failures. Yet each one of these failures appears to one participant or another in the process as avoidance of a major error; the opponents of a development project are usually as sincere and public-spirited as the project's supporters.

In only a few cases (nuclear power plants, for example) do the opponents who generate the individual failures favor the aggregate result. Hazardous waste processing facilities are probably the clearest example of this paradox: even in the three communities in Massachusetts that successfully obtained 1979 legislation preventing hazardous waste facility construction in their towns, only a tiny minority of citizens believe that hazardous waste should not be safely processed in appropriate facilities,[1] while the number of Bay Staters who believed that it should not be so processed in Massachusetts is only slightly larger. Nevertheless, as this is written, there are almost no such facilities in the state.

The fact that the participants on opposite sides of a particular dispute share a great many objectives—facility siting combatants are probably more nearly in agreement on overall goals than, for example, the political forces arrayed against each other in a social-welfare legislative battle—makes the experience particularly frustrating and embittering for all concerned. It is not surprising that the proponents of a new facility view the opposition as ignorant, irrational, and even anti-social, or that the opponents of such a facility so often view the developer as insensitive, selfish, and greedy.

Like most apparent paradoxes of political economy, this one appears to us resolvable by careful consideration of the incentives and interests confronting the parties. Far from finding the participants irrational, we are struck by the consistency with which parties in siting disputes act rationally and effectively to serve their interests as they perceive them. Thus, we think the failure of our conventional facility siting process lies in a decision-making and interest-balancing *structure* that frustrates the desires of the participants to cooperate or compete constructively, rather than in any defect in the intelligence or the character of the participants. Our view of the facilities siting problem is characterized by two basic propositions:

1. Inadequate mechanisms exist at present for the parties affected by a new facility proposal to share in the benefits the project will provide to society as a whole, or to effectively negotiate the size of their share.
2. Much of the facility siting debate is ignorant or ill-informed because the social, political, and economic structures by which information is made available obstruct its efficient use or generation.

In general, we find that people do rather well with the frustrating rules under which they are forced to act in facility siting disputes. But if we are to do better in disputes of this kind, the architecture of the arena itself must be substantially altered. Not surprisingly, we have fundamental criticisms to make of the conventional blueprints for such renovation because most of these blueprints proceed from the same misapprehensions about the source of friction and paralysis that gave rise to the unsatisfactory process in the first place.

We recommend a siting process—detailed in Chapters 9 and 10— applicable to a variety of different facilities that are typically characterized by negative local impacts and, at least geographically, positive society-wide benefits. The siting process we recommend is based on a critical review of current practice and proposed reforms (Chapter 4), an investigation of the strategic implications of making the project "pie" more easily divisible (Chapters 5 and 6), and a consideration of information and its use in public decision-making (Chapter 7). The theoretical analysis is motivated, exemplified, and supported by a series of case studies of facility siting disputes (Chapters 2 and 8).

The research that gave rise to this analysis was directly concerned with energy facility siting and focused on the New England experience. Some of the examples in the text, including six of the case studies, include or pertain to energy facilities. However, we intend the results to be applicable to disputes with the strategic and political/ economic structure suggested above and therefore to be much more general.

This is not the first book about facility siting. A large literature is in-

dexed under those keywords, and we have made no attempt to culti-
vate the same ground in the present analysis.[2] A sharp distinction,
however, divides the previous tradition from the work at hand. While
we are concerned with the debate over a proposal after it is made,
nearly every title and journal article on the subject of facility siting is
written as though "the siting problem" is to choose a site that op-
timizes a combination of such measurable and "objective" criteria as
fuel, transportation, power distribution, public safety from emissions
or other environmental insult, and so on. This engineering tradition is
epitomized in the admirable and extensive study by Ralph Keeney,
and we do not expect to advance the tradition of technical site selection from the high level to which Keeney has raised it.[3] (An important
recent exception to the pattern described above is the recent book by
Morrell and Magorian about siting hazardous waste facilities.[4] Their
findings are discussed in Chapter 4.)

Another tradition is exemplified, not by scientific publications or
books, but by legislation and regulatory practice; this is the tradition
of asserting government control over the actors in a process seen to be
delivering sub-optimal results. Because we are concerned with the process of implementing site selection and overcoming initial local opposition, we have considered this second tradition of statutory control
and regulation in Chapter 4.

The distinguishing characteristic of our work, then, is its focus on
the problem *after* the point at which one participant or another has
identified what appears to be a technically acceptable or at least
preferred site. We have taken this approach because the politics and
institutional difficulties of proceeding on a site that seems initially to
meet appropriate technical criteria are the rocks on which the process
has foundered. We know of no facilities that have gone unbuilt because no one could find the location that best met engineering criteria,
but many projects have failed because no criteria of that type were
convincing to a coalition having power to stop the project from proceeding, or because important criteria that could not be captured in an
engineering analysis were ignored when the initial selection was made.

In summary, we have restated the siting problem in the following
way: *there is a "technically best" location for a particular facility, and
at least a* prima facie *case can be made that it ought to be built
somewhere. We assume that title to the land can be obtained, whether
by taking or by purchase, and that the site meets specific regulatory*

criteria for environmental impact and public safety regulation. What now should be done to wind up with either a functioning facility on the site in a reasonable time or a decision that the project is ill-conceived? It is in the last stage of the siting process that the most expensive, embittering, and divisive failures of the public choice process occur.

FOOTNOTES

1. Public opinion in Massachusetts was surveyed systematically in 1981 by the Executive Office of Environmental Affairs (report unpublished).
2. See, for example, J. V. Winter and D. A. Connor, *Power Plant Siting,* Van Nostrand Reinhold, 1978.
3. R. Keeney, *Siting Energy Facilities,* Academic Press, 1980.
4. D. Morrell and C. Magorian, *Siting Hazardous Waste Facilities,* Ballinger, 1982.

2
The Traditional Siting Process

Public conflict over large developments seems to have become the rule rather than the exception. No matter what a developer proposes to build—highway, hospital, power plant, satellite tracking station, hazardous waste facility or dam—someone will oppose it. No matter how safe the proposed facility looks to its developer and government officials, someone will oppose it. No matter how badly society's general well-being depends on a new development, someone will oppose it.

Furthermore, opponents frequently win. If they don't stop a project at the local level, they try again through state license processes. If they can't win through the permitting process, they resort to the courts. If the courts don't rule in their favor, they may use civil disobedience and political clout. Public opponents of large projects are making a real difference in the success of development.

This opposition occurs at the end of a decision-making process that begins long before opponents are even aware of a proposed project, and which currently follows a similar pattern in efforts to site everything from small halfway houses for juvenile delinquents to large nuclear power plants. In this chapter, we sketch this process generally and illustrate it with three case studies.

THE GENERIC SITING PROCESS

Despite the variation among siting experiences, a common pattern breeds conflict and mistrust. Dennis Ducsik has called it the "Decide-Announce-Defend" model,[1] and it goes like this: In the first stage, the developer makes a series of technical choices with his engineer, market analysts, and lawyers. He typically has no interaction with local government nor those who would be affected by his decisions. Because most developers lack eminent domain power, they often keep these decisions secret until the appropriate land has been optioned, initial environmental reports made, and one particular site chosen as the best.

The developer then announces his technology and site package to the public. If he mentions alternatives, they often seem factitious. He appears to approach the public with a single firm decision camouflaged behind impossible alternatives. His strong position sets the stage for conflict.

Now the permitting process begins. The developer begins working his way through long and sometimes complicated application procedures for state, local, and federal permits. He must prepare and publicize information about the proposed project, and thus the public gets its first opportunity to be heard. People with strong concerns about the project and those who don't thoroughly understand it approach this opportunity defensively. They have no reason to expect the developer to change his mind, alter his project, choose another site, or heed the public's concern. In fact, they perceive themselves as having power only to delay or stop the project—because the developer has taken an apparently firm position, they must likewise be intransigent in order to protect themselves. In the end, this decision-making process breeds conflict and opposition, without providing constructive methods for incorporating people's concerns and resolving differences.

At the end of a process already far along, the developer thus faces a hostile population, composed of people who feel duped—informed of a project in the eleventh hour, and told by government and industry alike, "love it or leave." But in many siting cases the developer also feels duped. Even if he has approached local officials with the proposed project and sold them on the concept and its benefits, new voices of opposition are suddenly heard. Indeed, opponents often claim that the local officials are "in bed with the developers."

The Opposition

Although some opponents live in host communities, they just as often come from neighboring towns. These neighbors expect to receive nothing but public and private costs from a nearby development—more population, more traffic, more pollution, more noise; and while the host community government receives new tax revenues, nearby communities can anticipate no such gains.

Opponents organize easily. They typically live near each other, they know each other or are at least acquainted, and they share a simple, common perceived objective—to stop the facility (although they may have different reasons for wanting to do so). While they lack experience in public activity, and often find it necessary to work overtime in order to acquire the necessary skills, they are not without resources. Sometimes local opponents can often attach themselves to a politically active chapter of a national "proenvironmental" group as a means to their end.

A common factor in facility opposition is the use of informational and procedural requirements to delay or stop proposed projects. The Seabrook nuclear power plant occasioned the best example of this technique among our cases: opponents have used every possible opportunity to challenge decisions and to require additional information as tactics to delay or stop this particular facility. Even though the power plant is partially constructed, whether or not it will ever operate is still in question, as these delays have been significant enough to seriously jeopardize the developer's finances. Since those with concerns about a proposed project have little opportunity to influence it before the permitting process begins, it is not surprising—in fact, as we will see, it is to be expected—that they use procedural rights and informational requirements as a way to protect their own interests.

Another common theme throughout the stories of siting conflict is public mistrust and suspicion of developers. The public opposition seems to start off by doubting the developer's integrity and scrutinizing his initial behavior for evidence reinforcing this perception. Unfortunately, such evidence is often forthcoming: any inconsistencies between what the developer does and what he says he will do, any reticence in providing information, or any tendency to define the opposition's concerns as trivial or unimportant will encourage this mistrust.

Finally, we will see information playing a critical role in the evolution of opposition. Developers who provide only the information required by law often find that they are too late: people lack useful information when they want it (when they are forming opinions). Once opinions about a proposed project are formed, subsequent information provided by the developer is not likely to influence them: a doubting public will often construe a developer's early silence about his plans as a deliberate effort to deceive or to avoid taking responsibility for undesirable consequences. Indeed, we often see that such information is provided with the objective of satisfying legal requirements, rather than responding to the legitimate fears and concerns of the public.

We derive these impressions of the siting process and the nature of opposition from a wide variety of case histories about efforts to site everything from hazardous waste facilities to power plants—projects that would be good for the region but clearly not desirable *per se* as near neighbors. We have summarized three that highlight the typical approach to siting that produces conflict and ultimate failure. However, we do not claim that all siting procedures are exactly parallel to these—indeed, later in this book we summarize several stories that offer hope for improving upon the traditional process. But we think these three fairly portray the traditional process that has paralyzed development—large and small, public and private—across the country, especially during the last ten years.

THREE CASE STUDIES

Searsport, Maine[2]

Local officials of Searsport, Maine, have failed three times to attract industrial development to their shores. Only a few years after neighboring Wiscasset became the site for a nuclear power plant, the town of Searsport eagerly began a series of doomed efforts to get any facility constructed within its borders. First, Maine Clean Fuels tried to build an oil refinery, then Central Maine Power tried to build its second nuclear power plant, and at this writing Central Maine Power is trying to build a coal-fired generating station. None of these has reached even the pre-construction stage.

The Searsport story demonstrates how even near-perfect implementation of the conventional approach to development can lead to failure. When compared to the success in Wiscasset, Searsport's failure also points out important changes in the social and political climate for siting large facilities.

Maine Yankee/Wiscasset. In 1966, several public utilities joined Central Maine Power to form the Maine Yankee Atomic Power Company (MYAP) and initiated procedures to build the Maine Yankee Power Plant in Wiscasset, Maine. By 1972, the plant was built and operating, and since then has encountered only minimal operating problems. The only opposition (from Citizens for Safe Power, a local group) encouraged the Atomic Energy Commission (AEC) to regulate Yankee's operation practices, not to stop the project. Maine Yankee developers have maintained good rapport with Wiscasset, which has enjoyed an almost sevenfold increase in its property tax revenue, despite a rate reduction; MYAP pays almost 95% of that total revenue.

Searsport. The three proposed Searsport energy facilities (oil refinery, nuclear power plant, and coal-fired power plant) have all been designed for Sears Island, an uninhabited island owned by the Bangor and Aroostook Railroad in Penobscot Bay.

The Town Council's efforts to attract industry have been motivated by financial need: Searsport, unlike Wiscasset, receives little revenue from tourists or summer residents. In 1977, the town had a 21% unemployment rate, and average per capita income was $3,527. Town and state officials, and a majority of Searsport's 20,000 residents, favor "responsible" industrial development of the island, but each proposal has been thwarted by environmental opposition arising just outside of Searsport.

The Oil Refinery (1971-1973).   In 1971, Maine Clean Fuels proposed a 100,000 barrel per day refinery for Portland, Maine. The Portland City Council strongly opposed it, so Maine Clean Fuels revised its proposal to build on Sears Island. Although the local officials and residents favored the project, it foundered for two reasons. First, Maine Clean Fuels could not comply with state environmental standards. Second, coastal residents and out-of-state property owners applied strong political pressure to prohibit development of any oil refinery in Maine, alleging that rocky Penobscot Bay was too dangerous for regular oil tanker traffic.

The Nuclear Power Plant (1974-1977).   In August 1974, Central Maine Power announced Sears Island as its preferred site for a 1200 MWe (megawatt) nuclear-fueled electric generating plant. CMP used Maine Yankee as its model when promoting the Sears Island facility, and gave all interested Searsport residents an opportunity to inspect the Wiscasset facility. As CMP explained, it was attracted to Sears Island because of its good access, industrial surroundings, the strong support of local officials, and the fact that single ownership would ease site acquisition. In mid-summer 1974, Searsport changed the site's zoning to facilitate the project, and two weeks later CMP began constructing a meteorological tower on the site.

Problems arose almost immediately. CMP's procedures for informing the public about its plans created confusion and mistrust that motivated regional opposition. Inconsistent news releases confused the public about whether Sears Island was CMP's preferred site or simply one of five alternatives. Although CMP's actions clearly pointed to Sears Island as preferred—optioning property, constructing a meteorological tower, upgrading roads, responding quickly to zoning changes—CMP denied this until publicly embarrassed into doing so. When it became obvious that Sears Island was in fact (and had always been) CMP's preferred site, many local and regional residents felt deceived.

In general, the public was confused by CMP's actions, seriously questioned its intentions (without getting satisfactory answers), and felt that something was being "put over" on them. CMP had not voluntarily informed state officials about its plans, so the officials could not respond knowledgeably to citizen inquiries. In addition, CMP did not discuss its plans with town officials until *after* it had conducted enough investigations to choose the Sears Island site. Although CMP played by the rules and violated no regulations, its information policy created confusion, suspicion, and mistrust—conditions that strongly contributed to subsequent opposition and wariness on the part of state officials.

After this poor beginning, CMP sent a representative to the town on a weekly basis through the fall of 1974, and in January 1975 it opened an information office in Searsport, making information readily available to area residents. But by that time most people had formed an opinion about the facility and committed themselves to a position.

During a summer of confusion and suspicion, an opposition group gathered support in surrounding communities that would gain no tax benefits from the project and transformed the proposed project into a regional issue. They disseminated their concerns about safety, economic costs, and alternative energy sources. CMP believed it continually maintained an open policy, but opponents perceived them as deceptive and trusted neither CMP nor town officials.

The nuclear project eventually died because of a delayed Nuclear Regulatory Commission (NRC) ruling on CMP's rule-change application concerning the definition of a "capable [of causing earthquakes] geological fault." NRC staff unofficially reassured CMP that faults due to glacial rebound (evident on Sears Island) would not be considered "capable faults," but after a further two-year delay, CMP cancelled the nuclear project and revived plans for a coal-fired facility. CMP hoped to recover about half the eight million dollars already invested in the Sears Island site.*

Citizens for Safe Power for Maine contributed to the project's failure in two ways. It provided the only negative comment on the CMP's rule-change petition, and it created an atmosphere of public opposition that at least CMP, and probably NRC, considered when making decisions. Despite the NRC's informal reassurances, its foot-dragging and the timing and content of its decision indicate public controversy.

The Coal Plant (1979-1979).   In 1977, CMP petitioned the Public Utilities Commission for a Certification of Public Convenience and Necessity to construct a 600 MWe coal-fired plant on Sears Island, the plan long preferred by the site's owners, the Bangor and Aroostook Railroad. State officials questioned the need for this additional generating capacity and the project's ability to comply with the state environmental standards. In October 1979, the Public Utilities Commission rejected the project as unnecessary to fulfill future power demands.

Communication/Information.   Although CMP and Searsport town officials' interests appeared compatible, CMP's siting effort was not marked by effective communication with local and regional residents, nor by constructive response to environmental opposition. Each project was aborted so early that no Environmental Impact Statement has ever been written for these proposals. Many questions raised by state

---

* Shortly after announcing this shift, the NRC denied the rule-change petition but agreed to a case-by-case review.

and local officials and special interest groups would normally be covered by an EIS—but if ever such a statement had been prepared, it obviously would have arrived long after those affected had made critical decisions.

Conclusions.   Searsport town officials now look to their once-poor neighbor Wiscasset and see a rags-to-riches story which they have three times failed to replicate. They and the developers repeated the Wiscasset approach to siting, and failed. Town officials and residents have made it well known that they favor "responsible" development of Sears Island; like poor communities elsewhere, they have actively solicited development proposals. And developers have responded, working hard to satisfy the letter of the law. They applied for permits, talked to officials, provided information, and conducted studies all according to local, state, and federal requirements. Both they and the community assumed that "following the rules" would lead to success; however, in their case, as in the two cases below, the rules appear to have been written for a different game.

Seabrook Nuclear Power Plant[3]

More than thirteen years ago, Public Service Company of New Hampshire began the arduous process of trying to construct a nuclear power plant in Seabrook, New Hampshire. From the very beginning, Public Service has been adamantly determined not to deviate from its original plans, and environmentalists have been equally determined to stop the facility. Thus, for over nine years, the permitting process for Seabrook has been a battle of wills, fought with legal challenges, sit-ins, arrests, fence cutters, tear gas, and water hoses. No government ruling now obstructs the completion of Seabrook, but the lengthy delay has almost as effectively threatened the project's life. What began as a typical effort to site a large nuclear power plant has become a classic example of the effectiveness of public opposition and the failure of the conventional siting process.

The Facility and Developer.   Public Service heads a consortium of New England electric utilities constructing two 1194 megawatt (MWe) nuclear power reactors in Seabrook, a small coastal New Hampshire town five miles north of the Massachusetts border. The site was formerly the town landfill and is bordered on three sides by marshland. In 1969, Seabrook approved selling the landfill to Public Service for the power plant, and in 1973 Public Service began applying for necessary state permits. Construction began in 1976, despite lack of some critical permits, but was stopped several times due to environmental opposition. After seven years of opposition and court battles, Seabrook now has all permits and is scheduled for operation in 1985. But it is seriously threatened by financial difficulties.

Public Service claims it chose Seabrook because of its access to water, skilled labor, and transportation facilities; its geological suitability, easy site acquisition, low land costs, proximity to power demand centers, and its local permitting process. Environmental factors were not major criteria for site selection; in fact, Public Service planned Seabrook and arranged its financing entirely for engineering and economic reasons. When the environmental legislation of the early '70s produced a set of rules concerned with pollution control and ecological balance, Public Service made no effort to reevaluate its plans. First, Public Service had difficulty understanding that reasonable individuals might find the plant objectionable—it was, after all, a state-of-the-art "smokeless" facility, in sharp contrast to the "smelly, dirty" oil refineries that environmental groups had recently protested. Second, Public Service officials were committed to a facility design and location that seemed the least expensive alternative; any changes would create costly delay. And finally, Public Service officials found it difficult to accept the fact that new environmental laws had not only created new rules, but also empowered environmentalists to enforce them.

As opposition mounted, the company's determination to develop Seabrook as planned stiffened, and it became a single objective "to get the damn thing built." Public pressure resulted in correction of design faults, but these corrections neither addressed environmentalists' basic fears nor lessened opposition.

The Town. Seabrook is a small coastal town benefitting from a significant summer recreation industry and recent regional economic growth, but still not prosperous. Most town residents initially supported the facility because of anticipated increases in tax revenue and jobs. They expected a smokeless facility that would pay lots of taxes, that would not interfere with the use of the harbor, that would benefit clam growth with warm cooling water—that would, in short, provide nothing but benefits. Local disillusionment developed when noisy construction activities obstructed traffic, stopped access to the harbor, and contributed to a serious local water shortage. Although the town had previously made a "gentleman's agreement" with Seabrook about its water consumption, many residents thought Public Service arrogant and unreasonable when it refused to curtail water consumption during a severe shortage and used the courts to prevent town efforts to implement any restrictions.

Local dissatisfaction with the power plant has become even more evident since then. Non-binding referenda in 1976 and 1977 both rejected support for the facility, and several referenda in 1978 attempted to revoke the town's land sales agreement and regain access to the harbor. However, the town's tax rate has already been cut in half, and most residents seem to tolerate the facility for that reason.

A Battle of Wills. Opponents both inside and outside the town fought a sophisticated battle carefully planned and coordinated to maximize use of their limited resources and the legal system. However, by 1976 some people disillusioned with legal strategies had organized the Clamshell Alliance, a loosely knit federation of environmental groups and individuals, to oppose the plant through extra-legal means. As the legal tactics to stop or delay Seabrook construction neared exhaustion, Clamshell members began demonstrations and civil disobedience. Opposition never waned; it simply changed tactics to fit the case. (Opponents lost the last legal skirmish in 1978, ending seven years of legal and bureaucratic conflict.)

Most Seabrook controversy has, at least formally, centered on the plant's cooling system and its alleged threat to the aquatic environment. The original design called for an open-channel, "once-through" cooling system: cold ocean water would be brought into the plant, circulated to collect waste heat, and discharged through a pipe into the ocean at a higher temperature. Opponents charged that the warmer water would damage marshland and harbor ecosystems, so Public Service agreed to drill two tunnels through the rock beneath the plant and discharge water a mile offshore. Although opponents also attacked this plan, both the Environmental Protection Agency (EPA) and the Nuclear Regulation Commission (NRC) eventually approved a 7,000 foot discharge pipe, and courts have upheld their decisions.

Round One: State Permits.   The first legal skirmish began in 1973 when Public Service applied for two state permits. Environmental groups and the state's Attorney General opposed the facility, but Public Service did obtain preliminary state approval in 1973. The plant's opponents challenged this approval in court and lost; final state approval was received in 1975.

Round Two: The Nuclear Regulatory Commission (NRC).   In 1973, Public Service also applied for its NRC Construction Permit, and the NRC named eight intervenors for this application. At plant opponents' request, the NRC held hearings on this application in 1975. In the midst of these hearings, the NRC changed the presiding chairman; the opponents challenged this change. In 1976, 25% of Seabrook's financing changed hands, and at the opponents' request the NRC reopened hearings on Public Service's construction permit application. Later that year, the NRC granted the construction permit, subject to the EPA's approval of the plant's cooling system. The opponents immediately appealed that decision, and also initiated a series of court actions aimed at reversing the NRC's decision on several substantive and procedural grounds.

Round Three: The Environmental Protection Agency (EPA).   Meanwhile, action had begun over the EPA's decisions concerning Seabrook's "Section 316 permit," allowing its cooling water intake and discharge system. Public Service applied for its Section 316 permit in 1974, and in 1975 the EPA held hearings on the application and issued a tentative "determination" approving its "once-through" cooling system, but not the location of the intake structure. It then issued a second determination requiring Public Service to move the intake structure further out. Opponents argued against Public Service at both hearings, and requested adjudicatory hearings on both determinations. Eventually, they were joined by Public Service.

In early 1976, the EPA conducted adjudicatory hearings on both determinations. After the EPA studied the hearing record, it requested further information from Public Service, but was refused. So in November 1976, the EPA reversed both of its determinations. Public Service appealed to the EPA Administrator, who subsequently ruled in its favor in March 1977. The EPA denied opponents' request for hearings, and in June 1977 issued final EPA approvals. The opponents, who had been able to delay the approval for three years, immediately appealed to the First Circuit Court of Appeals in Boston.

Round Four: Back to the NRC.   Public Service then asked the NRC to reinstate their construction permit. In July 1977, the Atomic Safety Licensing Board (ASLB) voted to let work resume, but conditioned it on a favorable resolution of three issues before the ASLB (seismic activity, evacuation plans, and plant need). Opponents appealed this decision to the First Circuit. Meanwhile, the ASLB warned Public Service that they risked another suspension of their construction permit because the ASLB had ordered additional hearings on alternative site consideration and on the use of cooling towers. In November 1977, the ASLB ruled that cooling towers would be appropriate if the EPA said they were necessary. In February 1978, the intervenors asked the ASLB to stay construction on the basis that these findings were incorrect.

Round Five: The Final Resolution.   At this point in the story, the opponents were awaiting resolution of three legal appeals: two through the courts, concerning EPA Administrator Costle's decision and on the ASLB's ruling reinstating the construction permit; and one with the NRC itself. In June 1978, the NRC held additional hearings on the cooling towers, and in July suspended the construction permit pending the EPA decision. Meanwhile, in February 1978, the court ordered EPA Administrator Costle to reconsider his ruling favoring Public Service. After hearings in June 1978, Costle approved Public Service's EPA permits in August 1978. Finally, in August 1978, the court affirmed the ASLB decision reinstating the construction permit.

This last court ruling ended the final legal delay of Seabrook. But while the intervenors had been slowly losing the legal battle, the Clamshell Alliance had been accelerating its extra-legal tactics. Fourteen hundred demonstrators occupied the Seabrook site in 1978, determined to block construction of the plant: the Seabrook battle had simply shifted to a different front.

Conclusion.   Now 13 years from its first local approval, Public Service has very little certainty that its Seabrook project will ever be built. Although opponents have "lost" the legal battle, they may win the war because of Public Service's financial difficulties. These began in

1971, before active opposition, but the delay imposed by legal challenges has exacerbated the financial crisis considerably, as has a steadily falling growth rate in electric consumption.

The battle between Public Service and the Seabrook opponents was marked by an absolute lack of effort to compromise or settle out of court and by continually growing hostility and mutual distrust. From the very beginning, Public Service staunchly defended its announced proposal and made no effort to determine if the newly emerging environmental concerns should be heeded. Indeed, Public Service officials refused to believe that any aspect of their proposed facility might be challenged by reasonable people. Even environmental legislation promulgated shortly after their announcement resulted in no revision of their proposal. Public Service was unresponsive to concerns raised by either local residents or environmentalists, which fostered antagonism and hardened the opponents' determination to stop the facility. Public Service became a symbol for all that people perceived to be wrong with large developers. The result of this siting effort was highly determined (and still continuing) opposition to the Seabrook proposal, met by Public Service's fierce determination to overcome environmentalists as obstacles to development. With the wisdom of hindsight, these criticisms of Public Service's tactics seem airtight. But as we will see, the legal and conventional environment in which Public Service began the project seemed to encourage the ill-advised confidence in a narrowly legalistic approach that has been so frustrating to the company: the siting process as practiced consisted exclusively of licensing proceedings—yes-or-no decisions on well-defined proposals.

Wilsonville, Illinois Waste Facility[4]

In 1976, Wilsonville, Illinois, had a successful hazardous waste disposal facility. The new plant operated with minor incident and little public attention for approximately four months. Then, within two days, this public acceptance was transformed into adamant, near-violent public opposition. The conflict eventually involved the state Attorney General, the Governor, and both state and federal regulatory agencies. After 16 months of legal proceedings, the facility was closed, and a lengthy appeal process—not yet concluded—began.

The Wilsonville story is quite similar to other siting conflicts even though opposition began *after* the facility was sited and operating rather than before. The Wilsonville episode contains all the typical elements of public conflict over new facilities—lack of local control, legal and extra-legal delay tactics, misinformation and suspicion, and a small, localized and highly motivated public perceiving itself as being made much worse off by facility operation.

Facility Construction and Approval. In 1974, a former official of the Illinois Environmental Protection Agency incorporated Earthline, Inc. to invest in hazardous waste management facilities among other projects. The official began searching for a site near industrial areas, with good hydrogeology, and surrounded by undeveloped land. One location in Wilsonville seemed promising since it was partially covered by an unreclaimed pile of slag left over from an abandoned mine, and since village residents had previously used it as an open dump.

In 1976, the official applied for and received a state permit to develop a hazardous waste facility involving hazardous waste landfilling, acid-alkaline neutralization, chemical fixation, and short-term storage of recyclables. In four months, Earthline developed the landfilling and short-term storage facilities, and the facility opened for business in November 1976.

In the meantime, Earthline had taken several steps to secure local support for the facility. When it first applied for a development permit, it also sent a notification letter to the Wilsonville local officials and to several residents. This letter notified them of Earthline's intention to build a facility that would conserve precious resources, protect the environment, and reclaim the site; the facility would recover, treat, store and contain "industrial residues." The letter implied that there would be jobs for local residents. In addition, there was an open house for area residents the day the facility opened. In retrospect, it appears that the local residents did not fully understand that the proposed facility would be handling hazardous waste (although the developers maintain that the residents had been fully informed). People seem to have perceived it merely as a reclamation facility for industrial residue that would benefit their community and provide them jobs; hazardous waste dumping had not yet become a sensitive, nationally publicized issue.

A month before the facility opened, SCA Services, Inc. purchased Earthline. SCA Services retained the founder of Earthline as the consulting engineer for the facility, and made the owner of the land SCA's regional director.

During the first four months of operation, residents noted some problems with the facility, but in general accepted it. They complained about odors, and they were disappointed that the facility did not hire as many local residents as they had expected. There were a few reported spills. In addition, truck traffic traveling down a main street to enter the facility had caused some damage to local streets and property. Despite these problems, Wilsonville residents were either neutral or slightly positively inclined toward the facility.

Up to this point, Wilsonville residents had had little involvement with the facility. Earthline had largely determined the siting process—the state reviewed the application, made some alterations (i.e., it would not permit medium-term storage of recyclables), and approved a revised permit application. The local government had no say in the matter, since at that time Illinois preempted any local regulatory control over hazardous waste facilities. Earthline did notify the local officials about its proposed facility, but residents had little opportunity to analyze plans or suggest changes. They might have petitioned the Illinois Pollution Control Board to conduct a public hearing on the proposed project, but they were not aware of this opportunity and had no reason at this point in the process to be concerned. Although there is disagreement now concerning what information local residents did have, it seems clear that they did not fully understand the nature of this facility.

The Formation of Successful Opposition.   In April 1977, after four months of operation, Wilsonville residents read in the local newspaper that the Wilsonville facility would receive PCB-contaminated soils collected from a spill in Missouri. The public at that time was becoming concerned with the toxicity of PCBs, and local residents quickly opposed their importation. Shortly thereafter, a state senator held an "information meeting" in Wilsonville which intensified local opposition. Two days later, a local priest reportedly told parishioners in church that the facility presented a danger and should be shut down. By Sunday evening, when an angry armed mob gathered to stop the trucks importing the PCB-contaminated soil, local leaders had induced a retired circuit court judge to act as the village's special attorney to initiate legal action to stop the PCB importation on the condition that there be no violence. The mob dispersed, and the following day Wilsonville began legal action. In the meantime, SCA had cancelled the delivery of the PCB-contaminated soil planned for Monday because of the risk of violence.

Over the next 16 months, legal and administrative battles continued and opposition gained momentum. Initially, Wilsonville's suit to stop SCA from burying the PCB-contaminated soils at the Earthline facility was eventually joined by Macoupin County and the County Farm Bureau. A temporary restraining order was overturned, and the facility stayed open, but the contaminated soil in question never arrived. By the end of May, the state Attorney General had decided that the facility was not in the public interest and filed suit to close the facility entirely. He consolidated his suit with that of Wilsonville, and later amended it to request that SCA remove all waste buried at the site and pay $1.24 million in fines. Shortly thereafter, the Governor issued a 45-day moratorium on the issuance of new supplementary permits. More than a year later, in September 1978, the Governor prohibited the Illinois EPA from issuing Earthline's Wilsonville facility any more supplemental permits and prohibited agency personnel from participating in any more court actions on the case. Local opponents successfully mobilized other local officials, a state senator, the state Attorney General, and the Governor to support their position.

But the facility proponents also found support—mostly within the regulatory agencies and the industrial community. When Wilsonville filed suit against Earthline, Inc., the Illinois Environmental Protection Agency immediately filed an *amicus curiae* brief in favor of Earthline during its trial. Shortly thereafter, Illinois State Geological Survey personnel visited the site and, in November 1978, the SGS issued a generally favorable report on the site's hydrogeology. The U.S. EPA tried to join the suit, but was denied; eventually it joined as a friend of the court. Later, the U.S. EPA visited the site and determined that it was an acceptable site for disposing of PCBs.

Midway through legal proceedings, SCA/Earthline officials requested and held a meeting with local officials, and offered to negotiate an out-of-court settlement. They offered to settle all outstanding damage claims and pave the main street used by the trucks, but village officials reportedly responded that only the permanent shut-down of the facility and the removal of all waste stored on site could resolve the suit.

Several issues arose during the 16-month trial—the site's technical suitability, the health threat to nearby residents, adverse impacts on property values, and SCA's management techniques. Differing permeability data and differing predictions of significant subsidence caused residents to question the site's safety. Concerns over SCA's management ability arose from reports of personnel smoking on the site, reusing rather than burying emptied containers, inadequate records, and offensive odors.

On August 14, 1978, the circuit court ordered Earthline/SCA to close the landfill and remove all waste disposed there. Earthline/SCA appealed the decision and requested permission to remain open until the appeal was resolved. However, before receiving an answer from the Appellate Court, the village of Wilsonville dug a "culvert repair" trench across the access road to the facility, which effectively closed it. The lower court's ruling was upheld by the Illinois Appellate Court, and again on May 22, 1981 by the Illinois Supreme Court. In its decision, the Illinois Supreme Court recognized the need for such facilities, but claimed such a facility should be located "where it will pose no threat to health or life, now, or in the future." It held that the facts of the case indicated that the disposal site was located too close to the village and to abandoned coal mine shafts.[5]

The courts paid little attention to the conflicts between the state and federal government's regulatory process and the court's nuisance jurisdiction, and showed no deference to administrative agencies' expertise. One reviewer's comment pointedly summarizes the industry position:

> . . . A company can attach little legal protection to its state permits or any federal regulatory involvement. There is no assurance that the standards applied by the agency in granting a permit will be the same standards applied by the courts if nuisance cases are brought.[6]

It is not certain that the case can be appealed to the U.S. Supreme Court. Otherwise, the order to cease operations and exhume the site stands.

Inadequacies of This Siting Process. Despite Earthline/SCA's calm and trouble-free beginning, its siting effort faced stiff and successful opposition, which succeeded in closing the facility even after it was permitted, constructed, and operating. Several factors in the early chapters of this siting story laid the foundation for these difficulties. First of all, Earthline described the facility to the public as a place to reclaim "industrial residue." People did not associate it with hazardous waste or hazardous materials, any more than they considered their own industries "hazardous waste generating facilities." In addition, they expected the facility to provide numerous additional jobs for local residents. Initially, people perceived themselves as having something at stake in the proposed facility—e.g., jobs and a cleaner environment. These expectations seemed to carry them over their discontent about odors, minor spillage, and road damage.

But the report of the PCBs shattered their expectations and triggered a sudden and overwhelming belief that they had been deceived. Earthline/SCA lost its credibility, and its subsequent actions were not well-suited to restore it. Earthline's previous description of a facility that "recovered industrial wastes" seemed inconsistent with the newspaper accounts of a facility that would import and dispose of PCB-contaminated soils. Contradictory technical studies of the area increased the local perception that they had been duped.

In addition, some misinformation and public statements attributed to Earthline officials acted to increase public apprehension and further reduce Earthline's credibility. Some residents confused PCBs with PBBs, which had recently produced birth defects and deformities in cattle and required destruction of hundreds of Michigan cattle. A report also circulated that nerve gas was stored on the site; when that was proven wrong, the landowner was reported as saying that Earthline was free to store nerve gas if it desired. In addition, the Earthline manager was reported as stating that much worse materials than PCBs were being stored on-site. Thus, in the early months of the legal proceedings, residents had this "information" before them and no direct or reassuring information from SCA. Trucks traveled over and degraded the main village street, and the facility had produced many fewer jobs than people had expected.

SCA's immediate response to local opposition was to request that the regulatory agency keep confidential all remaining supplemental hazardous waste permits for the Earthline facility. Later, midway through the legal proceedings, SCA officials did approach local officials in an effort to negotiate an out-of-court settlement, but their offer was too late—by that time SCA had no credibility and people perceived that they had nothing to gain and a great deal to lose if the facility stayed. They had long since confirmed their own impressions of SCA and the Earthline facility, and their position was firm.

It is important to note that local officials had had no opportunity to become involved in the planning or siting of this facility, had had no local permit to issue, and had virtually no control over the facility, other than court proceedings, to restrict its operations or shut it down. While Earthline made an effort to inform local officials of its plans, the local officials had no formal authority to review the facility nor, at that time, any reason to believe such a review was necessary.

Conclusions.   When a parish priest and state senator began to question the acceptability of the facility and the disposal of PCB-contaminated soils, it is not surprising that residents reacted so strongly. The siting process had not built a basis of trust between the community and the developer; when problems arose, the developer did not seem to find it wise to respond in a way that would foster trust. Rather, he seemed to conclude that the community's lack of any legal right to approve or disapprove his operation meant that they lacked the power to interfere with his operation. The Wilsonville story demonstrates, on the contrary, that power is not limited to the authority granted through either the permit process or the legal system; it suggests that there may be no power great enough to force a community to accept a facility they strongly dislike.

SUMMARY—THE CLASH OF EXPECTATIONS

Despite the differences among siting conflicts, there exists a generic siting process that often doesn't work; at the core of that process is a fundamental clash of values and expectations. On the one hand, developers expect property development rights to be upheld, unless technical analysis or specifically defined procedures demonstrate that such development would clearly be detrimental to the public as a whole. In addition, they expect development of facilities to be beneficial to the local community, and they expect the community to perceive this. They see a responsibility as "good neighbors" to inform the community about their plans, but little reason to do more than that.

These expectations are on a collision course with those of residents. Property development rights take a backseat to the community's right to "control its own destiny." Residents often believe they have been misled in the past by technical analyses and licensing procedures designed ostensibly to protect the public and the environment. They expect many new facilities to be detrimental to the community or to their particular neighborhood unless they step in to control decisions.

As a result, the two major parties affected by a siting process, the developer and the community, possess expectations of each other that directly lead to conflict and animosity. Behavior that seems reasonable to each party appears ignorant or even willfully insincere to the other.

FOOTNOTES

1. Dennis W. Ducsik, "Electricity Planning and the Environment: Toward a New Role for Government in the Decision Process," unpublished Ph.D. dissertation, Department of Civil Engineering, M.I.T., Cambridge, Massachusetts, January, 1978.
2. This case is summarized from D. Sanderson and A. Messina, "Four Coastal Maine Development Efforts: Wiscasset and Searsport," in *Energy Facilities and Public Conflict,* M.I.T. Laboratory of Architecture and Planning, 1979.
3. This case is summarized from A. Weinstein, "Seabrook—A Case Study of Environmental Conflict," in *Nuclear Energy Facilities and Public Conflicts: Three Case Studies,* M.I.T. Laboratory of Architecture and Planning, 1979.
4. This case is summarized from the U.S. EPA, *Siting of Hazardous Waste Management Facilities and Public Opposition* (prepared by Centaur Associates), SW–809, 1979, pp. 303–316.
5. 7th Jud. Court of Illinois, 77CH10 and 77CH13.
6. W. C. Brashares, "Wilsonville's Legal Significance," *Waste Age,* August 1981, p. 38.

3
Principles of the Public Choice Process

The failures and near-failures in the previous chapter are not atypical of the siting process currently in use. This process has grown both by unconscious evolution and more recently, in response to the defects of *laissez-faire* practices, by purposeful reform. Unfortunately, most of the current reforms of the siting process, both implemented and under serious consideration, are based on fundamental misunderstandings of how people behave in the public choice process. Nearly all respond to one of four models of the siting problem, each of which is usefully caricatured—ironically—by the authors' professional conventions. In the following pages, we will review these misapprehensions and then describe the general behavioral principles that people seem to follow in siting disputes.

MISPERCEPTIONS OF THE PUBLIC CHOICE PROCESS

The Lawyer's Fallacy

People who see the world as a series of permits and injunctions often act as though the legal obstacles to doing something are the only ones. It is easy for them to view the siting process as a series of legal and jurisdictional tests, and to try to improve it by making it harder (public-interest law firms) or easier (developer's counsel) to pass those tests. A common fallacy is supported by this day-to-day experience: "Of course we'll have opposition; the whole world is made up of cases with two sides to the conflict. The way to deal with opponents is to beat them in court, or prove that you can." Developers have often approached a siting problem as though they believed: "If we do an extra-good, complete job on our environmental impact statement, and dot all the i's and cross all the t's in our license applications, and hire the very best counsel to defend our actions, then we will get all our permits, have any injunctions lifted, and obviously we can go ahead and build the project." The statement is almost true; if *may* were substituted for *can* in the last clause it would be a good partial guide to action. Unfortunately, not everything permitted is possible. Having a legal right to proceed does not in itself give one the power to build something.

The Engineer's Fallacy

Engineers spend their time thinking about things like the density of concrete and the price of steel—things about which all engineers agree. They work for corporations with unitary values. Their conflicts are rarely with each other and are most often with the limits to action imposed by the laws of a complicated but predictable and ingenuous nature. The basic philosophy of the profession is that if two engineers disagree about the best way to do something, a few hours with a computer and a blackboard will produce agreement on a single approach. (This is a distinctive quality: the philosophy of law does not expect a plaintiff and defendant to end a trial agreeing with each other.)

The engineer's fallacy that this professional orientation gives rise to is: "There is obviously a best place to build this project. All we have to do in order to bring opposition to our point of view is to perform a really complete, objective analysis of the project, showing that we have the best site and that it is good to build it at all. People will obviously accept this professional, complete, fair analysis and cooperate with the project." (Others may hear this, however, as "If we have any opposition, it must be because they don't understand the technicalities involved. The way to deal with them is to beat them up intellectually and to browbeat them with our professional integrity.")

But people can disagree with the result of a study even if they can't show *why* they aren't convinced. And while most projects are either profitable or unprofitable for a whole company, and all divisions of a company benefit from good projects, a polity is not a business, and some investments that are good for most people are bad for a few.

The Planner's Fallacy

Planners as a group have less well-defined professional boundaries than lawyers or engineers, and their approach to problems is still taking form. But some commonalities can be sketched. Planners see a world of groups (each of which has (1) some merit in its position on an issue and (2) a different narrow view) and a world of governments always about to do something to at least one of these groups. Planners spend their time struggling with conflicts that are difficult to resolve through the market, or for which market solutions are actually forbidden. They also tend to work on one case at a time, and want to succeed with the project at hand. The planner tends to think: "The reason opposition exists is that different groups have different values and experiences. The way to deal with it is by increasing public participation: get everyone together in public hearings; be sure that everyone's view is heard by everyone else, and that the government agencies in charge know how their constituents feel about things."

But planners are usually hired precisely because citizens *don't* want to spend a lot of time, individually, on every planning problem that confronts their town or state. And bringing everyone together to talk it out may reveal that people have not only different values but also different substantive interests; what is good for Anne may be quite expensive for Barbara. Finally, people do not always say what they believe when saying something else is more useful to them.

The planner's approach to facility siting is likely to increase levels of opposition when the facts are revealed, and to harden positions; it is not at all the same thing to present your views as to be able to alter the outcome of a process.

The Economist's Fallacy

Economists concern themselves with tradeoffs. They see a world in which people are forced every day to choose which of several alternatives provides them the greatest utility. While economists recognize that the vast majority of these choices are made implicitly—indeed, terms like "shadow prices" and "revealed preferences" are used to signal the non-conscious character of many of the choices—economists often assume that every decision can be reduced to its economic dimensions. Thus, they are prone to writing articles about the economics of churchgoing[1] and the economics of suicide[2] in which they analyze these decisions as value-maximizing economic choices.

This preoccupation with prices and costs leads some economists to think that the concerns of facility opponents can always be assuaged by providing money to replace amenities that will be lost if the facility is built. "If people are upset that the new airport will increase noise in the neighborhood, just offer them enough money and they will be happy." In practice, such offers are often greeted with open hostility and treated like bribes. In the eyes of many facility opponents, the offer of money in return for their acquiescence casts doubt on the sincerity of their beliefs. Thus, it may even intensify their efforts to convince the developer that he has underestimated the depths of their feelings. Experience suggests that everyone does not have a price for everything, and some impacts do not seem to be for sale, at least in the conventional sense. In Chapters 5 and 6, we take a closer look at the uses and limits of compensation.

The Conventional Wisdom

While the professional caricatures above are real (though simplified) attitudes, they are not associated exclusively with the professional categories we have used to personify them. The lawyer's fallacy, for example, affects the behavior of bureaucrats and engineers as well. For purposes of analysis, these misapprehensions—or incomplete views of the world, to describe them more accurately—can be subdivided and regrouped into seven propositions that most critics of the siting process say, or act as though, they believe:

1. Many, if not most, of the major facilities that developers or government agencies propose to build are worth having, and perceived as such, by society as a whole.

2. Most of the important problems in site selection and facility development can be anticipated and overcome by a thorough technical review: an unbiased and expert research program will identify the correct site and characteristics for the facility proposed.

3. Since we agree that we need these facilities and agree that they have to go somewhere, dispute and conflict can be resolved by tests of adequacy (permits) and a well-informed public debate (the political process).

4. The important non-technical obstacles to facility siting, in cases where the process has failed, have resulted from developer's failure to obtain the legal right to proceed with their projects—denial of permits or delay in permit granting, for example.

5. Legal mechanisms to remedy defects in the siting process will be used as the reforms' authors intended.

6. Most of the participants in the siting process mean what they say and say what they want.

7. The principal risk that the siting process, or development of the facility itself, will be turned to purposes inconsistent with public policy lies in the developer's desire for private profit and his failure to recognize the external costs of his proposal.

A SOUNDER VIEW

If the propositions listed above correctly described the world, the siting problem in its various manifestations would have been solved by implementing the existing set of "reforms in good currency." Unfortunately, most of these propositions are either naive or downright wrong. We set forth below more useful descriptions of the important qualities of the siting problem that will motivate the analysis in Chapters 5 through 7. Some of these appear platitudinous when stated simply, but they are repeated here since they are so often ignored in practice.

Preferences Differ

The first important quality of a siting dispute is that while we may all be in it together, we are not looking for the same results. Careless use of the word *we*, and of aggregates such as *the public* and *society*, conceal deep and important divisions among individuals who want very different outcomes from any particular siting dispute. Few facilities as proposed promise to help everyone; at least some people will be worse off if any project goes ahead. The existence of these differences is one reason for the poor record of "full public debate" and elaborate public information procedures; as often as not, full disclosure taken alone merely reveals to tentative opponents of a project that their expectations are qualitatively correct, and even that development will be worse for them than they expected!

Stakes Differ

Not only do different groups and participants have different desires for the project's outcome, but they also have different degrees of interest in it. Obviously, the developer of a new power plant expects profits, while his electricity customers expect reliable power. But even more important, people have different per capita stakes in any major investment. The project manager for the utility is more or less risking his entire career on the success of the proposal, while any single one of the utility's customers sees it as a matter of a few dollars annually on his electric bill. We will see in Chapter 5 that this difference in *per capita* stakes has the utmost importance for the design of a siting process in which efficient outcomes can be expected.

Almost as important as the difference in the *amounts* of benefit at risk for different parties in a siting dispute is the difference in *type* of benefit different parties will enjoy. Politicians and public officials are risking power, influence, and reputation, for example, while the stockholders of the developer have only money at risk.

Groups Are Not People

Just as the strategy of a siting conflict can only be fully understood by recognizing the different *per capita* stakes seen by different parties, the behavior of aggregates of individuals cannot be predicted by considering each group a unitary decision-maker. A most insidious fallacy is to impute a capacity for action, or other anthropomorphism, to a collection of individuals that have some quality in common, but that are not organized or formally associated. "Electricity Consumers"—those who will benefit from a new project by lowered utility rates—are not *consumers* in the same sense that the dues-paying, organized members of the Sierra Club are *environmentalists*.

Nor can even organized groups be treated as a single person: prediction of group behavior may occasionally be made by direct analogy to a fictitious individual situated as the group is, but this shortcut is risky. Groups and other organizations do not have desires or utilities, and the actions they can take are strictly limited by law and their own internal organization. What a group does is predictable or understood reliably only by reference to the goals and opportunities of the individual people who act for it or influence it. Furthermore, a group is not simply the sum of its parts; a group's goals and objectives may differ significantly from the summation of its individual members' goals and objectives. Group dynamics, personality differences among group members, and informal decision-making procedures manipulate and transform individual desires into a single statement. People will accept some amount of divergence from their individual ambitions in exchange for group acceptance, coherence, and support—much as people in a democracy accept election outcomes that differ from their individual preferences. Of course, extreme divergences will result in reduced group coherence and defections from the ranks.

Several characteristics can help predict the correspondence between individual and group goals and objectives. The smaller the group, the more singular the members' individual concerns; and the greater their geographic proximity, the more likely the group is to manifest a position closely parallel to positions held by individual members. We will return to this point in Chapter 5.

People Try to Get What They Want

As far as we can tell, the participants in siting disputes usually act rationally. They don't always understand the full set of strategies that they might adopt to get what they want, and their use of information and strategic planning is often imperfect—at least by measure of hindsight!—but we have found the common accusations of "irrationality" and "mindless stubbornness" so often fired back and forth in these disputes to be rarely justified. Nor do we think self-serving behavior is perverse. The world might be a nicer place to live, though probably much less predictable, if more people were altruistic, but it seems foolhardy to expect (and presumptuous to demand) that individuals or groups act contrary to their best interest—that they ignore the rewards society offers them for certain kinds of behavior.

It is this perception of human reasonableness that makes it possible to predict (for example) that, when the law gives the opponents of a project the right to delay the process by litigating the environmental impact statement, people opposing the project *for any reason whatever* will be in court trying to demonstrate the inadequacy of the impact statement to the best of their abilities. The siting process should be designed in expectation that opponents will use *every device available to them* to stop or delay the project, and that supporters will similarly seek out tools that might be used to serve their own goals. At the least, a reform or modification of the process should be analyzed not only to see whether it will serve the purposes for which it was designed, but also to see if it might be turned to other uses by any involved parties.

People Have Other Things to Do

Our discussion of the differences in *per capita* stakes at risk in a facility siting dispute leads directly to the recognition that there are few people to whom any particular facility is the most important thing in the world. Most people have limited resources to devote to opposition or support of any initiative; even wealthy people have only 24 hours a day to allocate among the pleasures and opportunities life affords. Urban planners are now familiar through painful experience with the difficulty of generating substantial commitments of time or resources to public issues, even where a neighborhood's very existence is threatened by a highway or development plan. The electricity consumer is, again, a case in point: to a first approximation, someone indifferent to nuclear power *per se,* who will save $10 per year if a new nuclear power plant is built, can be expected to devote *at most* $100 worth of time or other resources* to making the project a success.

Legal Authority is Not Power to Act

A variety of conditions are necessary to make it possible to build and operate a facility. Among these are ownership of the site or an equivalent property right such as a lease, appropriate zoning and permits, and other components of the legal authority to proceed. But these conditions are not sufficient—even in the aggregate—to allow a project to go forward. A developer, even with every permit and zoning amendment in place, can be stymied by a variety of extra-legal obstacles, (familiar from our case studies) including an endless sequence of temporary injunctions while litigation proceeds, direct action such as pickets and nonviolent obstruction, labor troubles, financing problems occasioned by lenders' uncertainty about the project's

---

* At a discount rate of 10% per year.

political future, slowness in government funding approval, and even the direct intervention of a legislature.*

If permits are not all issued, even though it may be obvious that they will be eventually, the project can be defeated by delay in issuing the remaining ones, especially if the project costs are increasing faster than inflation.

People are Aware of the Situation

None of these propositions is novel or, we think, especially insightful. In fact, they verge on banality, and the evidence for this is that in trying to get what they want, people in siting disputes *act* as though the preceding propositions do indeed describe other parties to the dispute! Not only will electricity consumers probably not band together and defend a project that promises very little of importance to any *single* member, but it would astonish everyone else if they did. Indeed, one reason this group does not spontaneously organize itself to protect its interest, as we will see in Chapter 5, is that each member of the group understands fairly well the incentives facing each other member.

APPLYING THESE PRINCIPLES

The remainder of this book will review the siting problem, generically and with reference to the case studies from Chapter 2 and other empirical evidence, by considering various critical actors in the process and the opportunities and incentives confronting them. We will find that a rather straightforward application of the above principles will suffice to predict the behavior of these groups and the people they comprise, and will also serve to inform the design of mechanisms that will work in the real world among the reasonable folks who live in it.

Along with this simple but sturdy mode of analysis, we are going to use two normative principles, and the reader should be aware that we subscribe to them:

---

*When a Massachusetts report on hazardous waste disposal selected three locations as well-suited to a facility, the legislature immediately passed legislation forbidding the use of those sites for hazardous waste disposal.[3]

1. *As far as possible, people should make their own decisions.* Our preference is to use *people* to describe a group of individuals and not an amorphous aggregate. We recognize, of course, that there are collective decision problems—situations in which, for technical reasons, everyone is going to suffer or enjoy the same outcome of the decision process, no matter how much we would like to provide individually tailored futures. Even an intransigent individualist must agree that we will *all* have to drive on the same side of the street if we are going to survive long enough to have other decisions to make. Since preferences differ, some people (the majority in an ideal democracy, for example) will inevitably be deciding for others (the minority). Furthermore, there are situations in which common action is enormously more efficient than individual choice: one reason we have a Food and Drug Administration is that the mismatch between (1) the "market basket" of food that would exactly match your preferences, and (2) what the government approves for sale, is much less costly to you than operating a private laboratory to test everything you eat for wholesomeness and cleanliness. Nevertheless, we see no virtue in collectivism for its own sake, and to the extent that decision-making and consumption choices can be decentralized without absurd administrative costs or inefficiencies, we think they should be.

2. *People shouldn't be punished for serving the public interest.* It is no denigration of altruism to require that social welfare not depend on it. For society to tell its members that a certain kind of behavior is (1) desired by the collectivity, but (2) will be punished when individuals display it, is a hypocrisy and an abuse of the citizens.

We will never achieve congruence of rewards in practice: some kinds of behavior, such as not littering, probably can't be obtained in any other way but by moral suasion and peer pressure. But to make the stated and accepted goals of society consonant with its reward system systems to us an unexceptionable objective.

We make the further claim for these two normative principles that they are widely accepted, at least in American society. And we infer from this acceptance that they have positive value as well: policies and practices that violate either one will be opposed by important constituencies, both in general and in particular cases; and in a democracy, this opposition will with greater or lesser success be turned to contravention of the policies themselves.[4] Entirely aside from our own preference that people should make their own decisions where possible, then, we caution that (1) the policy maker who interferes with people's independence in ways that are not widely perceived to be justified by efficiency or practicality does so at the peril of his policy, and (2) "rules of the game" that demand behavior costly to the person who exhibits it will be resisted and circumvented.

FOOTNOTES

1. C. Azzi and R. Ehrenburg, "Household Allocation of Time and Church Attendance," *Journal of Political Economy:* Vol. 83, 1975, p. 27.
2. D. Hammermesh and N.M. Soss, "An Economic Theory of Suicide," *Journal of Political Economy:* Vol. 82, 1974, p. 83.
3. Chapters 574 and 742, Mass. Acts of 1979.
4. See the discussion of "home rule" and state land planning in D. Morrell and C. Magorian, *Siting Hazardous Waste Facilities,* Ballinger 1982, pp. 49–52, as an illustration of the importance of people making their own decisions.

4
Conventional Reforms

The defects in conventional siting practice have not been a secret. Of course, deciding which aspects of current practice are problems and which are worth preserving has never generated a perfect consensus: for example, the asymmetry between opponents' ability to delay and developers' inability to accelerate looks like an unfair disadvantage to the developer; but to environmentalists it looks like a precious right by which the many are protected against the rashness of a few. As different interests have had the power to act, and as different views of the process itself have held currency, many reforms—some deliberately undoing the excesses of the last wave!—have been proposed and implemented. To put our own recommendations in context, we will review these, presenting them in generic categories and not seeking an exhaustive list.

DEFECTS OF SITING PROCESSES—A TYPOLOGY

At higher levels of abstraction, consensus increases: opponents in particular facility development cases seem to agree, as do we, that there are three ways the siting process can fail (though they disagree about which particular practices cause which failures). The reforms we review have been responses to one or more of the following types of failure: a feature of the siting process is a "problem" if it (1) decreases the efficiency of the process; (2) decreases the efficiency of the outcomes; or (3) decreases fairness or equity.

Problem 1:   Reduced Process Efficiency

A process is less efficient than another if it consumes more resources—time, dollars, emotional well-being—while producing similar outcomes. At least four conditions make a siting process less efficient.

Repetitious Testing.   First, the siting process often *requires* repetitious tests or reviews. For example, when different agencies must conduct separate hearings under different regulations, the same parties may cover many of the same issues in each. In other ways, the process can *indirectly* encourage redundant review. If a concerned public begins to doubt that developers and public agencies will fairly weigh the social, environmental and economic impacts of a proposed project, opponents will challenge as many decisions as their resources allow, forcing reviews and appeals.

Sequential Testing.   A second cause of inefficiency arises from the requirements for sequential testing. Deferring consideration of one issue until another is settled makes the overall process take longer than necessary and discourages analysis of multiple dimensions of the project. For example, Pittston Oil used a sequential and repetitive review process when trying to site an oil refinery in Eastport, Maine. It sought permits first from local agencies, then from the state and last from federal agencies. This approach deferred consideration of most environmental factors until late in the process, and also prevented lower levels of government from using the extensive environmental data produced by the federal environmental review process. In the end, the project failed because it did not comply with federal endangered species regulations.[1]

The conventional siting process indirectly requires sequential testing by leaving public participation until late in the process—after most decisions have been made without constructive public input.

Analyzing Irrelevant Issues.   A third type of inefficiency occurs when parties must waste time on irrelevant issues. Perhaps the best example of this shortcoming is the nonspecific and unmeasurable standards set forth in impact statement laws that lead to oversupply of inappropriate information. Developers and agency officials know that one likely strategy for delaying or stopping a facility is to sue on grounds that an environmental impact statement is inadequate: *i.e.,* it omits consideration of some adverse impacts. In order to reduce the probability of losing such a suit, agencies include as much information as possible in the EIS, and as a result spend time and resources on issues relevant only to litigation.[2]

Time-Consuming Individual Tests. A fourth type of inefficiency occurs when any test takes too long. Some issues that could easily be resolved with superficial analysis are given extensive, detailed study in order to make the developer less vulnerable to legal attack.

Issues that could be easily resolved with quick analysis and interaction before "posturing" occurs consume lots of resources if resolved late in the process. The traditional adversary licensing process delays public review until late in the siting process and requires that participants invest heavily in a single position *before* interacting. To resolve such conflicts requires significantly more resources than if discussion had been carried out before positions were fixed.

Problem 2: Inefficient Outcomes

Siting procedures can produce inefficient results by putting a facility at the wrong location, building it with the wrong technology, or building no facility at all when a compromise solution is actually better for all than the status quo. Many circumstances might lead to these results: standards that are too lax or too stringent, failure to consider enough alternatives, erroneous projections of costs and benefits, and poorly informed decision-makers. Posturing discourages negotiation and compromise and further reinforces a general perception that the system permits only binary choices to "support" or "reject" projects as proposed. In such an atmosphere, parties to disputes are not likely to explore tradeoffs to resolve their differences, so they are not likely to find intermediate results acceptable. Especially in cases where "no project" results, we suspect that a variety of compromises and more efficient options were overlooked.

Problem 3: Unfair Process

Fairness—equity in the economist's language—does not have the same kind of unambiguous meaning as *efficiency*. In the first place, equity is often assessed on an absolute scale, whereas efficiency only describes one option relative to another.* More important, different

---

*The "other" is in some contexts an ideal, but not necessarily attainable, set of prices and quantities, but the inherent relativism remains.

ethical systems will rank the same state of affairs in different ways, using different concepts of fairness.* Equity based on a concept of *procedural* justice bears on the justice of the distributional *process* used, rather than the results of the process. But equity can also imply *allocative* justice, which analyzes the distributional outcome of a decision as well as the process that produced it. We will usually use *procedural* fairness as an indicator of siting process inequities: (1) the process should not take something from anyone without paying for it; and (2) the process should in some sense equally consider (not necessarily *respond to*) all interests.

Current siting practice fails both of these tests of fairness. First, it often "takes something without paying for it," as in the "boom town" whose energy development consumes original residents' social and physical amenities (e.g., by overcrowding public services and causing social disruption) in exchange for little local benefit. In fact, the first public pressure for compensation arose in energy boom towns whose officials and citizens thought it unfair that people elsewhere should get lower-priced fuel at the expense of their rural lifestyle, peace of mind, and public services.

Nor does the siting process equally consider all interests. It is more likely to reflect the interests of developers, and strident or legally sophisticated special interest groups. It is not obvious to the underemployed people along the coast of Maine that failure to develop any type of facility on Sears Island represented a fair balance of economic as well as environmental interests. But environmentalists also feel they are playing with a deck stacked by public agencies for developers—that the process favors economic interests more than environmental concern.

These problems stem from four types of procedural shortcomings of the siting process: (1) the interests of certain people have been ignored; (2) participants were ill-informed; (3) even where the "right" people participated and used appropriate information, the wrong decision-making criteria were employed; and (4) previous efforts to improve the process have created unpredicted inefficiencies in the process.

The following pages briefly discuss each of these four shortcomings and the reforms designed to correct them, noting the common percep-

---

* These different concepts of fairness are discussed in more detail in Chapter 5.

tion of each shortcoming, the reform, and the effects of its implementation. We have categorized reforms according to the shortcomings each is designed to correct:

1. reforms expanding formal public participation and designed to guarantee that the process incorporates the interests of certain people previously ignored;
2. reforms leading to better informed decision-making;
3. reforms creating new regulations, designed to guarantee that participants use the "right" decision-making criteria; and
4. reforms designed to increase procedural efficiency.

In most cases, these reforms either did not have the corrective effect intended, or actually created new, equally serious problems. Subsequent chapters will suggest a different way of analyzing these shortcomings and alternative procedures for correcting them without producing these unanticipated side effects.

REFORMS EXPANDING FORMAL PUBLIC PARTICIPATION

Public Hearings

Provisions for increased public participation in the facility siting process were initially designed to give those affected by a proposed facility some chance to influence it: the goals were more efficient outcomes and, probably, a more equitable process. Reformers assumed that allowing more people to participate would favorably affect decisions by informing the siting process.

Many state and federal licensing regulations require *adjudicatory* hearings, trial-like proceedings where affected parties can *intervene* to contest proposals; very seldom are licensing hearings conducted in a format designed simply to solicit public comment on agency action.[3] Regulations restricting intervention in these hearings are typically quite liberal; for example, the Nuclear Regulatory Commission (NRC) must grant intervention rights to anyone "whose interests may be affected by the proceeding."[4] The NRC hearing process derives from one of the earliest federal regulatory requirements for public hearings: the 1957 amendments to the Atomic Energy Act required the Atomic Energy Commission (NRC's predecessor) to hold public hearings before issuing a construction or operation permit for a nuclear power plant. The hearings were expected to provide open, public discussion on potential hazards, thereby guaranteeing (1) that the facilities would be safe and (2) that the public would acknowledge their safety; hearings were mostly perceived as tools for public education.[5] A person can now participate in NRC hearings by making a *limited appearance,* simply issuing a statement of position, or by becoming an *intervenor,* a full party to the proceedings, who may make discovery, present evidence, and cross-examine.[6]

Most state siting legislation also requires some sort of public hearings: some designate the participants; others specify which parties must be notified; and others provide for hearings only upon public request.[7] For example, the Washington Energy Facility Site Evaluation Council conducts contested case hearings near the applicant's proposed facility site, and solicits comments of those opposing any aspect of the proposal.[8]

As long as the public, government, and developer shared similar concerns, hearing procedures appeared to function as planned. But beginning about 1968, intervenors began raising social and environmental concerns not previously considered in the licensing process. As a result, adjudicatory hearings became a less appropriate tool for the public to influence development decisions. Some citizens felt that decision-makers did not readily incorporate their concerns, or they felt that decisions were actually being made *before* hearings took place. They concluded that the adjudicatory hearing process was "more a hollow ritual than an effective means of citizen involvement,"[9] and they were often right. For example, a utility building a nuclear power plant has to invest extensively in a preferred site and make a firm commitment about technology by the time it files an NRC application, in order to meet projected demand and to get in line for equipment purchases. In other cases, developers have to make extensive site-specific, data-gathering investments early on in order to merely provide a satisfactory environmental impact report.[10]

The adjudicatory hearing process has other defects. First, the contest is lopsided; project opponents (relatively) lack financial resources, technical and legal expertise, and appropriate information. Nor do adjudicatory hearings afford citizens the opportunity to address generalizable concerns or join a constructive two-way conversation.

But the most important defect of the hearing process is the adversarial and non-constructive relationship it fosters between the developer or agency and the public. Contested case hearings and adjudicatory hearings embody a litigious process in which parties can only fight, not cooperate. Often, public hearings merely afford the parties the opportunity to jockey for position in the litigation that inevitably follows. The skilled advocate uses these hearings to build a record for appeal. Cooperation typically comes, if ever, only *after* the adjudicatory process has proven unsuccessful, and *after* people have already invested heavily in a single position.

Some agencies have taken steps to facilitate easier public participation by (1) increasing participation in rule-making proceedings where general safety issues are settled, (2) allowing intervention immediately after accepting an application, or (3) funding intervenors.[11] However, the last two approaches still limit participants to adversarial responses to *final* plans.

In summary, the fundamental reason public hearing requirements have so little improved the siting process—the Seabrook disaster, for example, has been orchestrated around endless formal public hearings of one kind or another—is that they ignore most of the principles presented in the previous chapter. People have better things to do than commit large amounts of time to the business of government. The hearing process, appropriate to a licensing decision rather than to negotiation, relates only to obtaining the legal right to act, which as we have seen is not complete power to act. And it takes no account of the fact that peoples' stakes in a decision differ widely.

Public Interest Advocacy

State siting laws have seldom improved the conditions for constructive public involvement; they typically restrict participation to the eleventh hour in the siting process. Very few states require public hearings on utility long-range forecasts; only a few states combine early site disclosure and early public participation (e.g., Maryland and Florida). Several states appoint one or two public representives to decision-making boards on the assumption that they, with public hearings, will satisfy any needs or demands for public participation. Another solution has been the formation of citizens' advisory councils (in Wisconsin, Minnesota, and Kansas) to give the public some direct influence in the process.[12]

Using a different approach, other states have sought to increase public participation by appointing an official as a "public counsel" representing the public interest. Washington has a "counsel of the environment" charged with advocating environmental concerns in the licensing proceedings. Both New Hampshire and Massachusetts have designated their attorneys general to represent the public's environmental concerns.[13] Such reforms seek to increase the relative weight of previously underrepresented public interests by making one official responsible for their concerns in the existing siting process. However, they do nothing to alter the noncooperative, adversarial nature of the process, and do not provide for early public influence over the outcomes. Public counsel, like intervenors, can only react to the agencies' and developers' already-firm decisions. Even state siting laws that include early warning of sites and development plans usually delay public participation in the decision-making process. California rejected a proposal to create an "environmental advocate" and adopted a less radical reform. A 1974 California statute creates a "public adviser" position, with more responsibility than the typical public counsel, to facilitate participation and to integrate it into the decision-making process.[14]

Most important, appointment of a "public interest advocate" implicitly ignores the fundamental source of the siting conflict: preferences differ from person to person, and there is no policy that is unambiguously in the interest of the whole public. The integration of different preferences and stakes is the role of representative government and negotiations; thus, constructing a "public advocate" outside the electoral process, with undefined constituencies and responsibilities, ignores the problem instead of solving it.

Participation Reforms: Review

Most efforts to reform the siting process by increasing public participation have done little more than increase public access to courts. They have inadvertently made the process less efficient and less fair, and have increased the probability of inefficient outcomes. Statutory comment periods, more liberalized standing provisions, and adjudicatory public hearings have fostered a highly adversarial atmosphere and discouraged cooperation and negotiation among interested parties. While these reforms raised expectations about popular ability to influence the siting process, public influence was "too little and too late"—entry into the process at the site-approval stage occurred after key decisions had been made and after both developers and agencies had invested heavily in particular positions and decisions.

Intervenors often find themselves no match for project proponents in adjudicatory hearings or court proceedings—their lack of expertise, or financial resources and professional skills puts them at a clear disadvantage. Disillusioned and mistrustful of a process that seems to provide them no opportunity to influence outcomes constructively, many environmentalists and local groups conclude that their only option for avoiding what they perceive as dangerous or damaging results is to use the various participatory procedures to stop the project entirely. They face an all-or-nothing situation, feel threatened and outmatched, and are highly motivated to "fight to the finish."

At the same time, developers are threatened, frustrated, and confused by the increased opposition; following the "rules" appears insufficient to assure success, so developers become determined to protect decisions in which they have already heavily invested. The participatory process and litigation have encouraged adversaries to become more entrenched, since it limits effective influence to trial-like, adversarial proceedings challenging already-made decisions.

The efforts to encourage or even force increased public participation in the decision-making process are especially disappointing because their goal is so unexceptionable. Most of the problems that participation strategies have caused result from use of highly formalized mechanisms to encourage participation, combined with a complete lack of certainty that participation, when it occurs, will have consequences such as modifying the project. We think it likely that public participation of a meaningful and useful type will not only occur, but will be demanded, by interested groups if the decision-making process is modified to allow it. Such participation is useful, and obviously so, to the potential participants, and the siting strategies recommended in Chapters 8 and 9 are so conceived.

REFORMS TO INDUCE BETTER INFORMED DECISION-MAKING

It is commonly perceived that public officials, the general public, and developers do not have enough information about the likely social, economic, and—especially—environmental impacts of proposed facilities to make wise decisions. There is also general suspicion that those providing the information are misinforming both the public and the decision-makers, either intentionally or unintentionally. How can we avoid discovering in a decade that we have done far-reaching and irreparable environmental or social damage?

Before decision-makers can reasonably conclude what type of facility, location, or operation practices are best, they need information covering all types of impacts and covering the more important impacts in greater depth. The provision of *enough,* accurate information for the political process to make a decision based on the "real" consequences of a proposal has become a major goal for reform.

Current reform in information supply is exemplified by the impact statement requirements in the National Environmental Policy Act (NEPA) and similar state acts (SEPAs). Most of these have successfully increased the volume of existing information, but have not solved the problem, since a variety of circumstances—timing, complexity, format, and source—render such information either inaccessible to or unusable by the lay reader. Information requirements have also become tools of opposition; if you don't like a project, challenge its impact statement. As a result, developers have become more concerned with satisfying legal requirements than fostering well-informed decision-making through the provision of useful information.

National Environmental Policy Act

The National Environmental Policy Act (NEPA), enacted in 1969,[15] requires all federal agencies to develop and use decision-making procedures that appropriately consider environmental as well as economic and technical factors. It also requires that all major federal actions significantly affecting the human environment be accompanied by a statement that describes (1) the proposed action's environmental impacts, (2) its unavoidable adverse effects, (3) alternatives to the proposed action, (4) irreversible and irretrievable commitments of resources, and (5) the relationship between short-term uses of the environment and maintaining long-term productivity. This Environmental Impact Statement (EIS) must be circulated in draft form to the public and among all federal agencies either having jurisdiction over the proposed action or having special expertise concerning expected impacts.

NEPA's requirements for environmental impact statements, public comment periods, and consideration of alternatives were expected to improve the supply of available information concerning environmental impacts of proposed projects. Also, decision-makers were expected to consider this new improved information when making decisions, thereby increasing the relative importance of environmental and social variables in the decision-making process. (Most state environmental policy acts are patterned after the federal act, and will not be described separately. Their special importance lies in the fact that they bring an enormous number of projects—typically, anything requiring a state subsidy or permit—into an impact statement process.)

Environmental Impact Statements

Environmental impact statements have significantly increased the volume of available information concerning proposed facilities. However, the documents have tended to be long, complicated, poorly referenced, filled with unsupported conclusive statements, and very technical. Nor does information satisfying NEPA requirements always satisfy decision-makers' needs, since it addresses different concerns or arrives too late to be of assistance.

A Washington state siting case illustrates these problems with information requirements. The Energy Facility Site Evaluation Council (Siting Council) is responsible for certifying all power plants; its mandate calls for the encouragement of power plant siting and the protection of local community interests. In order to protect community interests, the Siting Council determined that it needed more information than was typically provided concerning social and economic impacts on local jurisdictions, and adopted a guideline requiring all applicants for state certification to provide information on probable social and economic impacts of their proposed facilities. When the developer in one case technically satisfied this requirement, the Siting Council still had little confidence that the power plant construction would not create fiscal problems for the surrounding jurisdictions, so it required him to monitor the social and economic impacts and to negotiate and honor any claims made by taxing districts demonstrating adverse fiscal impacts due to power plant construction. But despite the availability of Environmental Impact Statements, monitoring reports, and socio-economic analyses, several taxing districts funded their *own* analyses of projected impacts before negotiating claims with the developer—in their own eyes, even the many volumes of required data from others were obviously not appropriate to their needs.[16]

A major component of NEPA is the requirement to explicitly consider alternatives. The environmental impact statement is to review credible alternatives to the proposed project and to demonstrate, through comparative analysis, why the proposed choice is the best. However, in practice, there is no way to guarantee that the alternatives listed by the developer are the true "next-best" alternatives, and as we have seen, a developer's process for choosing a site and facility design often produces three or four projects with very marginal differences among them. Most developers try to minimize costs, and thus want to avoid unnecessary analysis. In their internal decision-making process, to which the public is not privy, they choose one project (site and facility) to analyze in detail. They will nominate alternatives, as required by law, but the existing siting procedures and political environments actually discourage developers from revealing their true alternatives for several reasons.

First, developers have incentives to "save" their real options for later projects and to put forth either reasonable but not seriously competitive alternatives, or "dogs" whose only value is to make the preferred choice look best.[17] This strategy satisfies the legal requirements but limits the risk of having authorities recommend anything but their preferred site. Furthermore, developers face political and economic penalties for early site disclosure, especially if they do not have eminent domain power. By revealing sites in their inventory for consideration (i.e., their true alternatives), they risk public opposition at alternative sites before they are prepared to handle it. More importantly, a developer without taking power must secretly option the land at several sites (to avoid being "held up" by landowners) if he is to present alternative sites publicly. Taken together, these factors create strong incentives for developers to avoid discussing viable alternatives in their environmental impact statements.

Unanticipated Outcomes

The major unanticipated effect of NEPA has been its value as a bargaining tool for those opposing proposed projects. NEPA requirements, vaguely worded, have become a ticket to sue; information's value to decision-making becomes secondary to its leverage potential in litigation. Even if they don't expect to win a case, opponents can use litigation to delay a project, in hopes of either discouraging the developer from continuing, or rendering the project uneconomical. Where developers are extremely sensitive to the costs of delay, litigation under NEPA requirements has allowed opponents to pursue *de facto* legislation, by agreeing to drop a case if developers will conform to more stringent environmental protection standards than required by law.[18] And the legal process provides opponents an additional benefit—it can win them publicity and additional public support, and serve to further educate the public concerning their causes. In response, developers perceive these uses of litigation as "blackmail" and respond with equally strategic moves, such as announcing potentially controversial sites long before they are needed, in hopes of diffusing and exhausting opponents early on. All in all, such uses of litigation and their responses foster an adversarial atmosphere that, once established, produces a long-lasting and non-constructive spirit of controversy.

The Council on Environmental Quality Regulations

In 1970, the Council on Environmental Quality (CEQ), under an Executive Order, issued the first guidelines for the environmental impact section of NEPA; they were revised in 1973. The guidelines set non-discretionary standards for federal agency decision-making; but many agencies viewed them as advisory, and court interpretations gave them varying weight when evaluating an agency's compliance with NEPA. These inconsistent agency practices and legal interpretations impeded federal coordination, made participation by outsiders more difficult, and caused unnecessary duplication, procedural delays, and paperwork. Thus, the Environmental Impact Statement had become an end unto itself rather than a means to better decision-making.

A 1979 executive order directed the CEQ to issue regulations for all nine subdivisions of Section 102(2), rather than just the subdivision covering Environmental Impact Statements.[19] The regulations, unlike the guidelines, are binding throughout the federal government for environmental review procedures. Most of the new CEQ regulations were designed to reduce the amount of unnecessary paperwork and can be read as efforts to improve the supply of appropriate information.[20]

The regulations require that agencies keep the length of an EIS to 150 pages (300 pages for exceptionally complicated cases), emphasizing real alternatives and avoiding detailed analysis of peripheral matters. They must all use plain language, follow a clear format, include summaries, and use consistent terminology. Agencies can prepare statements jointly with other state and local agencies, thereby avoiding duplication of efforts and written analyses, and they can incorporate other material by reference, rather than duplicating everything in the statement itself. They may combine the EIS with other planning and decision-making documents where useful. These regulations replace those in about seventy other federal agencies, and thus reduce duplicated reports and provide more consistent reviews through the federal government. In addition, agencies must consider the environmental analysis as early as possible in their decision-making procedures.

The most far-reaching reform is probably the "scoping" requirement for a meeting of interested parties before the EIS is written to agree on its subject coverage. As soon as practicable after deciding to prepare an EIS, the lead agency makes public notice of its intentions and invites representatives from all affected parties (including those likely to oppose the proposed project) to participate in determining (1) the significant issues deserving detailed analysis, (2) insignificant issues deserving only a brief statement explaining why they are not significant and referencing them to coverage elsewhere, (3) assignments for preparing segments of the statements to other agencies, (4) other related environmental assessments, (5) any other environmental review and consultation requirements, besides the EIS so that they can be conducted simultaneously, and (6) the timing of the EIS preparation with respect to the agency's planning and decision-making schedule.[21]

Massachusetts has adopted a quite similar scoping requirement under its Massachusetts Environmental Policy Act (MEPA).[22] Experience to date indicates that the scoping process can constructively involve people with different and even conflicting concerns early in the process, thus reducing the incentive for, and the need to use, litigation as a means of public participation or as a method for obtaining useful information.

The importance of these scoping requirements should not be underestimated. The value of the scheme lies in its reversal of the incentives to demand irrelevant information: an opponent demanding more information than he really can use at the time of scoping imposes little delay on the process as a whole, whereas litigation after a statement is written can extend the process and increase the total project costs—an effective mode of opposition. With a formal prestatement scoping process, a *post-facto* intervenor must show that he could not have anticipated his demand at the scoping time in order to have the statement rejected, and this is a difficult hurdle. The result is to make it in the participants' interest to demand the information they really want, and not to use the impact statement process for obfuscation.

Information Reforms: Review

The 1979 CEQ regulations represent a significant advance in managing the impact statement process and implicitly recognize that the first round of reforms to improve the use of information in facility planning were imperfect. Unfortunately, the fundamental premise that "decision-making can be improved by forcing party A to reveal information to party B under the authority of party C" is based on a fundamental misunderstanding of the nature of information and its use in decision-making processes. This misunderstanding is widespread, and the issue is rather complicated; consequently, we have devoted Chapter 7 to an extensive discussion of the use of information and how it might be managed in the siting process. At this point, it suffices to note that three major failures of the impact statement process remain with us.

1. No amount of enforced disclosure of information can compel decision-makers to use what has been revealed; people making decisions and allocating their own resources are much more likely to rely

upon information that they have obtained for themselves from sources they already trust.

2. The formal requirements for information disclosure, like all formal requirements of law, create legal rights that project opponents can use as a means to delay and manipulate the process, entirely independently of the substantive result those rights were designed to secure.

3. Finally, impact statement legislation has up to now been designed without taking account of the fact that preferences and stakes for different parties to a proposal differ fundamentally, and it also ignores the principle that people have other things to do with their time than learn everything possible about a new project.

REFORMS ALTERING DECISION-MAKING CRITERIA

A third category of reforms directly altering decision-making variables includes the following: more stringent environmental standards, "demonstration of need" requirements, site banking and inventory procedures, and "local override laws."

More Stringent Standards

New environmental controls include stringent standards designed to obtain efficient outcomes by regulation, ensuring that a project failing one or more public interest tests will not be allowed to proceed, despite its private or narrow benefits. These regulations include several federal laws: the Energy Reorganization Act; the Clean Air Act and subsequent amendments; the amended Federal Water Pollution Control Act, 1972; the 1976 Resource Conservation and Recovery Act; the 1973 Endangered Species Act; and many state environmental and facility siting acts.

Portions of many state statutes are patterned after a Model State Utility Environmental Protection Act, developed by the National Association of Regulatory Utility Commissioners in 1970.[23] Well over half the states require an energy facility developer to file a formal "demonstration of need" statement, supported by power supply and demand forecasts subject to agency review and approval and occasionally to public hearing procedures,[24] and these states prohibit power plant construction unless the demonstration of need is approved.

Such requirements are intended to decrease the probability that unsafe, environmentally unsound, or unnecessary facilities will be built. While the requirements seem to have accomplished at least part of their aim—that environmentally dangerous facilities not be constructed—they have had another, unintended result: very few facilities are being built at all. People opposing facilities for many different reasons can use the environmental requirements as tools for stopping the facilities. Again, we see a familiar pattern: anyone expecting a proposed facility to impose significant large costs on him (including non-environmental costs), faced with a "go/no-go" decision, seeks to avoid the costs by stopping the facility any way he can. New environmental requirements provide important leverage for that purpose, and environmental groups attract many non-environmentalists using their organization and legal activities to protect themselves and their interests.

A factor contributing to this unexpected outcome is public mistrust of the "system": despite ever more stringent standards many still doubt that the requirements are tough enough (others, including many in industry, think them too strong). Others fear that "clientele capture," a mutually supportive relationship between developer and regulatory agency, exists and means the standards will not be adequately enforced. Mistrust of the system motivates opponents to challenge permits granted under these requirements, and with adversarial behavior rewarded, it ensures that these challenges do not commonly take the form of negotiation and compromise.

Developers don't trust the process to support them when they have properly followed all the regulations, and are wary about negotiating with environmental groups that cannot control the behavior of individual members. Regulation typically provides many additional methods for stopping or delaying construction of almost any major project, but no ready methods for resolving differences in a less costly (and more efficient) manner. Thus, in this particular decision-making environment, the more stringent regulations, combined with mistrust, increased legal leverage, and incentives for adversarial interactions have resulted in less efficient outcomes, since all options, other than no project at all, have often been eliminated.

Government Site Selection

The frustration of both project opponents and developers with the current regulatory process has, in some states, given rise to acceptance by both sides of government assumption of the site selection process itself. This assumption can take either of two forms: (1) under the first model, the government selects sites for facilities not yet proposed and goes through as much of the review process as possible before a developer has expressed interest; (2) under the second model, typically used for hazardous waste facilities, the government enters the site selection process by taking over the productive activity itself.

Inventories. At least four states have initiated procedures to inventory sites suitable for energy facilities after review of their environmental qualifications. Their objective is to assess sites without the pressures for a single "best" proposal discussed above, and to place the review before the project announcement so that it won't delay important developments. For example, an Oregon agency may designate entire areas as either suitable or unsuitable for additional facility sites.

Two New York state agencies have site inventory responsibilities: the New York Public Service Commission, Office of Environmental Planning has conducted a 12-county pilot survey for potential power plant sites, and in 1968 the New York Atomic Space and Development Agency received responsibility for developing a land-bank for nuclear sites that would be leased or sold to electric companies.

A 1971 Maryland statute[25] created what is probably the best known state site inventory program: every year the state's Public Service Commission must (1) evaluate electric company supply and demand forecasts, including their existing and proposed sites, and (2) prepare a ten-year plan of possible and proposed sites for the state's Secretary of Natural Resources. The Secretary then conducts preliminary environmental evaluations, disqualifies inappropriate sites, conducts detailed analyses of the remaining sites, and purchases enough sites to maintain a four-to-eight-site inventory. Once the process identifies a site, the Secretary must either purchase it or remove it from consideration within two years. Utilities can purchase either state-owned inventoried sites or other non-inventoried sites; however, if a utility seeks state approval for a non-inventoried site, the Public Service Commission can substitute acceptable inventoried sites should the non-inventoried site prove inadequate.[26]

Critics of the Maryland process fear that ownership will jeopardize the state's neutrality by giving the agency a vested interest in developing its own sites. In addition, utilities still choose sites for development, and they can easily ignore the state's sites and proceed through the licensing process with their own sites. The process's success rests on the difficult political balancing required to maintain the trust and confidence of the different parties; the process won't work if the utilities see it as "too environmental" or if the environmentalists see it as "too development-oriented."

A Minnesota program, initiated in 1973, overcomes many of these defects.[27] The regulatory authority itself maintains an inventory of potential sites, which it reevaluates annually by established, formal criteria. After publishing an initial list of sites, utilities must annually submit a five-year development plan which identifies preferred and alternative sites for each plant scheduled for construction within the coming five years. Any sites not on the agency's list must be justified according to the established site review criteria. Then the regulatory agency, not the utility, makes the final site choice when a utility indicates a need for a new site.

The Minnesota approach avoids state ownership (the agency lists but does not purchase the sites), provides early site review, gives the state the responsibility of choosing the site, but still allows the state and the utility to conduct separate but simultaneous site review procedures.

Unfortunately, the state site inventory process has not had a chance to demonstrate its merits, since the existing mechanisms, designed for energy facility development, were implemented just about the time that falling demand for electricity caused most utilities to put their expansion plans on hold indefinitely.

Some tentative experiments in government site selection in the area of hazardous waste facilities are not encouraging. In at least two cases, a government search for hazardous waste facility sites has been attempted—one in the Delaware River Basin region (eastern Pennsylvania, New Jersey, and part of New York State) and one in Connecticut. Both used an apparently rational process of (1) public development of a list of criteria for sites and (2) a search of the state for sites meeting the agreed-to criteria. Tentative efforts of the same kind are under way in other states; all are meeting similar problems.

It's relatively easy to achieve broad political consensus on a list of criteria ("no hazardous waste facilities in wetlands," "no hazardous waste facilities in densely populated districts," etc.). However, such a list of exclusionary criteria implies a map, and whether the government or someone else draws it, the map appears at some point in the process and focuses residents' attention on those parts of the state that have *not* been excluded by the criteria on the list. In the Delaware River Basin case, application of the accepted siting criteria restricted the search for a chemical landfill site to a narrow strip of suitable soil roughly paralleling the New Jersey Turnpike. People who lived in this small region of New Jersey have shown greatly increased interest in the hazardous waste facility development process and enthusiastically advocated the application of new criteria, not previously identified, that would exclude one or another parts of this target area. There is also widespread suspicion that the entire selection process was designed initially to target this (industrialized) region of the state.

In Connecticut, the criteria ruled out the entire western part of the state for one reason or another, and residents of the (more rural) eastern part have banded together to oppose the whole process. The general rule seems to be that rationalistic site selection by successive exclusionary judgments serves only to focus political opposition in the relatively small part of the state remaining after the exclusion process, while the broad consensus agreement on the particular criteria being used seems impossible to maintain after its implications become known.

Morrell and Magorian have considered the issue of state preemption of siting authority, especially in the New Jersey context. A principal conclusion of their investigation, with which we concur, is that the belief that state preemption of local power will accelerate the siting process for hazardous waste facilities or improve its success rate is a myth. The principal bases for their conclusion are (1) that it encourages public mistrust of the processes themselves, and (2) that public trust of the siting process is not merely a moral desideratum, but a practical essential for getting things built and operating.[28]

State Override

Another regulatory reform starts from a very different point of view by giving some state agency a veto over other state or local rulings, putatively to keep "narrow interests" from interfering with actions in the best interest of the public at large. A principal contribution of Morrell and Magorian's study is to distinguish between what we have called "Government Site Selection"—state preemption of the siting process—in which a state agency finds and approves sites independently of local authority, and override, in which local decisions may be reversed—but only after they have been taken, through a local process—by the state.[29]

Under the Michigan Hazardous Waste Law and the Massachusetts and Washington Energy Facility Siting laws,[30] a single state agency can reverse a denial (or approval) on the part of a particular government agency or a local government body. In the case of hazardous waste, the motivating fear is that no hazardous waste facilities will be built, even though some are needed by society as a whole, because communities consistently refuse to host them. The Michigan law provides for a Hazardous Facilities Board (at the state level, but including local membership for each case) to make an up-or-down decision without appeal on a hazardous waste facility proposal; it supersedes any decision of a local agency.

An alternative model, exemplified by the Massachusetts Energy Facility Siting Law, constitutes a state agency as an "appeal court" with the power to reverse siting decisions by other state government agencies or by local authorities.

The response to state authority has been almost exactly contrary to designer expectations. State agencies having override power are reluctant to use it; we know of no case in which state override has been attempted explicitly, much less advanced a particular siting proposal. Officials realize that if they try by law to force a community to accept a facility that it strongly opposes, they will simply have another bitter battle at a different level. Where use of local override has been reared, the siting process has become more conflicted and more heated.

The expectation that state (or federal) power alone will deal with local opposition is the purest manifestation of the lawyer's fallacy in siting process reform. An outraged local constituency has many hurdles to put in the way of a developer it wishes to discourage, including the threat of extra-legal opposition (lying down in front of the bulldozers), political opposition (introducing exclusionary legislation in the state legislature, picketing the governor), and legal strategies in the federal rather than the state system. Those obstacles that are based in law, such as zoning prohibitions and the denial of local permits, are only part of the complete set of potential obstacles a community can present—but they are the only ones a state legislature or the federal government can override. The use of override mechanisms thus has the effect of removing only some of the tools at a community's disposal while increasing its level of outrage and sense of mistreatment and therefore increasing the likelihood that other, equally effective, obstacles beyond the reach of the state override process will be put in place.

Very complicated strategic/political problems arise in the design of the override process. The Michigan Hazardous Waste Facility Siting Council provides an interesting example. The Council is composed of three state officials, four representatives of the community in which the facility under review is to be sited, a chemical engineer, and a geologist (the last two from the state university system). The attempt in constructing a board like this is to have "all interests represented," in the expectation that the various interests will then have an opportunity to sit down together and reason the process out to a satisfactory conclusion. In practice, this governmental mechanism rarely functions in the way expected.

In the case of the Michigan board, the problem lies in the fact that the voting pattern of this council is predictable from the beginning of the process. The four local representatives will presumably vote against a project that does not have strong local approval. The three state officials will obviously vote in favor of it if it meets statewide public safety requirements—after all, this is the whole reason for the board's existence. In the case of a hazardous waste facility, it's reasonable to assume that a chemical engineer, who believes in chemical technology and is professionally committed to rational disposal of industrial waste, would vote in favor of a well-conceived proposal. Thus, the geologist is, for *any* controversial proposal, in the position of making a single-handed, up-or-down decision. The strategic position he will confront should make any reasonable person think very hard about accepting the job; at the least, it would be wise for him to have tenure in his academic position.

Even when the representation of interests is more complicated and the board's voting patterns are less predictable, siting boards run into a more general difficulty: exactly because the representatives have been appointed as representatives of particular interests—an environmentalist, an engineer, a representative of local government, etc.—they are much less free to trade and compromise than they would be if they were members of an agency with more general powers and more diffuse responsibilities. A siting board member who happens to be very much concerned about environmental protection will hold out for stringent environmental controls in any siting board debate; but if he's identified from the day of his appointment as being "the environmentalist" on the board, it's likely to be impossible for him to make any compromise or agreement that could appear to flout the wishes of his publicly identified constituency.

The fundamental defect of increased state legal authority as a "solution" to the siting problem is that all the authority the state has is insufficient. Any attempt to use this inadequate tool is likely to stiffen the resolve of opponents to use the remaining weapons at their disposal, such as direct political confrontation. On the other hand, it is obviously inappropriate to leave all facility siting decisions in local hands when statewide or national benefits are at stake. We find Morrell and Magorian's conclusions persuasive, at least in concept: (1) State siting authority, even with local participation through hearings, etc., will make matters worse instead of better. (2) An opportunity for some entity with greater-than-local responsibilities to override local decisions after they have been made, is one important component of a workable siting process. To respect both of these conditions at once requires careful design of the siting process; in their words, "there is no easy substitute for the balance of state and local authority over siting these controversial facilities."[31]

EFFICIENCY REFORMS

A fourth category of reforms includes efforts to increase the efficiency of the overall siting process. A confusing, complex, and often overlapping set of local, state, and federal regulations govern the approval of facility sites; new regulations result in more administrative proceedings, which consume much time and other public and private resources. Each statutory reform requires additional hearings, permitting procedures, and public information; each allows new appeals, and each incrementally adds to the cost and time involved in applying for permits. Reformers from both industry and the public sector have begun to agree that many of these procedures are repetitive and that the overall process needs streamlining.

For example, when New England Electric System sought approval of a fourth-fossil-fuel unit at its existing Brayton Point facility in Massachusetts, more than 300 formal interactions took place between the utility and public officials during three-and-one-half years. The Boston Edison Company needed 46 different permits or approvals from 17 different federal, state, and local jurisdictions prior to construction and initial operation of their Pilgrim 1 nuclear plant in Plymouth, Massachusetts. A report from New England Power (subsidiary of New England Electric System) estimates that preparing permit applications for a hypothetical coastal coal-fired generating plant in Massachusetts would cost over four million dollars, take three-and-one-half years, and require permits from four federal, eight state, six local, and two regional agencies.[32] Assuming all goes well, the utility can expect to receive permits within a year-and-a-half after submitting applications, stretching the site approval process to five or six years, beginning after the utility's own site search.

A variety of private and public organizations have recommended reforms for process efficiency, including the Council of State Governments, the President's Office of Technology Assessment, and the National Association of Regulatory Utility Commissions. For example, the Council of State Governments' Model State Utility Environmental Protection Act was designed to produce more efficient outcomes, although its recommendations focus on procedural efficiency.* The enacted state reforms incorporate a consolidation of reviews, ranging in degree from simply broadening the authority of a single existing agency to creating an entirely new agency with all review authority.

Expanding Public Utility Commission Powers

A common statutory reform in eastern states broadens the review authority of the Public Utility Commission. For example, in 1969 Ver-

---

* It recommends a one-step siting process to balance decision-making—allowing the development of reliable, economic energy supplies while protecting the environment. It also recommends procedures to expedite the judicial review process of regulatory commission decisions.

mont empowered its Public Service Board to certify for all new generation and transmission facilities that additional power is necessary and that construction will not adversely affect other public interests (aesthetics, environment, public health and safety, and historic preservation).[33] This streamlining solution leaves intact the fragmented regulatory process that fosters haphazard administrative review without providing a mechanism for balanced final judgments (i.e., an overall cost-benefit analysis).

One-Step Regulatory Process

A second approach, more often found in western states, creates a one-step siting process that consolidates all review and permit authority (typically including local authority) in a single agency or council. This agency has the responsibility of balancing competing interests, and often has preemptive authority over all other state and local regulations. However, determining the responsible agency presents a major implementation problem. Requiring an existing agency to conduct new review procedures based on considerations previously outside its domain encounters institutional barriers; it is difficult to effectively change the factors influencing an existing bureaucracy's decision-making process—especially when it means incorporating factors conflicting with its previous mandate. Some states have vested the authority in a newly created special commission or council representing all regulatory agencies; however, this solution also has its drawbacks, since representatives may feel compelled to act as advocates for the factors they represent, rather than collectively so as to balance factors. A third approach is to invest the authority in a new agency, but revenue constraints due to states' current efforts to reduce expenditures and overlapping jurisdictions can render this approach ineffective.

Many states have developed one-step siting procedures under a variety of structures. For example, Washington has developed a one-step process implemented through the newly reorganized Energy Facility Site Evaluation Council representing all 14 state regulatory agencies; it prepares a Site Certification Agreement presenting all conditions necessary before either construction or operation can begin. The legislature had initially created a three-step process, but 1977 amendments transformed it into a single-step process and granted the

Council preemptive authority. The procedure has worked well to the extent that the Council can consider all factors—economic, social, and environmental—when writing the certifications: the Council has required at least one developer to compensate local taxing jurisdictions for adverse fiscal impacts, as a condition for facility operation. However, the Council has faced difficulties in implementing its mandate since the legislature has provided it a very small budget.

In combination with other essential reforms, a consolidation of the state-level permitting process into one forum appears to us to be a promising mechanism for improving the siting process.[34] At the least, it allows worthwhile tradeoffs to be made between the different interests that are currently reviewed in different fora. It may also save a great deal of time by avoiding sequential review and repetitious testing of project proposals. It has not, however, been the unqualified success that supporters hoped for; one important reason for this is that developers frequently prefer a sequential testing process that avoids the necessity of doing all the anlaysis required for a project at once; it's often cheaper for a developer to submit his project to sequential licensing, because if he fails one test, he can stop further expenditures on the project and save the cost of analysis and litigation of all the subsequent tests. If he can arrange the schedule so that his most difficult tasks come first, he will be able to devote the least possible resources to the testing and licensing process for those facilities that turn out to be impossible or ill-advised.

More importantly, one-step siting reforms have often been presented as solving more problems than they can possibly correct; often they are presented as a local override mechanism to remove legal obstacles to facility development, but instead produce greater rather than reduced siting conflict for the same reasons discussed under local override above.

Additional Streamlining Efforts

Other streamlining reforms make no shifts in authority but simply change operating procedures. Since the lengthy Storm King power plant controversy in New York involved only a single agency, some reformers concluded that consolidating authority, by itself, is insufficient and must be accompanied by other changes. Some states have promulgated new timetables for the review and permit process, not only requiring agencies to act on permits within a specified amount of time (typically between six months and two years) but also enforcing the deadline with a default provision. For example, California specifies that an application is approved *unless* the Energy Office rejects or qualifies it within two months. Another type of reform tries to make the intervention process more efficient by adopting more stringent criteria for intervenor status, by requiring detailed specifications of intervenors' contentions, by limiting discovery rights, by excluding repetitive or irrelevant testimony, and by consolidating representation of similar interests. A third streamlining effort shortens the review process; New York provides direct review by the highest appellate court.

Another type of reform seeks to reduce redundancy. Often the same issues are argued repetitively in overlapping jurisdictions, sometimes with contradictory results. In order to eliminate redundancy, some agencies are pursuing the possibility of holding joint hearings; for example, the Massachusetts Energy Facility Siting Council has decided to hold some of its hearings jointly with the Nuclear Regulatory Commission. Still another proposed reform would separate overlapping jurisdictional functions in nuclear facility approvals by allowing the state to rule on the need for additional facilities and the Nuclear Regulatory Commission to determine compliance with safety standards.

Efficiency Reforms: Review

While these reforms may have increased the efficiency of the *formal* procedures, they have not resulted in a more efficient process all-in-all—successfully siting public facilities takes more time than it did previously, largely because these reforms overlooked critical factors in procedural inefficiencies, especially those affecting the actual procedures rather than just the statutory ones. Many of these reforms reduced both local governments' and concerned citizens' leverage over the process by reducing the number of reviews necessary, the number of agencies involved, or the sheer volume of different procedural requirements, and thus effectively reduced the number of ways concerned citizens could challenge the decisions being made.

Some environmentalists and other interest groups fear that consolidation of authority will reduce the overall importance of environmental and social concerns, especially when the authority is embedded in an existing agency previously unconcerned with these issues. A plethora of reviews by different agencies represents to them a series of hurdles that have acted as a check against approval of "bad" facilities—fewer hurdles suggest increased probability that "bad" facilities will be approved. As a result, opponents have felt pressured to step up the magnitude and sophistication of their activities. Many environmentalists favor the longer, more complicated process, since it gives them time to develop the technical, legal, and financial resources necessary to battle the developer and agency more nearly as equals.

SUMMARY

The variety of siting process reforms described in this chapter for the most part represents well-intentioned and reasonable efforts to improve a process widely agreed to be not working. That these reforms have not been successful in correcting the defects of the process is evidenced by the fact that many of them were already in place for the cases described in Chapter 2. It's true that none was intended to completely correct all the defects of the siting process. But we think their failure, and the failure we expect for those that have not been fully tested yet, has more fundamental roots. The central defect of these reforms is that each is based on one or another of the widespread misapprehensions about the siting process itself, or about how people behave in it, described and criticized in the previous chapter. If the theory behind a reform does not correctly describe the real world, the process will not change in the way its designers intended, and the effects that do occur are as likely to be damaging as beneficial.

The siting problem is a complicated one and facility siting decisions seem to manifest some of the most frustrating and paradoxical characteristics of social behavior. Accordingly, we devote the next three chapters to a careful review of the three broad areas in the siting process—or (equally important) excluded from it under current practice—that seem to give rise to the most important problems. In Chapter 5 we will discuss the strategic orientation of the parties to a siting decision and demonstrate the importance of an explicit mechanism for compensating concentrated interest groups for the injuries they may suffer from a project that is socially beneficial in the large. In Chapter 6 we will discuss the theory of negotiation and the types of problems that must be anticipated before such compensation can be negotiated effectively by the parties to a siting dispute. And in Chapter 7 we present a careful discussion of information and its role in public decision-making. These chapters are necessarily rather theoretical, although we have tried consistently to embody the insights that they present in a practical and applicable form. They are the intellectual basis for our recommendations that the siting process be recast into a negotiating framework that allows each party to obtain the information that he thinks he needs, and allows all parties to explicitly balance the different kinds of benefits, to different interest groups, that different versions of a single project might provide.

FOOTNOTES

1. A. Streeter, "Pittston-Eastport: An Energy Impacts Evaluation," in *Energy Facilities and Public Conflict: Four Case Studies,* Laboratory of Architecture and Planning, M.I.T., Cambridge, MA, 1979.
2. E. Bardach and L. Pugliaresi, "The Environmental Impact Statement vs. the Real World," *The Public Interest,* Fall 1977, pp. 22–38.
3. Dennis W. Ducsik, "Electricity Planning and the Environment: Toward a New Role for Government in the Decision Process," unpublished Ph.D. dissertation, Department of Civil Engineering, M.I.T., Cambridge, MA, January, 1978, p. 232.
4. A. Weinstein, "Bases for Legal Opposition to Energy Facility Development," Laboratory of Architecture and Planning, M.I.T., Cambridge, MA, 1979, p. 24.
5. Ducsik, *op. cit.,* p. 233.
6. Weinstein, *op. cit.,* p. 24.
7. *Ibid.,* p. 39
8. Rev. Code of Wash. 80.50
9. Ducsik, *op cit.,* p. 234.
10. *Ibid.,* p. 220
11. *Ibid.,* p. 337
12. Weinstein, *op. cit.,* p. 39.
13. Ducsik, *op. cit.,* p. 339.
14. 1974 Statutes of California, Chapter 276, Public Resource Code §25222; see also Ducsik, p. 342–343.
15. National Environmental Policy Act (U.S.C. §4321 et seq. as amended).
16. This case is reported in detail in D. R. Sanderson, "The Washington Public Power Supply System Compensation Agreements," Laboratory of Architecture and Planning, M.I.T., Cambridge, MA, 1979.
17. Ducsik, *op. cit.,* p. 228.
18. *Ibid.,* p. 36.
19. United States Executive Order #11991, May 24, 1979.

20. 43 *Federal Register* 230 (November 29, 1978).
21. *Ibid.*, p. 55993
22. 301 CMR: 10.05
23. Weinstein, *op. cit.*, p. 38, fn.
24. *Ibid.*, p. 41.
25. Ann. Code of Md. §§3–304, 305.
26. Ducsik, *op. cit.*, p. 320.
27. Minn. Stat. Ann. §§116 C. 51–70.
28. D. Morrell and C. Magorian, *Siting Hazardous Waste Facilities,* Ballinger 1982. pp. 90–106.
29. *Ibid.*
30. Mich. Comp. Laws Ann. §§229.501–.551 (Supp. 1981); Mass General Laws Ch. 164 §69H; Revised Code of Washington 80.50.
31. D. Morrell and C. Magorian, *op. cit.*, p. 103.
32. Arthur J. LaCroix, New England Power Service Company, "Siting of Coal-fired Electric Generating Facilities in New England," presented to the New England Business and Economic Association, Inc., October 13, 1978.
33. Ducsik, *op. cit.*, p. 278.
34. But for discussion of the difficulties of permit consolidation at the local level, see Fred Bosselman, Duane A. Feurer, and Charles L. Siemon, *The Permit Explosion: Coordination of the Proliferation,* Urban Land Institute, Washington, D.C. 1976.

5
Compensation and Strategy

We have argued generally that the defects of the existing siting process, and the failures to be expected from conventional reforms, are due to misunderstandings or oversimplifications of the interests and likely behavior of the parties to siting conflicts. Accordingly, a close look at the people and organizations that make decisions in such conflicts will have two useful consequences: (1) ill-conceived strategies can be identified as such and abandoned and, (2) more importantly, such a description will lead to workable and effective reforms for the siting process.

In the remainder of this chapter, we will discuss the decisions facing certain of these participants—especially the decision to commit resources on one side or another of a siting dispute—and the incentives that face these participants as they decide. We will be concerned at first with the local opposition, and will see that an efficient siting process demands a program of compensation to fundamentally change the alternatives they face. The importance of this compensation is one of the central insights of the present study. Our primary argument is that such compensation is important on efficiency grounds, both as a means of making it possible to build worthwhile projects and also as a way to reveal the undesirability of many that should not be built.

We will then turn our attention to diffuse opposition. Such groups are strategically situated differently from local opponents, and a compensation program will only occasionally serve the same purpose in the face of diffuse opposition as it will for overcoming local opposition. (We will see in Chapter 7 that the management of information and the use that can be made of it by the diffuse opposition can be much improved.)

But compensation, of course, has an equity side as well, and we will also discuss the issues involved in compensation on grounds of fairness. The last section of this chapter will focus on different mechanisms for determining the amount and type of compensation. We conclude that compensation is best determined through negotiation among the parties to a dispute; the next chapter discusses why and when negotiation is a useful tool.

COMPENSATION AND FACILITY NEIGHBORS

Local Opposition and the Importance of Side Payments

Our central proposition here is that compensation payments of some sort are essential to a strategic alignment in siting disputes that favor desirable outcomes. A theoretical analysis is presented in the article, "Not on My Block, You Don't: Facility Siting and the Strategic Importance of Compensation."[1] Here we present the argument discursively.

If a powerful government agency could know all the benefits and costs of locating a facility in various locations and could choose the optimal location on the basis of a comprehensive benefit-cost analysis, resource allocation would be efficient. Unfortunately, there is no such agency, no such knowledge, and no such simple choice. Siting decisions are influenced by political pressures of many kinds exerted by many different groups, and these pressures are not proportional to the total benefits each group would gain from alternative social choices.

In particular, the *per capita* costs that a facility threatens to impose on a small number of people—especially the social costs imposed on people who live near the site—tend to be large for groups that are numerically small. For example, in the case of a hazardous waste facility, it is the neighbors who bear the risk of accidents; it is the neighbors who will have to live with disruption during construction; it is the neighbors who will have to listen to the traffic generated by the facility; and it is the neighbors who bear the risk of any diminution in property values that may result from construction of the facility.

Because they have so much at stake, each of these neighbors is likely to be willing to invest substantial resources to see that the facility is defeated. The neighbors will attend meetings, lobby regulatory officials, form opposition groups and hire lawyers if necessary to stop the project. In contrast, each of the many beneficiaries of a project—

customers, company stockholders, and so on—has only a very small stake in the decision. These people are far less likely to invest resources to defend the proposal than are facility opponents. And although the total benefits at stake may be larger for the diffuse beneficiaries, local opponents will be more motivated to take action because of their higher *per capita* stake in the outcome.

As we observed in Chapter 3, groups are not people; Mancur Olson has shown why many groups do not act as individuals would if faced with the same alternatives the group as a whole confronts. The actions of individual members of a group are predictable and we know that the likelihood of individuals taking action decreases as (1) the size of their group increases and (2) the amount at stake for each individual decreases.[2] This means that the neighbors for whom a project is costly on net are likely to invest significant effort in opposing it, while the more diffuse group of beneficiaries is likely to remain inert, reflecting the rational expectation of each member that his own action will not affect the result.

Two results are to be expected. First, each proposed site will be in danger of defeat by local opposition even if local costs are exceeded by diffuse benefits. Second, and consequently, decision-makers will apply an indeterminate devaluation to local opposition: if projects that are good (all things considered) are as vigorously attacked as the bad, a responsible government agency is correct in discounting such opposition as a discriminant among locations, and it will respond only to those groups that have the power to force acquiescence. Projects will wind up in the right place only in those cases in which might is proportional to right; in our case, only two alternatives will produce this result: (1) the political process must be altered to give government agencies the will to act so as to maximize total welfare, the power to override any political opposition, and (much the hardest part) the wisdom to perceive correctly a wide variety of economic, social, and environmental costs; or (2) we must begin to compensate the local victims of public and quasipublic investments so as to alter their strategic incentives. The former is impossible and the latter merely difficult, so we propose to compensate victims of localized nuisance costs, just as we already compensate those who suffer tangible costs when their property is physically invaded or taken by eminent domain.

Why is compensation a useful way to respond to local opposition? It's central importance is that compensation payments of various kinds, reduce the difference in welfare that neighbors expect to experience with and without the project, and thereby reduce their motivation to oppose the project. People who think a new facility will leave them much worse off than they would be without it are strongly induced to take action against it; people who each have a little bit to gain from its completion are only weakly motivated to support it. When the losers are few in number and known to each other, they also have the ability to act, while a large number of beneficiaries cannot easily organize themselves to take action. As we have seen in our examples, many of the tactics open to opponents cannot be countered by government action (picketing, litigation, political opposition), while the project developer—the only high-stakes, well-organized project supporter—is limited by law and public pressure as to the force he can bring to bear.

In many cases, therefore, organized local opposition can be expected to prevail independent of the value of the project. The only practical response to this structural "tilt" in favor of local opposition power is to change local motivation to oppose. Compensation does this by reducing the costs each neighbor expects to suffer should the facility be built. In many cases, compensation is also important on grounds of equity; this issue is somewhat complicated (we discuss the equity considerations below), but most people would agree that if people are damaged by a new development, they should be made whole if possible. Compensation also has an efficiency importance that is not as widely appreciated; if developers are obliged to actually compensate those they injure, they will be more likely to take account of those injuries in their planning than if they are merely instructed to "consider" social costs. Indeed, if a private developer doesn't plan for compensation that he must eventually pay, he could go bankrupt, just as if he had ignored construction or material costs. Thus, a program of requiring compensation payments will make facility planning more efficient, in the scene that all costs and benefits will be better accounted for.[3] Such payments may not always be worth their administrative costs on grounds of fairness alone, but if their omission means that a valuable project is cancelled entirely for want of a community willing to accept it, a strong efficiency argument is applicable. We think compensation for costs incurred by a new facility's unwilling neighbors is essential to the existence of a strategic situation conducive to good, as well as just, public decisions. Furthermore, the assumption that "costs average out in the long run" does not apply to the strategic issue.

The case for compensating the neighbors of noxious facilities is buttressed by noting some important qualitative reasons why neighbors are likely to exert power out of proportion to their numbers of aggregate risk, and should therefore be compensated.

1. The prospective neighbors of a new facility are easy for an organizer to identify, if only because they live in a known location. Most of the facility beneficiaries are dispersed throughout the region and united only by characteristics, such as occupation or wealth, that are hard to infer from visible evidence. The people who will suffer from the new plant are all lined up behind their front doors, waiting to be canvassed.

2. The members of the group are known to each other by sight: in socially coherent neighborhoods, they often know one another very well indeed. This acquaintanceship network encourages peer-group pressures, if only implicit, that discourage "cheating" or slacking in the common effort.

3. Without compensation, neighbors face costs that would take them below their original asset positions, while project beneficiaries face only opportunity costs (the failure to advance beyond their original positions). As economists say, "utility curves are typically concave downwards"; each unit of cost to losers can be expected to loom larger than a unit of foregone gain to the winners.

4. Any suspicion or resentment of government on the part of the public at large is readily turned to the advantage of opponents; public intervenors are easy to characterize in the popular media as the actions of a faceless, insensitive bureaucracy riding roughshod over the "little people."[4]

Types of Compensation

Since the strategic effect of compensation rests on reducing net costs that neighbors expect to feel from a new development, anything that has this effect is *compensation* in the sense we mean. In some cases, money payments will work; in other such payments are ill-advised, while other kinds of benefits work well. We will see several types of compensation in later chapters, especially in the case studies in Chapter 8, but some examples can be offered here.

Money. A developer can offer payments of money to local governments—i.e., tax rates for citizens might be reduced, or services increased—or he can offer to pay residents directly. Money compensates for many kinds of costs in other contexts: the publishers of this book happily accept money compensation for their costs of printing and distributing it, and the authors were compensated for their time in writing it at least partly with money. Even injury and loss of life are compensated with money, though in such cases it is usually not a willing exchange but merely the best we can do after an accident.

Conditional Compensation. Some costs of development are feared but not certain; property value losses are an example. A developer might, accordingly, guarantee property values, or offer other kinds of insurance, as forms of compensation.

In-Kind Compensation. Some kinds of costs can be balanced by compensation in kind; if a project is built on land used for hunting or picnics, the developer might acquire other land and develop it for outdoor recreation to balance the loss.

Protection. Health and safety impacts of development are sometimes compensated by providing specific protections; a hazardous waste incinerator operator might find that a host community would be reassured by a new fire engine or special training for the fire department for handling chemical fires. Similarly, a project might be monitored especially closely to identify risks while they can be corrected, and the developer might pay for this monitoring.

Impact Mitigation. Finally, some negative impacts of a development might be reduced or eliminated directly, as when a developer replaces once-through water cooling for a power plant with a cooling tower, increases a stack height to disperse pollutants, or adds stack-gas scrubbers to a coal-fired boiler.

Particularly because simple money payments are often inappropriate (recall the economist's fallacy from Chapter 3), the variety of compensation alternatives is important to consider. A formalism will help to organize the possibilities. The expected net cost of a new facility to a neighbor can be portrayed as

$$\text{ENC} = \sum_i P_i C_i - \sum_j P_j B_j - M$$

where

ENC = expected net costs
P_i = the (neighbor's) probability that cost i will be imposed on him
C_i = the cost of impact i
P_j = the (neighbor's) probability that benefit j will be provided to him
B_j = the value to him of benefit j
M = money payments he will receive

The developer's purpose for compensation is to reduce ENC; different kinds of compensation act on different elements in the equation above. P_i is reduced by some kinds of mitigation and by protection; other kinds of mitigation reduce C_i; conditional payments like insurance make P_j larger, while in-kind compensation increases B_j for non-money kinds of benefits.

COMPENSATION AND DIFFUSE INTEREST GROUPS

What about geographically diffuse opposition? Many facility siting disputes—Seabrook is an example—have pivoted on the opposition of non-residents of the site community, and such opposition has not infrequently prevailed over strong local support. When such opponents can organize themselves, the strategic situation would seem to call for compensation of some sort, based upon an argument similar to that presented in the preceding pages. Unfortunately, we have less sanguine expectations for compensation in this context.

Certainly diffuse opposition, especially "environmental" or what we may call "ideological," such as nuclear power opponents, is unlikely to be moved by offers of money. In the first place, such offers suggest selling a principle, and acceptance may hopelessly compromise the groups' leaders. In the second place, it is impractical to deliver money compensation to the groups' members or to condition it on their cooperation.

However, certain specific kinds of compensation can still be useful. In-kind compensation, which replaces what the project destroys with similar—not just equally valuable—benefits can be a practical device; recreation land might be offered (by purchase of development rights, for example) in return for the occupancy of countryside by the project. Also, the impacts of a project might be directly ameliorated. For example, one company successfully dealt with opposition to a dam in Wyoming by assuring that low river flows threatening a whooping crane refuge would be prevented by purchasing water rights sufficient to assure unchanged net flows at the critical downstream location (see Chapter 8). Other examples of what has come to be called "environmental mediation" have recently been coming to light, and each exemplifies a compensation agreement of some sort.[4]

The relatively straightforward exchange of benefits for amenity that can be offered to local opponents of a project will not translate directly into a strategy for dealing with environmental opposition. But a conceptually similar approach, where the opposition's fundamental principles are not challenged by a project, can be taken. Chapter 6 discusses such strategies.

COMPENSATION AND COOPERATION

An explicit program of compensation for neighborhood impacts has a further value in promoting negotiation, as opposed to confrontation, in the resolution of siting disputes. In simplest terms, it provides a middle ground between the positions of the opposing parties. In Figure 5.1, we illustrate the decision facing an opponent of a project that he feels will injure him. He can oppose it vigorously from the start; if he does so, the project will fail with probability p_1 leaving him where he was when he started, while with probability $(1 - p_1)$ the project will go ahead despite his opposition and he will suffer a loss of, say, 10 units. If he negotiates with the project's proponents, when compensation is impossible, the same two outcomes are available. Obviously, in this case, whether he negotiates or opposes depends on whether p_1 is equal to p_2. Commonly, a participant will reasonably assume that a willingness to negotiate will make p_2 smaller than p_1, by

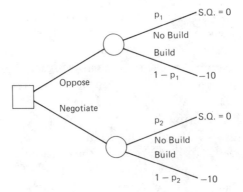

Fig. 5.1 Decision tree for a neighbor of a proposed unattractive new facility. The facility promises costs to him of 10; unless p_2 is larger than p_1 —an unlikely state of affairs—he is likely to oppose the new project.

indicating weakness, so he has nothing to lose and something to gain by adopting a strategy of intransigent opposition.

If the same participant is faced with a situation in which some compensation might be paid, the situation changes significantly (Figure 5.2). Suppose, for example, that while negotiation might lead to one of the two polar outcomes already discussed, it might also lead to a compensation payment of 13. He then faces a decision in which, depending on the value of p_3 (the probability that a negotiation strategy will lead to this outcome), the negotiation path might seem much more

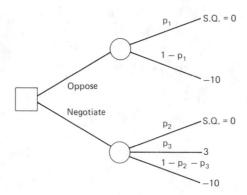

Fig. 5.2 Decision tree for decision-maker (of Figure 5.1) with the possibility of compensation that might provide payments worth 13 if the facility is built. The "oppose" branch of the tree is no longer certain to be the most attractive one.

attractive; certainly he can't wind up any worse off than if he opposes vigorously. Opposition, however, forecloses for him the attractive outcome of having the project go ahead with a compensation payment that leaves him even better off than he is at present.

Recognition by both parties that compensation might be paid for local impacts, then, introduces a new dimension into the "lumpy" set of alternatives that a siting dispute usually offers the parties: it makes outcomes possible whose values are in between the polar "build" and "no-build" cases, and, depending on the amount of compensation, makes it possible for both parties to be better off at the end of the negotiation, rather than allowing only one to gain at the expense of the other.

We have seen that a compensation program for local impacts will correct the strategic situation, allowing local opposition to be transformed into support (note again that we have not assumed that any traditional avenues of opposition open to potential neighbors will be foreclosed—or that their wishes should be overcome by authority; it is of the essence of compensation that local opposition is dealt with by making people more willing to have the project go ahead, rather than by forcing them to accept it against their will). It will also induce at least some of the parties in a dispute to negotiate, rather than to dig in their heels. Both of these results bear on the efficiency of the process; a third efficiency consequence of compensation is that it makes more of the social costs of the project in question visible, and, in fact, measures them in units that are probably comparable with usual measures of project cost and benefit. If the social costs that have to be compensated in order for the project to proceed are so high that the project shows net benefits, we will have made visible the very valuable information that the project isn't worth having.[5]

FAIRNESS AND COMPENSATION

The argument to this point has justified compensation payments mainly for reasons of efficiency: they allow good projects to proceed (by correcting strategic imbalances) and prevent bad ones from happening (by revealing their full costs). It might appear that compensation ought to be paid when practical for the simpler reason that it's morally proper to do so, but in fact, this justification is weaker than the efficiency arguments: the difficulty hinges on the imprecise and conflicting meanings of *fairness* or *equity*.

Some ethical systems determine fairness without considering any individual's status in life. It is "unfair" to take something without paying for it, even if the poor take from the rich; after an auto accident, at-fault poor people are liable to pay the damages of those they hurt, no matter what the victim's resources. Used in this way, "fairness" depends on a concept of *procedural justice* which analyzes the justice of the distributional procedures used, rather than the result of those procedures.[6]

Allocative justice, in contrast, requires analysis of the distributional outcomes of a decision, rather than the process that produces them.[7] If those hurt by an energy facility tend to be wealthy and those benefitting tend to be poor, it is probably not equitable, by this standard, to take from the poor to compensate the rich.

By any reasonable procedural standard of equity, compensation is not just appropriate but obligatory. However, allocative justice may not support compensation payments if they aggravate an unjust distribution of resources—for example, if the poor compensate the well-off. A familiar argument among policy analysts pits those who would test every program by an allocative criterion against those who think policies should be narrowly focused on efficiency, leaving allocative justice to be served by specific redistribution policies such as a graduated income or wealth tax.[8] On the whole, we favor using compensation in siting disputes for efficiency purposes without trying to serve allocative goals. But the idea of compensation is easily confused with income redistribution; in the following pages we present a careful discussion of the different grounds by which a compensation program might be justified.

Consider a project that might give rise to three kinds of results affecting populations A, B, and C (see Table 5.1):

Type I: The current status quo: no facility gets built, thereby leaving people neither better nor worse off than before the project was proposed.

Type II: With this project, there are no losers. The project is net beneficial to society, and no one suffers a net loss; some reap net gains. In our hypothetical case, A gains, and B and C suffer neither loss nor gain.

Table 5.1 Net Benefits for Alternative Projects

CATEGORIES OF AFFECTED PEOPLE	NET PER CAPITA BENEFITS FOR EACH TYPE OF PROJECT			
	I	II	III	IIId
A	0	2	3	3
B	0	0	−1	−1
C	0	0	0	−d
Total Net Benefits	0	2	2	2−d

Key:

I — No facility built
II — Project with net benefits and no losers
III — Project with net benefits and some losers
IIId — Project II with "demoralization costs" calculated (see page 85)

Type III: The project is net beneficial to society as a whole, although some individuals come out losers. As represented in Table 1, A makes substantial gains, B suffers a small net loss, and C suffers neither loss nor gain.

To design a siting process, we ask ourselves which type of project we usually want to produce. At least initially, we reject alternative *I,* given that the others have positive benefits. Alternative *III* looks acceptable because society gains, but we are concerned about the losers. We notice that merely by compensating B with part of A's benefits, we create alternative *II,* with someone better off and no one worse off. If we can change our project from one of *type III* to one of *type II* by compensating losers, should we? Three decision criteria, discussed below, can help us choose among these three types of projects.

Criteria for Choosing Alternatives

Our task is to choose among the three alternatives: *I, II,* and *III.* Note that the problem is not choosing a specific project but disclosing how projects will be chosen—in particular, the agreements, and conditions that accompany the decision. (If we decide that, in general, alternative type *II* (with compensation) is preferred to alternatives *I* and *III,* we will face another decision concerning the characteristics of the preferred compensation process.) The rationale for choosing type *II* will illuminate the preferred type and amount of compensation.

At least three different criteria can be used to compare the preferred alternatives.

1. *P: Pareto criterion.* A choice is Pareto-preferred to another if it makes at least one person better off and no one worse off.

2. *N: Net benefits criterion.* The distribution of costs and benefits in the short-run is unimportant, as long as the decision is net beneficial; compensation must be possible but need not take place; costs and benefits are expected to "average out" over many projects.[9]

3. *E: Equity criterion.* Allocative justice; we determine fairness by examining the distributional impacts of our decision.

Figure 5.3 shows the three alternatives, *I, II,* and *III,* and the three criteria, *P, N,* and *E,* for choosing among the alternatives. Each arrow points to the alternative preferred under the criterion it represents. Where an arrow points both ways, the decision implied by the criterion cannot be used in general, but depends on the case at hand.

P: Pareto Criterion.   By the Pareto Criterion, a decision is taken if it makes some people better off and no one worse off. Alternative *II* is preferable to alternative *I,* since A's benefits increase and neither B's nor C's decrease. Unfortunately, this criterion does not help us decide which of the three alternatives is *most* preferred: *I* is not Pareto preferred to *III,* since A would be made worse off; *II* is not Pareto preferred to *III,* since A would again be worse off; nor is *III* Pareto preferred to *II,* since B would be made worse off. A siting process that meets the conditions of Pareto optimality is usually impossible to implement, since redistributing benefits to hold *all* parties harmless is almost always administratively intractable. In addition, the Pareto criterion does not help us choose one process over another as long as the net benefits of different alternatives are equal and remain unchanged; in redistributing the same amount of benefits, someone must lose benefits for another to gain.

E: Equity Criterion.   To choose among these three alternatives by an equity criterion, we must be able to demonstrate that the preferred alternative leads society close to our image of a "better world" than

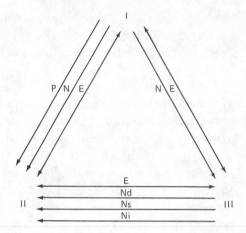

Alternative Projects

I: No build
III: Net-beneficial project,
with some losers
(without compensation)
II: Net-beneficial project,
with no losers (with
compensation)

Criteria:

E: Equity criterion, using allocative
theory of social justice
P: Pareto criterion
N: Net benefits criterion

Criteria, applying special considerations

Nd: Net benefits criterion, considering
demoralization
Ns: Net benefits criterion, considering
social costs
Ni: Net benefits criterion, considering
strategic value in implementing
project

Fig. 5.3 Criteria for weighing the value of compensation when siting energy facilities.

either of the two rejected alternatives. If we look at compensation without examining individuals' positions in life (i.e., income, wealth, opportunities, etc.), we won't know whether the people we pay (B) were wealthier or poorer than those whose benefits we reduce (A). Should B be rich and A poor, then *III* is probably *more* equitable than *II,* since it distributes the benefits to the needy (A). Should A be rich and B poor, then *III* is probably *less* equitable than II, for the same reason. Without looking at such characteristics of A and B, we don't know whether paying compensation increases or reduces social equity; without knowing *more* about A, B, and C than the way in which the project affects them, we cannot base our choice on equity.

We should avoid using the facility siting process to increase equity, *unless* that objective is clearly consistent with an overall social welfare program. Distributional equity considerations involve the whole polity and not just a limited group of people who happen to live near a potential facility site; equity programs should be catholic. We could increase the welfare of nearby low-income people, at the expense of a "rich" power company, but this would give their welfare a higher priority than the welfare of equally deserving people living elsewhere. Furthermore, if consumers pay the price for this overcompensation, then poor as well as rich will shoulder the additional cost. Efforts to improve equity on a project-by-project basis could easily reduce overall equity, unless we can be certain about the incidence of these additional costs.

Equitable compensation may imply more compensation than is efficient, and may in any case be more costly to improve welfare through overcompensation than through other social programs. Overcompensaton associates more apparent costs with a project than actually exist. It could make an otherwise net beneficial project appear net costly and thus get rejected; even the equity gain would then be lost. The complexity of equity justifies leaving it to broad, national programs and discourages it as an element of siting decisions.

N: Net Benefits. By the net benefits criterion, a choice increases social welfare if it is *net* beneficial—the gainers *could* compensate the losers so as to (1) leave the losers no worse off than they were before the choice is made, and (2) still have some benefits left over—whether or not such compensation will be paid. The alternative with the highest net benefit is preferred, no matter what the distributional characteristics; in the long run, social costs and benefits are expected to "balance out." By the net benefits criterion, *both* alternatives *III* and *II* are preferable to alternative *I*. However, it does not help us choose *between III* and *II,* since they have the same net benefits.

Considering Demoralization Costs

Our discussion has centered on whether or not transfer payments increase equity, and whether or not the process allows an efficient project to be built. However, another efficiency problem lurks beyond a particular siting decision, because of the precedent it sets. If we build a facility without compensating losers, then we reinforce the expectation that, *in general,* losers will go uncompensated. Since people are usually risk-averse, they avoid some choices that threaten them with an uncompensated loss—even when such choices are actually "fair bets." Thus, today's siting precedent reduces the efficiency of future decisions and thereby produces *demoralization costs*.[10]

Demoralization costs are reductions in future net benefits that arise because *today's* decision increases the risk associated with a *future* choice. A theoretical risk creates demoralization costs if it is great enough to cause unaffected people to choose differently than they would have otherwise.[11]

In our hypothetical situation, alternative *III* creates demoralization costs: it sets a precedent that some people come out losers when facilities are built. People don't know now whether they will fall into category A, B, or C in the future. If people think they *may* come out losers because of a proposed facility, they will act differently than if they know they *would not* come out losers. Assuming they are risk-averse, they will avoid using their resources in the most efficient way by choosing safer options.

For example, assume 100 families prefer buying a particular new home in Site City; they face the decision depicted in Figure 5.4. For each family (and society), investing in a Site City house is a more efficient choice than investing in an Urban City house. When an energy facility is proposed for Site City, they face the decision depicted in Figure 5.5. There is a 99 percent probability that the facility will not harm their preferred home—a .99 chance that they will receive benefits (payoffs) of 1. However, there is a 1 percent probability that the facility will pollute heavily and they will not be compensated; this would reduce the payoff from the choice to -10. For each family considering a house in Site City, the expected payoff to them from living there has been reduced from 1 to .89 ($1 \times .99 + -10 \times .01 = .99 - .10 = .89$). However, even with the threat of a heavily polluting energy facility, the value of choosing the Site City house (.89) is still greater than that of the Urban City house (.80).

If people were risk-neutral in their decisions, then we would expect each family to go ahead with its plan to live in Site City, since that choice has greater expected benefits. But because people are risk-averse—they avoid choices involving substantial amounts of risk and uncertainty—they calculate their presumed *utility* in the worst case (-20) as less than their actual costs (-10).[11] The expected *utility* of a Site City choice (.79) appears less to them than an Urban City choice

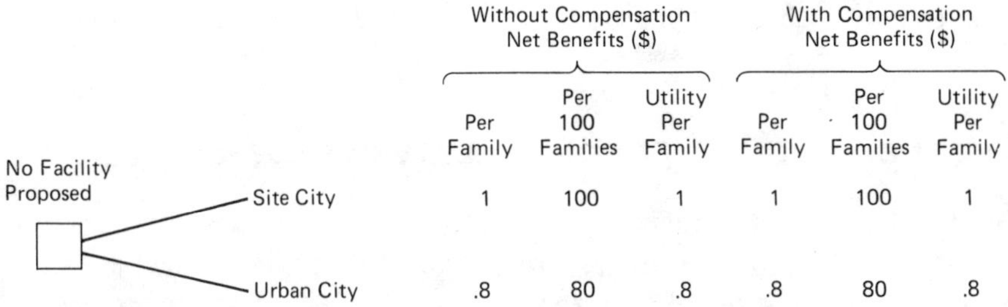

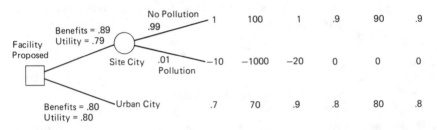

Fig. 5.4. Social choice without demoralization costs.

Fig. 5.5. Social choice with demoralization costs.

(.8); they will choose the house in Urban City and thus get less house for their money. In this case, society's demoralization costs equal 9; 100 Site City choices would give society 9 more units of benefits than 100 Urban City choices.

If society had handled similar cases in the past by paying compensation for facility costs (for example, by paying one family 10 units of benefits out of other families' gains) such payments would be expected in Site City. They would increase Site City's expected *utility* to .901 per family; the payment changes the per-family expected net benefits from 1 to − 10 to .9 and 0. Even with compensation, society is better off if the 100 families choose Site City, but they will do so only if they can count on compensation.

Alternative *III* thus imposes a cost on society equal to the reduction in social benefits attributable to risk avoidance in *future* decisions. If the true benefits from alternative *III* are reduced by d, the demoralization costs, as represented by column *IIId* in Table 5.1, even by the net benefits criterion, alternative *II* (NB = 2) is now preferred to both *IIId* (NB = 2 − d) and *I* (NB = 0), since compensation reduces risks for all people affected by a future facility. In Figure 5.1, note the arrow *Nd* representing the net benefits rationale with demoralization costs considered.

HOW CAN COMPENSATION BE DETERMINED?

Our foregoing argument—that compensation for development impacts should be a central feature of the siting process—leaves unanswered the question of how the amounts and types of compensation for a given project should be determined. Unfortunately, there is no entirely satisfactory or neat prescription for this process. We think it best that the parties to a development proposal negotiate the compensation package directly, but other alternatives are possible.

Site Auctions

In the paper presenting the strategic value of compensation, O'Hare suggested as a conceptual example that facilities might be "auctioned" off to the one community among several candidates whose bid for compensation, added to construction and operation costs on that site, gave the lowest costs for the project.[12] While we still find the idea to have merit, the legal apparatus needed to implement such a perfect market-clearing mechanism is intimidating to contemplate, and several practical problems remain to be overcome. At this writing, it remains an idea awaiting development before it can be implemented. The object of putting things where their net costs are least remains the appropriate goal of facility siting, but it has to be sought by more incremental means.

Legislated Compensation

Rates of compensation can be estimated and prescribed in legislation. One example, and it is an imperfect one, is the Massachusetts law specifying a payment of one dollar per ton of waste processed to towns hosting solid waste resource-recovery facilities.[13] (Its legislative history suggests that it was not intended to be a compensation mechanism exactly as we have conceived it.) Inflation, differences between communities and local tastes, special characteristics of different projects, and project-specific political alignments make it seem improbable that a legislature could anticipate the value of impacts to communities well enough to specify compensation that is even approximately correct.

Administrative Compensation Awards

If compensation legislation cannot be generally set, might a government agency determine it case-by-case? According to one model, taxes on the developer's activity are collected by the state and then distributed to affected communities as compensation: Montana distributes half the revenue from its coal severence tax this way. Alternatively, a regulatory agency, such as one empowered with a local override power (Chapter 3) could specify compensation as a condition of siting approval. There is nothing intrinsically wrong with such a process; presumably, the community would apply to the agency for a lot of compensation and the developer would argue for a small award. But it requires that community representatives trust the agency to make an award that they will consider fair, and it suffers from all the problems of government attempts to determine taste, values, and costs without a free market to guide it. It is also an invitation to real bribery, or abuse of the developer by agency members seeking political gain.

Negotiated Compensation

The deals that best satisfy both parties are typically those that they negotiate for themselves. If this generally applies to facility siting— and we think it does—the best way to know how much compensation is enough, and what kinds should be offered, is to let the developer thrash it out with the community directly. The main advantage of this assessment mechanism is the difficulty of conceiving anything else that can deal with problems like the following model case:

> The developer of a hazardous waste treatment facility has designed a plant that he considers extremely safe and proposes a very safe operating plan. The prospective neighbors are not much afraid it will have an accident, say an explosion, but they expect that potential buyers of their houses years in the future may fear explosion—or fear a hazardous waste plant generally. When the buyer turns up, the seller will be in no position to offer objective evidence

about how safe the plant is—after all, he will be trying to sell his house.

The neighbors would appeal to a siting board for increased safety measures, say a fire control system, that will cost the developer a lot of money before he has started to make a profit from his plant, and that will offer only modest assurance about future home buyers' attitudes. The appropriate deal instead is probably for the developer to offer to insure property values, which go directly to the neighbors' real concerns and costs him little up front. He doesn't expect the guarantees to cost him much in the future, either, because *he* expects to run a facility that will quickly establish a very good safety record.

Making this sort of deal requires head-to-head negotiations so that the parties can feel out each other's real concerns without having to perform for third parties. Furthermore, direct negotiations assure the parties from the start that they can influence the outcome directly and effectively; this assurance is likely to discourage the intransigence or stonewalling that would be rational if a bureaucrat were liable to impose an unsatisfactory settlement after an obscure and uncertain process.

SUMMARY

The discussion in this chapter has ranged widely, but specific results can easily be highlighted. Our principal conclusion is that the facility siting process ought to include an explicit negotiating process for compensating those injured by a major development, especially neighbors of the project.

The reasons for this compensation are several; most are aspects of economic efficiency interpreted broadly. In the first place, compensation will often mean the difference between being able to proceed at all with a well-conceived (net beneficial though locally costly) project and failing completely; this is a strategic reason. A second strategic reason is that demoralization costs follow uncompensated injury; compensation today can obtain efficiency tomorrow. Finally, compensation reveals costs that might otherwise go unconsidered; inefficient projects are more likely to be abandoned.

Whether compensation is fair depends on what equity criterion is to be applied. As a procedural device, it is fair; as an allocative mechanism it may or may not be, depending on the case. The efficiency criteria, consequently, are the principal support for our recommendation. Grossly inequitable compensation programs should be corrected by other mechanisms that do not incur efficiency costs.

In the next chapter, we will look closely at the conditions under which negtiations can occur; one of these is that the parties have useful access to information about the issues on the table, and in Chapter 7 we study the management of information. These considerations allow us, in Chapters 9 and 10, to present informal and formal mechanisms, respectively, under which the facility siting process can avoid the pitfalls and failures of the past.

FOOTNOTES

1. M. O'Hare, "Not on My Block, You Don't—Facility Siting and the Strategic Importance of Compensation," *Public Policy,* vol. 25 (1977), pp. 407–458. Parts of this chapter are excerpted from that article, with permission of the publisher.
2. M. Olson, *The Logic of Collective Action,* Harvard University Press, Cambridge, MA, 1965.
3. For discussions of compensation's importance in portraying social costs for efficient decision-making, see D.G. Wilson, "Pollution and Solid Waste Disposal," Boston Development Strategy Research Project, M.I.T, Department of Urban Studies and Planning, 1972; and B. Yandle, "Externalities and Highway Location," *Traffic Quarterly,* vol. 24 (1970), p. 583.
4. Wisconsin Center for Public Policy, *Using Mediation When Siting Hazardous Management Facilities—A Handbook for Citizens, Developers, and States,* U.S. Environmental Protection Agency, 1981.
5. J. Cordes and B. Weisbrod, "Governmental Behavior in Response to Compensation Requirements," *Journal of Public Economics,* vol. 11 (1979), p. 47. Presents evidence that compensation requirements do induce government agencies to make more efficient decisions (decisions that account for the real compensated costs).
6. For a thorough analysis of procedural justice, see R. Nozick, *Anarchy, State, and Utopia,* Basic Books, New York, 1974.
7. For a thorough presentation of allocative justice, see J. Rawls, *A Theory of Justice,* Harvard University Press, Cambridge, MA, 1971.
8. A. Hyllund and R. Zeckhauser, "Distributional Objectives Should Affect Taxes But Not Program Choice or Design," *Scandanavian Journal of Economics,* vol. 81 (1979), p. 264.

9. For more discussion of net benefits maximization principle, see R. Zeckhauser and E. Schaefer, "Public Policy and Normative Economic Theory," in *The Study of Policy Formation* (R. Bauer and K. Gergen, eds.), Free Press, New York, 1968; and R. Haveman and B.A. Weisbrod, "Defining Benefits of Public Programs: Some Guidance for Policy Analysts," Report #144, Institute for Research on Poverty, University of Wisconsin, Madison, Wisconsin, 1975.

10. F. I. Michelman, "Property, Utility, and Fairness: Comments on the Ethical Foundations of 'Just Compensation' Law," *Harvard Law Review,* vol. 80 (1967), p. 1241.

11. For an introduction to utility and risk-aversity, see H. Raiffa, *Decision Analysis: Introductory Lectures on Choices Under Uncertainty,* Addison-Wesley, Reading, MA, 1970. Books and articles concerned with statistical decision theory treat this matter in detail.

12. M. O'Hare, *op. cit.*

13. 16 Mass. G.L. §24A.

6
Negotiation

In the previous chapter, we showed that compensation for social costs is desirable, primarily for reasons of efficiency and strategy: both developers and opposition groups have something to gain from negotiating compensation agreements. Developers of net-beneficial facilities stand to cut project delay and legal expenses,* and if the compensation payments are large enough to more than offset social costs, local opponents may actually become *desirous* of the facility.

Notwithstanding these opportunities for mutually beneficial exchange, we do not observe developers and opposition groups rushing to negotiate compensation agreements in practice. While such agreements do exist (some are described in Chapter 8), they are still the exception rather than the rule. This state of affairs is curious: usually when two people each have something that the other wants, they are seized by an irresistible "urge to make a deal." Indeed, the inclination to trade is so powerful that the government is often hard put to prevent people from engaging in mutually beneficial exchanges that are illicit (e.g., the markets for heroin, prostitution, insider stock market information, etc.)

In this chapter, we review the theory of bargaining to better understand the practical obstacles to negotiation of compensation agreements.[1] This discussion will also illuminate the case material presented in Chapter 8, and improve our policy recommendations.

---

* If the project is net-costly, the developer, by definition, will not be able to offer adequate compensation to offset the social costs imposed by the facility. In such cases, a compensation requirement will help defeat an ill-conceived project.

CONDITIONS NECESSARY FOR EXCHANGE

Four conditions must be present before two parties (or two organizations) will voluntarily engage in exchange. First, each party must possess something to trade. Second, there must be some possible "deals" that leave each party better off than non-exchange. Third, each party must be confident that the other will honor its promises and commitments. And fourth, each party must believe all of the above conditions to be true. Failure of any of these conditions may thwart exchange.

The first condition appears easy to satisfy; it is not. In theory, all but the completely powerless have assets that can be offered in trade. In practice, however, for an asset to be "tradeable" the offeror must be willing and able to part with it, and the offeree must value it. Occasionally, these two subconditions are in conflict. For example, the potential support of a charismatic opposition group leader may be highly valued by a developer, but the power of the opposition leader may be asymmetrical: he may be capable of directing the energies of his following against the developer but incapable of delivering the support of the group.* Many leaders of modern protest movements have found that they cannot rein in their aroused groups. Similarly, a public utility financially capable of paying compensation as an inducement for facility opponents to support a project may be legally barred from doing so. In general, for an item to be tradeable it must be both valued by the opposition and alienable by the party offering it in trade.

The second condition might be thought of as an efficiency condition. The essence of exchange is that it leave the trading partners better off: a developer is unlikely to offer compensation unless he believes that the benefits it will bring, such as avoided project delay, will outweigh the costs of the compensation agreement. Similarly, facility opponents will not trade with the developer unless they believe that the package of compensation and other amenities offered by the developer more than outweigh the residual costs imposed by the facility.

Thus, the prospects for a deal may be improved either by increasing

---

* Schelling notes that the inability to act may actually strengthen the bargaining position of a "weak" party.[2] In the example above, the opposition leader who is incapable of delivering the support of his group is less able to compromise than the leader who is capable of delivering support. Once the developer recognizes such "weakness," agreement can only come through moderation of the developer's position.

the costs of non-agreement to either party or both parties or decreasing the costs of agreement. A developer can make non-agreement look costlier to opponents by convincing the opposition that he is capable of building the facility notwithstanding their opposition. He can make agreement look less costly by sweetening the settlement that is offered. Similarly, opponents can increase the cost of non-agreement to a developer through tactics that demonstrate that they can, and will, delay construction forever if necessary; they can decrease the cost of agreement by moderating their settlement position.

The third condition only matters if the exchange cannot be consummated simultaneously or in separable phases. In general, one is reluctant to enter into a transaction unless he believes that his negotiating partner will carry out the other end of the deal. If the exchange can be consummated simultaneously, then performance rarely becomes an issue. For example, the custom of paying for retail goods on delivery reasonably guarantees to both the merchant and the cutomer that which each party has bargained for. If the purchase price is not tendered or if the goods are not up to specification, then either party may void the exchange. In those instances where simultaneous exchange is not possible, society has created a number of institutions that either guarantee future performance, or render the parties indifferent to performance. These include contractual remedies for damages or specific performance, performance bonds, sureties, escrow accounts, guarantees, and insurance.

The last condition is extraordinarily important in understanding the dynamics of bargaining. The positions taken by negotiating opponents are influenced less by reality than by their *perception* of reality. Even if an objective observer should find that exchange would leave both parties better off, a deal will not be forthcoming if one party believes that it will work to his disadvantage.

WHY WE DON'T OBSERVE MORE COMPENSATION AGREEMENTS IN PRATICE

Condition 1: Possession of Something to Trade

The first condition often is not met in practice for a number of reasons. First, developers who fall prey to the lawyer's fallacy (Chapter 3) fail to recognize what they have to gain from negotiation. They systematically underestimate the power of the opposition by assuming that potential opponents can only exercise rights granted to them by law. Thus, a developer may assiduously court the local zoning board, while ignoring the concerns of what may appear to be a powerless community group. To get the attention of the developer, the community group is often forced to flex political muscle by applying pressure to the zoning board itself, by urging the legislature to impose new regulatory requirements on the developer, or by pursuing extra-legal tactics such as "lying down in front of bulldozers" in order to delay the project. In general, facility opponents usually possess a much larger arsenal of delaying tactics than most developers recognize. Consequently, developers often underestimate the returns from negotiating with what appear at first glance to be relatively powerless opponents.

Second, even a developer who recognizes the power possessed by opposition groups may not recognize that this power may be turned to his advantage. Facility opponents often appear to be irrational, inflexible, and unyielding. Only the shrewd developer can distinguish between positions taken out of ideological fervor and commitment—from which retreat is unlikely—and the posturing and hyperbole that merely precede serious negotiation and bargaining. If a developer is seriously interested in testing the willingness of his opponents to trade, then he must package alternatives in a way that encourages compromise. As we noted in Chapter 5, if opponents perceive that only two alternatives are under consideration—the status quo and the project as envisioned by the developer—they will have little incentive for anything but obstruction. Unless a developer has something to trade (compensation) opposition groups will have little incentive to negotiate. And similarly, unless opposition groups make it clear that under the right circumstances they would be willing to drop their opposition (or throw their support to the developer) a developer will have little incentive to negotiate.

Third, the developer who recognizes the gains to be had from negotiating with the opposition still faces an interesting strategic problem: with whom does he negotiate? In theory, the developer should invest in compensation to the point where the last dollar expended on compensation yields exactly one dollar in reduced project expenses, the reduction in expenses coming from foregone project delay. Having stated the obvious, we still have not helped the developer very much. He still does not know whom he should compensate first or last. One is tempted to suggest that he allocate his compensation expenditures by compensating the individuals (or institutions) in question in order of the ratio of benefits to costs. In other words, the first person compensated should be the one who will most reduce project delay per dollar of compensation. But this approach is not particularly useful unless the developer has very good knowledge of the shape of both the marginal benefit and cost curves for each possible investment in compensation. In practice, this knowledge is extremely difficult to obtain, if only because the shapes of the curves vary as a function of the developer's actions.

Expenditures for compensation are intended to neutralize the potential opposition of those compensated. Unfortunately for the developer, however, such expenditures often also influence the preferences of the groups that have not received compensation in a rather perverse way. To the extent that compensation rewards individuals or groups that are obstructionist, it may actually encourage other groups or individuals to exercise legal or political leverage over the developer in the hope of receiving similar rewards.* Thus, the mere act of entering the marketplace bids up the price of avoiding delay.

In effect, the developer faces a rather unusual "commons" problem. To potential project opponents, profits that might be redistributed through compensation represent a "common property resource"; it is impossible to prevent each potential opponent from acting in an obstructionist manner so as to lay claim to a portion of the money available for compensation. Not surprisingly, people will exaggerate the degree to which they oppose the project, and thus quickly exhaust the common. Thus, a developer may rationally decide not to compensate because every method he has at his disposal for identifying the shape of the marginal cost and benefit curves for investments in compensation may render compensation non-economic.

Finally, even when trading partners can be identified (for example, when the opposition consists of a well-organized environmental group or a city or town) the developer may find that their support is not for sale. Many environmentalists, for example, will refuse to exchange en-

---

* A developer willing to compensate individuals to obtain their support is in a similar position to a developer trying to assemble a large parcel of land from a group of landowners; public knowledge of his actions may drive the price of the land up to a point where the project is no longer economic. Unlike the real estate developer, the developer interested in compensating to avoid project delay cannot easily hide his intentions.

vironmental degradation for other amenities, because such an exchange conflicts with firmly held ideological beliefs. Some people believe that natural objects such as trees, animals, rivers, and mountains have value independent of the value placed on them by mankind.[3] According to this philosophical position, man is a guardian or steward for natural objects; his superior intelligence imposes a duty on him to protect the right of these objects to exist, even if he does not value them himself. It is inconsistent for an environmentalist who sees himself as an agent of nature to willingly exchange damage to the environment for compensation or other amenities directed at humans. If the environmentalist truly believes the agency theory of intervention, he will consider the offer of compensation akin to a bribe that would induce him to abandon the interests of his principal. Only if the compensation is directed at the environment itself (e.g., the developer offers to reforest the land, or restock a stream, or create a wildlife preserve) will the environmentalist go along.

Environmentalists are not the only people who may characterize compensation as bribery. In almost every non-economic discussion of compensation for development impacts we have witnessed, someone has proclaimed such a strategy to be a thinly veiled effort to "buy off the opposition" and hence, immoral. (Interestingly, when opponents of a facility suggest that they might be willing to live with it if the developer sweetened the pot a bit, the developer often characterizes the request for compensation as "extortion.")

It is difficult to explain why offers or requests for compensation are greeted with moral outrage. The characterization of compensation as a "bribe" is flatly incorrect: a bribe is a *secret* payment to an individual that influences a decision that is supposed to be made according to criteria other than the personal utility of the decision-maker without revealing the influence. Since we expect the public's participation in the political and legal process to be motivated by concern for individual utility, efforts to influence this utility cannot be characterized as bribes. Moreover, reluctance to entertain trades of one type of amenity (e.g., quiet, uncongested streets, clean air, etc.) for another (e.g., money, a park, a wildlife preserve) is particularly puzzling in light of the fact that people appear to make such tradeoffs all the time. For example, the family that chooses to buy a large house on a noisy street typically does so because it values space more than it values quiet. Nonetheless, people may be willing to make some kinds of trade implicitly even though they find the same deals repugnant when offered explicitly. For example, heavy cigarette smokers are thought to lose five to seven years of life on average because of their habit. Most such smokers would refuse any amount of money for the loss of five years of life. Yet these same individuals often admit that they would willingly give up smoking if someone offered them enough money, say $100,000. When confronted with the inconsistency between the finite value they place on the benefits of smoking, and the infinite value they place on its costs, most smokers just shrug and go on smoking. The general point is worth emphasizing: in many cases environmental amenities, especially those associated with human health, many not be tradeable because the process of placing an explicit valuation on them is morally offensive to those involved.

Condition 2: Exchange Leaves Both Parties Better Off Than Non-Exchange

The efficiency condition can be violated in at least two ways. The first is a trivial restatement of the condition itself; sometimes no option exists that would leave both parties better off than non-exchange. The second way this condition may be violated is more subtle; if many different groups or individuals must agree on what it means to be "better off," consensus can be thwarted if each group or person has a different marginal rate of substitution between the disamenities to be visited upon them and the compensation offered in their stead. For example, some members of a group may prefer to receive cash, while other members may prefer a recreational facility donated by the developer. Unless the group can achieve consensus, a deal is not likely to be forthcoming. This problem does not arise if the developer is capable of recreating the status quo. For example, if the only adverse impact of the proposed facility is to increase the demand for fire services in the community, the developer could recreate the status quo by endowing the purchase and operation of additional firefighting equipment. In effect, the status quo is a focal point from which any departure requiring consensus is difficult.*

---

* The importance of the status quo as a focal point is illustrated by an apocryphal anecdote from Germany. When a strip mining project approaches a town underlain by lignite, the law requires that the town be moved and reconstructed. Notwithstanding the fact that such a move provides an opportunity to correct several centuries of accumulated city planning mistakes, the towns are usually reconstructed as they originally appeared. The explanation is that residents can never agree on a single way to modify the town plan, even though each finds the existing plan defective in one way or another.

Condition 3: Agreement Will Be Honored

In practice, contracts are the primary vehicle used by developers and facility opponents to guarantee future performance. Thus, in return for compensation, a developer would seek a contractual pledge from facility opponents to forbear from pursuing litigation or political opposition to the facility. If potential opponents are very numerous, it may be impractical for the developer to negotiate individual contracts with each opponent. Instead, he may be forced to negotiate with an organization that represents the interests of the many opponents—an environmental group, for example. A contract negotiated by such a group, however, is not binding on the individual members of the group unless they actually signed the agreement themselves. It is only binding on the group in its organizational capacity. Consequently, a disgruntled member who dislikes the deal struck with the developer may always resign his membership and pursue legal or political opposition against the facility in his own name.

The legal principles just described may frustrate the negotiation of some compensation agreements. Recall our behavioral principle, "Groups are not people" (Chapter 3). The preferences of diffuse groups are not homogeneous; people adhere to beliefs with varying degrees of conviction. When a group takes a position opposed by a significant minority, it may encourage the minority to leave the main group and form a new interest group to champion the minority position. For example, Friends of the Earth split off from the Sierra Club in 1969 due to ideological differences over nuclear plant siting. Similarly, when the Massachussetts Wildlife Federation struck a deal with the developer of the Pilgrim II nuclear plant to abandon its opposition for a wildlife monitoring program funded by the developer, two subgroups threatened to withdraw from the Federation, one because it believed the original opposition to be unwarranted and the other because it found the settlement unacceptable.[4] Consequently, if a developer wishes to insulate himself from lawsuits by negotiating a compensation agreement, the agreement must be acceptable to all coalitions within the negotiation group that have the financial, legal, and organizational resources necessary to maintain a suit.*

---

* Not everyone can bring a lawsuit. A plaintiff must first demonstrate that he has legal standing to sue. That is, he must be able to demonstrate that a legally recognized injury has been suffered and that he is among the injured. In recent years, however, the courts have relaxed the barrier

When developers negotiate with cities and towns, a similar problem arises. Many states have common law rules that limit the capacity of local governments to enter into contracts in which they agree to confer regulatory approval (a zoning variance, for example) in return for compensation offered to the contracting government. The rationale for this rule is that the government should be free to act in the public interest at all times and that private contracts which constrain the government's future choices are against public policy. It is this rule that continues to frustrate contract zoning in many jurisdictions. In practice, the rule may leave a developer uncertain as to whether a government may actually fulfill its promises even if the developer lives up to his part of the bargain. For example, a new mayor unhappy with the deal struck by his predecessor may rely upon this rule to withhold the agreed regulatory approval, thus unraveling the prior agreement. If the uncertainty introduced by this "no contract" rule is sufficient, it will discourage developers from entering into agreements with local governments.[6]

Condition 4: The Parties Perceive the Above Conditions to Be True

As the discussion at the beginning of this chapter suggested, the bargaining position of any party will be shaped by his or her perception of reality, not by reality itself (whatever that is) or an expert's perception of them. Consequently, in practice we may observe people opposing a hazardous waste processing facility because they fear the facility may someday spontaneously explode even though any engineer will agree that such an explosion is chemically impossible given the properties of the materials being processed. Developers love to swap stories about how irrational fears often constitute the basis of facility opposition. Usually such stories are immediately followed by the refrain, "if only people understood the impacts as well as I, they would not oppose us."

We find this situation perplexing. Notwithstanding efforts by the government to inform the public through public meetings and impact statements, and notwithstanding efforts by developers to educate the uninformed, people still complain that they lack the information

---

posed by standing requirements to suits based on claims that an environmental impact statement was deficient or that the relevant regulatory authority followed improper procedures in approving the facility.[5]

needed to intelligently evaluate the consequences of a new facility. In fact, it often appears that efforts by the government and developers to close the information gap often make matters worse, not better. Public meetings are divisive, impact statements are unreliable, and information proffered by a developer is characterized as self-serving and not to be believed. If people cannot determine to their own satisfaction how a new facility will affect their lives, they are unlikely to voluntarily enter into compensation agreements. In such situations, the parties are more likely to argue endlessly over the extent of the impacts than they are to bargain intelligently over the level of compensation to be paid for those impacts. In the chapter that follows, we explore the role of information in the bargaining process in more depth.

SUMMARY

Parties to a siting dispute have good reasons to negotiate a deal, but important obstacles must be overcome before they can do so. These obstacles can be removed, in many cases, by actions on the part of one or another party, or by government in setting the rules of the game. The rarity of negotiated settlements in current practice is both cautionary—reminding us that compensation will not just happen because someone points out how useful it is—and instructive—allowing us to identify the specific reforms that would encourage it. These reforms will be detailed in Chapters 9 and 10.

FOOTNOTES

1. For an extensive discussion of negotiation, see R. Fisher and W. Ury, *Getting to Yes,* Houghton Mifflin, Boston, 1981, and H. Raiffa, *The Art and Science of Negotiation,* Harvard University Press, Cambridge, 1981.
2. T. C. Schelling, *The Strategy of Conflict,* Oxford University Press, New York, 1960.
3. C. Stone, "Should Trees have Standing?—Towards Legal Rights For Natural Objects," *Southern California Law Review,* vol. 45 (1972), p. 450.
4. "The Pilgrim II Nuclear Power Plant," in L. Bacow and D. Sanderson, *Facility Siting and Compensation: A Handbook for Communities and Developers,* M.I.T. Energy Laboratory, August 1980.
5. For a full discussion, see R. Stewart, "The Reformation of American Administrative Law," *Harvard Law Review,* vol. 88 (1975), p. 1699.
6. This problem is reviewed at length in D. Kretzmer, "Legal Problem of Binding Communities to Compensation Agreements for Adverse Effects of Energy Facilities," Laboratory of Architecture and Planning, M.I.T., 1979.

7
Information

If people are to bargain intelligently over the distribution of benefits from a facility, they must know what the facility will do, how it will operate, and how it will affect the natural and human environments. Moreover, because negotiations are likely to encompass mitigation measures, this must be known for a number of different versions of the proposed facility. For example, neighbors of a coal-fired electric generating station, will want to know how the quality of their air is likely to be affected by each of such possible pollution control measures as low-sulfur coal, electrostatic precipitators, and flue gas desulfurization.

Presently we try to generate this type of information through the environmental impact assessment process. The federal government and many state governments make available to the public reams of information about impacts associated with major developments. Notwithstanding these efforts, actors in the siting process still commonly complain that they lack access to the "right" information. They criticize impact statements for being too long, unreadable, late, and not responsive to the needs of information consumers. When impact statements are read, they are often not believed. Charges of bias are common. Moreover, in many cases, the impact assessment process itself has become a focal point for opposition: if you don't want a new regional landfill (or prison, airport, or low-income housing project), good tactics require that you (at least) challenge the legal sufficiency of the environmental impact statement.

In this chapter, we examine several unique properties of information that give rise to the problems described above. After we have explained why our existing mechanisms are unsuited to the task of informing the siting process, we will outline an improved information process.[1]

UNDERSTANDING THE FAILURES OF IMPACT ASSESSMENT

To understand why the impact assessment process has been subject to such intense criticism, we must first understand something about the nature of information, because it is fundamentally different from most other goods we consume. We rarely consume information for its own sake. Rather, we desire information because it helps us make a decision. For example, most people would care little to know to the foot the exact location of a new highway. For the homeowner whose front lawn may be condemned to make way for it, however, such precise information is enormously valuable because it will help him decide whether to support or oppose the project. This brings us to our first important observation about information.

Observation 1: Each User of Information Has His Own Information Requirements

Everyone involved in the siting process is interested in different things. In general, each wants to know how a new development will affect him personally. Thus, a fisherman may be interested in the impact of a new oil refinery on fishing, a banker may want to know how it will affect local economic conditions, and a parent of school-aged childen may be interested in whether the influx of new workers and their families will overcrowd the town's schools.

Information demands vary not only by content, but also by quantity. For example, people who have already made up their minds are generally not interested in obtaining new information. Information generally is not valuable if it merely reconfirms a prior belief: the banker may not waste his time reading another report on the likely impact of the refinery on local employment if he already has a good idea what that impact will be. (If the report corrects an erroneous opinion, it may be very valuable. Unfortunately for the banker, however, he cannot tell how valuable the report will be until after he has read it.) Finally, we note that people may not be interested in consuming information if they believe that their opinion is unlikely to make a difference even if they change their minds. The parent concerned about the impact of the refinery on school enrollment may rationally decide not to read a report on the subject if she believes that the oil refinery is unstoppable no matter what she does.

Such differences explain why impact statements are simultaneously criticized for being too long and too short. By assembling "all the information" about a project into one massive document, an impact statement tells each person a lot about aspects of a project that affect him very little. And since an impact statement generally is not written to respond to the needs of any particular group, it often does not provide enough information to satisfy the needs of any one individual. The EIS tells a parent too much about the problems of bankers and fishermen and not enough about the problems of parents.

Complicating matters still further is the difficulty writers of impact statements have in knowing whether they are doing a good job by observing the consumers of their product. Usually, when a producer manufactures something that consumers find undesirable, he is stuck with a large and growing inventory which signals that his product is not meeting the test of the market. But unconsumed information does not create physical inventories. Since the EIS writer cannot observe whether the information he is providing is being consumed, he cannot tell when he should alter his practice to be more responsive.

Instead, impact statement writers respond to the demands of courts that ultimately certify the legal sufficiency of the document. Thus, we wind up with long, boring, unreadable documents whose organization reflects the requirements of the law that mandate their production.[2]

The impact assessment process is also criticized for producing biased documents. Frequently, both sides of a siting dispute make this criticism and call for "better" or "more objective" analysis. What most parties in this debate fail to recognize is that a certain amount of bias in impact assessment is inevitable. This brings us to our second major observation about information.

Observation 2: Objectivity is in the Eyes of the Beholder

Assessing the future consequences of a new development is necessarily a value-laden process. Each step in the process demands judgment by the analyst, and it is the exercise of this judgment that renders the analyst vulnerable to charges of bias. For example, a common criticism is that the analyst has cast his net too narrowly—i.e., he has not described all of the consequences of the proposed project. But consider the problem faced by the analyst who possesses scarce resources and a finite amount of time. Which impacts should he address? Frequently the potential range is limitless; construction of a new power plant, for example, will obviously affect the local natural environment. It may damage flora and fauna and contribute to air pollution. But the plant will also have some less obvious effects. The influx of new construction workers may bid up prices and rents in neighboring communities. The increased mining required to provide coal for the plant may stimulate economic growth in a distant mining region. The additional mining may also adversely affect the health of miners in the area. The cheap power made available by the plant may encourage additional development in nearby rural areas with consequent social and environmental impacts.

It is possible to keep working back through this range of probable impacts almost indefinitely, as causes unravel like a knitted fabric. Given limited resources, we cannot examine all potential impacts. We must somehow seek to identify the most important impacts. But as the previous discussion has already noted, each group participating in the siting process is likely to have a different view of what is important. To the extent that the impact statement slights any of these views, it is open to charges of bias.

The need for judgment is not limited to defining the boundaries of analysis. Virtually every aspect of impact assessment, from specifying alternatives to predicting impacts to balancing competing interests, requires the analyst to make subjective decisions and to exercise judgment.[3] If these decisions reinforce the parochial interests of a particular group in the siting process, the group will view the analysis as "objective." If not, the analysis is likely to be criticized as biased. Thus, we should not be surprised that the mechanism we use to inform the siting process often raises more questions than it answers. We have designed an information process to produce a single correct answer but failed to recognize that the questions we ask of this process defy purely objective responses. If little turned on this analysis, people might accept it uncritically. But in practice, the stakes are sufficiently large that close scrutiny should be expected.

Moreover, we note that even if such analysis could survive such scrutiny unscathed, it still would not be persuasive to those disadvantaged by the recommended outcome. The person who has the misfortune to live next to the site of the nation's first high-level radioactive waste repository is unlikely to feel good about the siting decision even if it is supported by a thorough, objective, technically sound study prepared by the National Academy of Sciences. If decisions impose social costs on people, we should expect them to protest notwithstanding the quality of the supporting analysis.

While an impact statement may be closely read by people (or their lawyers), seeking to block a particular project, it is generally true that the public at large ignores such documents. Even statements that are well written, well indexed, and that contain little technical jargon don't attract an audience. This situation is puzzling and frustrating to people who write the documents but perfectly understandable in light of another unique property that distinguishes information from other goods.

Observation 3: The Value of Information is Difficult to Ascertain Prior to Consumption

In deciding whether to purchase a particular good, a consumer usually compares the benefits provided by the good with its costs. For most purchasers, this comparison is made very quickly with little explicit analysis. The value of the prospective purchase is usually ascertained by reference to past experience ("I really enjoyed the last meal I had at that restaurant"); experiences of others who share tastes ("My brother ate there and said it was very good"); by observing the consumption patterns of others ("That restaurant always has people waiting to get in, so it must be good"); or by seeking expert advice ("The restaurant critic for the *Times* gave it four stars"). Most of these strategies for ascertaining the value of a product work poorly when the product in question is information.

In terms of frequency of consumption, the decision to read an impact statement is more like buying a house than deciding where to have your next meal; most people don't have occasion to do it very often; hence they don't have a large range of past experience to draw upon.* Even if they did, they would find that impact statements (and the decisions they inform) differ sufficiently that it would be difficult to assess the value of the next impact statement from past experience. More-

---

* Even the homebuyer has spent his life in houses, his own or other people's.

over, while a consumer may be able to evaluate the quality of the consultant who drafted the statement, he still will not be able to determine whether the information contained within will be useful without first reading (consuming) the document.

Since the value of the same piece of information will vary substantially from consumer to consumer because of different interests, prior knowledge, and so on, it is difficult for an individual to rely on the experiences of others in deciding whether an impact statement is worth reading. Similarly, because consumption of information is not observable in the conventional sense, one cannot assess the value of information by judging its popularity. Finally, it is hard to rely upon the judgment of a critic in deciding whether to read an impact statement because even if such a critic existed, he could only evaluate the technical merits of the document, not whether it is informative given the background and interests of the consumer in question.

If consumption of information were costless, the difficulty of ascertaining the value of information prior to consumption would not be a problem. At a zero price, all information (including information that was only marginally beneficial) would be consumed. But consumption of information is not costless, even if the money price of obtaining the document is zero. It takes time to consume information and given the uncertain value obtained in return, the rational consumer may decide that time devoted to the decision in question would be best spent trying to influence the likelihood of his preferred alternative. So instead of reading a long report that describes the noise impact of a new airport, one may be wise, instead, to write his congressman to protest the decision to site a "noisy" airport nearby.

A TYPOLOGY OF INFORMATION CONSUMERS

If consumers underinvest in information for the reasons noted above, how do they come to hold the beliefs that they do? In our case studies, we have identified six types of information users. We cannot estimate the frequency with which each type is met, but every one is encountered in almost every real dispute. Though the categories overlap, they will serve as useful behavioral pattern summaries.

1. Some participants behave in a way that could be called rational even in the narrowest sense. These *fact respecters* form their opinions,

insofar as they can, on substantive information concerning a proposal at hand and expect to do their own analysis of the data they collect.

2. *Expertise takers* adopt opinions (usually a "favorable" or "unfavorable" view) of a particular proposal from other individuals who presumably have special expertise in the area of concern. While these participants think rational analysis appropriate to the decision, they do not expect to perform the analysis themselves. They accept the result of an analysis performed by someone whose conclusions they have already determined to accept.

Within this category, two types of expertise takers can be distinguished. The *rational* expertise takers select the expert they will attend to on the basis of specific criteria, probably taking into account education, employment, access to information, honors, and distinctions. Another type of expertise taker looks for an expert with some *official* approval, perhaps an agency of government. A participant of this type is more likely to be impressed by the Staff Director of the President's Commission on Energy Safety than by one professor of nuclear engineering among many others.

3. Another type of participant forms his opinion as an *attitude taker;* again, two classes can be distinguished. *Ideology takers* weigh more heavily outcomes that reinforce their previously established ideology. For example, a project widely promised to provide more jobs will be favored by those who think unemployment is an important goal to serve. We shouldn't be surprised to find attitude takers of this type ready to accept a project which promises high employment, even if the promise can be demonstrated to be unlikely of fulfillment. The distinguishing characteristic is that a desire "that the things that happen be good ones" swamps the participant's interest in "whether the good things will happen at all." (While most of the information users in this list are arguably acting rationally, ideology takers may not be: if their approach is simplified to "caring about values rather than probabilities," it seems to be irrational in the same way as an effort to determine which blade of a pair of scissors does the cutting.)

4. Another type of attitude taker, a *leadership taker,* adopts the position of a publicly visible individual whose ideology is known to be sympathetic on other issues, but without a review of the facts of the case at hand.

5. A fifth important category of participants can be called *majority viewers.* Members of this group take their positions from the "pre-

dominant" view of certain groups of individuals; when a bandwagon comes by, they jump aboard. The particular majority chosen may differ from one person to another. For example, some people will adopt the opinions of their friends or peer groups; if three out of four people in the carpool oppose a new power plant, the decision-maker will oppose it also. Another kind of majority viewer looks for the dominant view in a local or national polity; the sentiment at town meetings or the results of a public opinion poll will influence such a participant to join the revealed majority.

6. Participants in the last category take their opinions from an individual or individuals on entirely personal grounds. These *personality takers* are to be distinguished from the *leadership takers* described under number 4 by their lack of interest in expressly ideological or public interest concerns; they follow a particular opinion leader because they "like him" in an irreducibly personal rather than ideological or rational way.

Every one of these approaches to information use represents an effort on the user's part to balance the cost of obtaining information of various types and at various levels of detail against the benefits to be obtained by doing so. They are roughly ordered on a scale of decreasing predicted value of analysis: the fact respecters invest the most resources in obtaining data, making their own models, and doing their own analysis; the expertise taker invests—perhaps once for several decisions—in an evaluation of experts, and then uses the experts' conclusions; majority viewers and personality and leadership takers commonly use easily obtainable information about sources of opinions and then adopt conclusions at second hand. Not only individuals, but also agencies and firms can be placed in one of these categories; government agencies usually have special responsibilities to behave like fact respecters (and also to collect data on preferences of affected populations).

Discussing the interpretation of a survey research project studying voters, Popkin *et al.* constructed a model of voters' use of party affiliation and ideology in obtaining information about a particular candidate's future performance that recognizes the efficiency problems we have described:

> . . . the voter is using his vote as an investment in one or more collective goods, made under conditions of uncertainty with costly and

imperfect information. As an investor, the voter is concerned with outputs and because the outputs are collective goods there is incentive to be a free-rider and pass the responsibility to others to inform themselves. Combined with the costliness of information, this leads to the use of information cost-saving devices like party, ideology, or demographic characteristics despite the voter's focus on the candidate himself and not just his party.[4]

The argument has a close parallel in the debate over citizen participation in planning decisions. Planners have vigorously and successfully advocated allowing parties "most affected" by various public decisions to be involved in the planning process, only to be perplexed at the tendency of people to display "apathy" towards the opportunities so created. What often happens is that the project or proposal "most affects" the planners (in fact, it occupies their whole attention!) and a few special interests, and its consequences for the community are so widely diffused that the value of involvement for any individual is probably quite small. The *individual* members of the community in such cases are not well advised—at least as regards their respective self-interests—to invest much effort in being informed or in other participation.

Recognition that much information is a public good, and a less frequently explicit realization of the efficiency (for the many individuals who see only modest gains and losses at stake) of ignoring public choices, is presumably why we delegate some decision-making to governments in the first place. In cases in which it's not worth anyone's while *in particular* to invest much effort in a problem, but in which much is at stake for the society *as a whole,* we invent, fund, and empower a government agency to perform expert evaluations and make choices. These services have probably failed, as accused, but the principal failure is one of imperfectly obtaining or integrating information about preferences, and not one of depriving the people of influence.

Interesting indirect support for this perception is found in such studies as Stewart and Gelberd's demonstration that public officials predict the judgments (preferences) of relevant interest groups very badly, suggesting ignorance that could only damage their ability to serve their decision-maker function.[5] Regulatory agencies are to some extent "captured," of course, but accusations of favoritism also affect planning agencies, and government units such as legislatures with very broad constituencies. In such cases, the institutional design errors that cause the wrong interests to be served are more subtle than simply allowing a concentrated interest group to shoulder the public interest aside.

An important class of such errors is the design of information management systems for public choice that ignore the properties of information elucidated above. A public involvement process constructed as though everyone is a fact respecter will not work in the real world as the designer expected it to. But even if an affected party involves himself in a public decision and is willing to commit enough time to make a difference, there are paradoxical properties of information that will discourage its use. One of these is the positive feedback implicit in opinion information: as we demonstrated above, to the extent that someone has formed a strong opinion on an issue from information already processed, the likelihood that further information will contradict what he already knows is small and therefore the expected value of obtaining any is reduced. Again, this is not irrational. In fact, such devaluation of future information is the only logical result consistent with the fact of having an opinion, which in turn is just what a responsible person should have if he has processed some information!

There are two factors in opinion change, however, which may be less rational, at least to the extent that social conventions are occasionally dysfunctional. First, the decision-maker with a partly formed opinion may, consciously or not, foresee anxiety if new information contradicts what he has heard to date; he may stop taking data simply to avoid this discomfort. Second, many people find it costly to change their minds at all, especially from publicly revealed positions. The reason for this is partly related to efficiency issues of the type Popkin *et al.* discuss[6] and partly deep within Western values that exalt "strength of will" and "decisiveness" and suspect their absence when someone changes his mind.*

Finally, the nature of the available information itself will have a great bearing on the likelihood that someone uses it. Consider our hypothetical citizen, confronted with a report that will take more time to read *in toto* than he thinks worth committing.** First, the analysis

---

* An elected official in a contested seat will presumably try to make his entire set of positions consistent over time so that voters can use them as signals.
** It should be realized here that we are not assuming a conscious or explicit analysis. Every time the reader fails to read a newspaper story he is acting on an analysis of exactly this kind: "Knowing what this story has to tell me won't be worth the effort it requires."

might generate descriptive data about the project as part of a sequence moving from simple to detailed. For example:

1. The project will injure some wildlife.
2. The species affected will be birds, rather than animals.
3. Central estimators for the number of each species killed are: *etc.*
4. The variances of these estimates for each species are: *etc.*
5. New technologies available with probability 0.2 will reduce these estimates by 8 percent on the average.

If absorbing the five items listed above exceeds someone's efficient information processing time, the last fact adduced will never be consumed since its understanding requires that the first four be appreciated. If consumers know that information is being supplied in this fashion, however, not much harm is done other than the waste of the analysis that generated item number 5.

But suppose information is supplied with increasing degree of accuracy, not merely precision, as with the following:

1. This project is harmful to birds and other living things.
2. Actually, it's only harmful to birds.
3. In fact, it makes fish poisonous to eat and the effect on the bird population will be temporary.

Processing information of this kind is likely to make a decision-maker's overall judgment about the project swing back and forth as he consumes it. Furthermore, there is no particular sequence in which it must be consumed, since understanding one item is independent of understanding the preceding item. One would be as well off to read only the last (most authoritative) report as to read the entire sequence. The order of provision is important for reasons opposite to the former example: we would like to know which paper came out last so that we can be sure to read it. If research and public investment could be organized so that only the last (best) research is done, that would obviously be preferable to simply doing more research at any given time—if we had the last paper available we would not go back and prepare the first ones. But conflicting sources of information of this kind are typically not provided to the consumer (however they are generated) in any sequence or ordering. What the individual decision-maker sees is a quantity of information, separated into parts that he can expect to be more or less independent, *each of which will turn his decision in a different direction,* and to process all the information would exceed his rational time budget for the project.

Such a consumer is in a very difficult situation indeed. He must either overrun his rational investment of analysis or run a serious chance of missing most or all of the valuable information available to him if he stops after having processed what he has time for. It is easy to construct cases in which the rational response of the consumer is to do without information entirely, adopting his opinion from someone else or even choosing at random. He may also excuse himself from participation in the decision-making process entirely.

A common way to overprovide information is typified by an environmental impact statement that is ineptly or inadequately summarized and indexed; the user would take the time to read the part that matters to him, but can't find it. His dilemma is familiar to anyone who has confronted a long reading list for the first time on the night before an examination. Just as the rational strategy for the unprepared student may be to go to the movies hoping for the best but resigned to the worst, the decision-maker will often be acting efficiently if he washes his hands of the problem entirely rather than foraging at random in an encyclopedic document.

OPPORTUNISTIC USE OF INFORMATION

Up to now, we have mostly treated information consumers as though their interest in information is entirely due to a desire to be efficiently informed. In doing so, we have allowed the ball to slip partly out of sight: except for the incidental case in which obtaining information is fun in and of itself, all this informing is merely instrumental to obtaining public choices beneficial to the consumer. We mentioned one use of information for reasons other than self-enlightenment, propaganda: one participant in a dispute might obtain information only so as to be able to persuade another with it. But information can be turned to even less informative purposes.

Participants in public choice who have formed firm opinions as to the merits of the alternatives available are principally concerned with getting what they want. A variety of ways to do so are available; one of these is often to demand more information about the project. This strategy is especially effective in the form of a lawsuit or administrative appeal on the adequacy of an environmental impact statement; redrafting the statement and including more impacts can impose delay on a project's developer that can sometimes stop a project cold through cost increase, and sometimes form part of a multi-pronged strategy to defeat it. The legal process by which information is managed provides levers that participants have incentives to pull for reasons unrelated to information's typical use. The analogy to dilatory or bullying use of discovery in litigation is direct. Frieden describes such uses of environmental protection levers to avert local population growth.[7]

The importance of such opportunistic uses of information is evidenced by Bardach and Pugliarese in their description of the effort invested by public agencies in anticipating exactly such attacks on impact statements.[8] The reason this opportunism is so often successful is that the amount of information in a signal cannot be assessed without reference to the receiver's probabilities, and these probabilities are subjective and, therefore, not observable from outside the receiver's head. An information user can thus claim to be underinformed without the independent review possible, for example, when a purchaser of a commodity claims to be short-weighted.

POLICY IMPLICATIONS

Focus on the Demand Side

Supply-side strategies for information provision—like EIS laws—require someone to guess what someone else would find useful to know. The unique properties of information described earlier suggest the difficulty of doing this well; the likelihood of opportunistic information use cautions against trying to have it supplied efficiently by regulation.

This conclusion challenges the entire impact-statement process as currently practiced, and the challenge is a powerful one. It's hard enough for an information consumer to obtain the information he should; for someone else to anticipate his needs and those of other differently situated parties with different interests is simply hopeless. The only chance an agency has to supply what the various interested parties care to know is to supply everything it can—but the result will be to provide too much information for any but the most profoundly affected party, and it will not be worth the major investment of effort required to get anything out of it! As we have seen, overprovision of information is not only wasteful, but also can easily decrease the amount of information used by many parties acting rationally.

The new Council on Environmental Quality guidelines for EIS's recognize the problem of information overload, but only with the greatest crudeness (a 150-page length limit).[9] As long as party A is compelled to provide information for B(1), B(2), B(3), etc.,—especially at the beginning of a dispute—he will err seriously one way or another. Resources committed to informing participants in a public choice process should be concentrated on the users themselves.

Furthermore, trying to push a string, as impact-statement requirements of law do, has consequences more serious than waste; someone can *pull* on the string and deflect the information search towards ends that have nothing to do with information. In particular, we have become accustomed to intervenors in the public decision process demanding in court that an agency provide more information in the EIS; it may be that the agency guessed wrong about what the public wanted to know, but the same events can be explained as intervenors using the opportunity as a means to delay the project, and the latter interpretation has in many cases poisoned the well of constructive debate.

Reorientation of our attention to information demand rather than supply has two subsidiary implications for information providers.

Government Should Provide Only Public Good Information

For a particular proposed project, most information about the futures to be expected from different alternatives is valuable to only a minority of affected parties. There are a few things everyone wants to know, however; among these are an initial identification of the *kinds* of impacts the project's alternative versions might cause (to allow specific impacts to be predicted by the parties respectively concerned with them), and descriptions of fiscal impacts on a government (since these are spread by the tax system over all citizens of the polity). Also, basic research (for example, to develop *techniques* of fiscal impact prediction) is correctly understood to be a governmental responsibility. But there is no advantage to expansion of government's role; the information it provides will be poorly matched to consumer demand for all the reasons we have seen. The information that people will gather for themselves will be better suited to its purpose.

This principle does not unduly restrict the role of government in making public decisions better informed. While it has no business providing information that does not meet the conventional test for public goods, it can often be appropriate for a unit of government to subsidize potentially affected parties to obtain their own information,[10] and government management of the decision process itself can have profound effects on information use.

Package Information by User Rather Than Subject

The fundamental question a decision-maker asks of a proposal is "what does it mean for me?" He knows who he is, but he usually seeks information at least partly because he doesn't know what is subsumed in the *what* in his question. An ideal source for citizen use would allow a reader to look up his own characteristics ("plumber, more than three children, income between $15,000 and $20,000, good health . . .") and find descriptions of his future life with and without the proposal in question: how his health would change, what would happen to his taxes, etc. (The advertiser understands this principle, and includes in his commercial message signals that his pitch will be useful for its intended receivers.) If information is organized by subject, on the other hand, the user either has to know at the start that his taxes, for example, might change and that he should look under "fiscal effects," or he must browse at random, at a cost that may well exceed what he is wise to invest. Short of the ideal, there is much room for achievable improvement on the conventional planning report, with chapters on "environmental impacts," "fiscal impacts," "economic impacts," and so on. At the least, information can be presented so that it can be used in a variety of "bite" sizes.

Because it is so difficult to know how much information a document or other record contains for the next user, much less how valuable it will be to him, and because differently affected parties have different rational information processing budgets, information is much more likely to be used if it is provided with a conscious recognition that different users will use it in different ways. A modest example would be the use of thorough indexing and summarization of impact statements; a document (not an EIS) deserving emulation is the

New England River Basin Commission's study of oil development on the New England coast. It offers its results in at least three levels of detail, with imaginative cross-referencing and "road maps."[11] Current practice works in almost exactly the opposite direction, perhaps because the operational criterion for an impact statement is that it withstand a court test of its completeness imposed by someone who is looking specifically for faults rather than trying to use it.

Discourage Staking Out Positions

The planning process should be designed to discourage parties from taking positions, especially binary "pro" or "con" positions, until the last possible moment. After people adopt such positions they are unlikely to invest time or effort in using information, and a planning process in which the various parties take firm sides and try to bargain each other towards a "total victory" position will ensure poorly informed participants. Furthermore, many projects, especially industrial developments, don't allow intermediate positions as usually formulated: half a nuclear power plant is not a feasible compromise. If the feasible actions are widely separated, there is little to bargain about, since one "side" or the other will obviously end up near-total losers. In such cases, it is especially important to keep the possibility of persuasion alive. If everyone agrees that a certain solution is pretty good, no one feels like a loser—but if the parties have taken sides early on, such an outcome will be especially difficult to attain.

The existence of majority viewers and personality takers, in the formulation earlier in this chapter (see pages 104–106), gives special importance to public figures and local leaders in this regard. In facility siting conflicts, for example, a proposal can be permanently derailed if a local official takes a position in opposition to a new proposal early in the debate: in the first place, he often cannot gracefully change his mind, and in the second place, a bandwagon of opposition can develop that soon carries a great many people who are no longer processing information.

Keeping participants uncommitted depends on the gross structure of the planning process, and in particular on two factors:

1. Many different alternatives should be on the table early, and for as long as possible: one of the wrong ways to build a prison or hazardous waste landfill is to choose a single "best" site and advocate it.

2. The alternatives should be described with as many parameters as possible that can be adjusted over a wide range of values: another wrong way to site an unpopular facility is to present a fixed design on a take-it-or-leave-it basis. Sometimes continuously variable parameters, such as local compensation for disamenity (see Chapter 5) have to be purposely built into the design.[12] If the only possible outcomes of a dispute are "a power plant" or "the status quo," someone who favors the status quo will have to expect overwhelming evidence contradicting his current view in order to rationally invest in more information. But if compensation, or some other dimension of the project, allows for more outcomes distributed between these poles, a modest amount of information favoring the pole opposite his can be expected to move him to a feasible, nearby solution. A modest amount of such information is much more likely than overwhelming evidence, so the decision-maker will have incentives (1) to process more information at any point and (2) to suspend judgment as to exactly where along the "scale" he wants to take his stand until he has more data.

Don't Depend on an Objective Analysis

A tradition of social choice is embodied in the study by a "blue-ribbon" or "expert" or "broadly representative" commission, or an engineer's technical evaluation of alternatives. This tradition may be the modern expression of oracular or priestly decision-making, or it may be a new development; in any case it produces the same schismatic effect, but more frequently. Appeal to an expert evaluation, or trust in an "objective" impact statement, is grounded in the expectation that the resulting study will be perceived as objective, and treated as objective, by the participants in the debate. This expectation is confounded so universally that we can propose a general principle exactly contrary:

There is no report or study on a controversial matter that will be used by the paticipants in debate as though it were objective.

The empirical evidence for this proposition is ubiquitous; if the reader has a counter-example (we do not) he should compare it to the library of supporting evidence that includes the Warren Commission Report, every site-selection study for a controversial facility, and the report of the President's Commission on Obscenity.

The results should not be surprising, for several reasons. In the first place, many controversial issues cannot be settled with an outcome that leaves everyone better off than the *status quo ante,* much less with a solution that is better in every way than all others. This means that some interests will think themselves worse off under the proposed solution than they would be otherwise: motivation therefore exists to attack the report. The means are usually at hand as well: (1) complicated problems are at best analyzed under uncertainty and on the basis of arguable assumptions; (2) experts achieve their expertise by involvement in that industry or practice under study on one side or another, and bias is easy to assert; (3) preferences are difficult to assess, and an expert study deliberately removes log-rolling from the political process that was invented to balance interests. A study commission's balancing formula, if any, has no constitutional authority,[13] by which we mean a profound commitment by individuals in society to accept the outcome on the basis of the process used, whether or not they like the result it gave at that time. And finally, one faction or another will present the report as evidence for one side—a seizure which afflicts the document itself with the appearance or suspicion of hidden bias.

The policy implication is accordingly that public choice mechanisms should not require objective information in order to function properly; there is no operational definition of "objectivity" and hence no such information. Current practice induces waste: much useful information is ignored by the parties it might best serve because it is mistrusted. Such mistrust is more likely to vitiate the information if the provider makes claims to objectivity. Because of the acceptance of the "capture" theory of regulators, or because of a more general mistrust of government, this fate often befalls impact statements. Designed to nourish information-hungry citizens, they are more often dismembered by litigants. In fact, the parties to the dispute often have more influence with frankly self-serving statements and reports, since a user can correct them for known bias and doesn't fear deception by indeterminate distortions.

If tendentious information had a formal place in the decision process, it would be less important to try to select or produce "objective" material; trials exemplify decision processes in which *all* information is presented to favor one side or the other, and explicit confrontation is trusted to separate truth from falsehood. One obvious way to provide this place is to enable each party to obtain his own information, noting that the public good information that a central authority might provide is most often (but not always) of the type that will not attract challenge.

The foregoing paragraphs complete the general recommendations we have developed for siting reform. In Chapters 9 and 10 we combine the result of the last two chapters into specific siting procedures that align the interests of the various parties with the public interest in fair, informed, and efficient siting.

FOOTNOTES

1. The complete theoretical presentation of this chapter's analysis is given in M. O'Hare, "Information Management and Public Choice," in J. P. Crecine, ed., *Research in Public Policy and Management,* vol. I, JAI Press, Greenwich, Conn., 1981, part of which appears in this chapter. A shorter version appears as "Improving the Use of Environmental Decision Making," *Environmental Impact Assessment Review,* vol. 1, no. 3 (1980), p. 229. Also see L. Bacow, "The Technical and Judgmental Dimensions of Impact Assessment," *Environmental Impact Assessment Review,* vol. 1, no. 2 (1980), p. 109.
2. E. Bardach and L. Pugliarese, "The Environmental Impact Statement Versus the Real World," *The Public Interest,* Fall 1977, p. 22–38.
3. L. Bacow, *op. cit.*
4. S. Popkin *et al.,* "Comment, What have you done for me lately? Toward an Investment Theory of Voting," *American Political Science Review* **70** (1976), 753–778.
5. T. R. Stewart and L. Gelberd, "Analysis of Judgment Policy: A New Approach for Citizen Participation in Planning," *AIP Journal,* January 1976, pp. 33–41.
6. Popkin *et al.* (1976).
7. B. Frieden, *The Environmental Hustle,* Cambridge, MA, M.I.T. Press, 1979.
8. E. Bardach and L. Pugliarese, *op. cit.*
9. U.S. Council on Environmental Quality, "National Environmental Policy Act: Implementation of Procedural Provations: Final Regulations," *Federal Register,* vol. 43, No. 230—Wednesday, November 29, 1978.
10. R. M. Steeg, "Federal Agency Compensation of Intervenors," *Environmental Affairs* vol. 5 (1976), 697–719.
11. New England River Basins Commission, *Onshore Facilities Related to Offshore Oil and Gas Development,* 1976.
12. M. O'Hare, "Not on My Block, You Don't," *Public Policy* vol. 25 (1977), pp. 407–458.
13. E. T. Haefele, *Representative Government and Environmental Management,* Baltimore, MD, Johns Hopkins, 1973.

8
Compensation Practice in Facility Siting

This chapter presents five case studies that trace the steps taken by many different types of parties to reach agreements about proposed facilities, and illustrates the practical problems that arise when designing and implementing compensation procedures. Although not all the cases involve formal negotiations, they all include some offer of compensation or mitigation. Offers were made for a variety of different reasons, took many different forms, were initiated by different types of parties, and had very different effects on the siting process. The following *Overview* highlights the experiences presented in the cases that follow.

OVERVIEW

1. Grayrocks. As originally proposed, the Missouri Basin Power Project (MBPP) dam would have reduced the North Platte River's flow to a level threatening whooping crane breeding grounds in neighboring Nebraska. Nebraska and four conservation groups sued MBPP under NEPA and the Endangered Species Act. During efforts to negotiate an out-of-court settlement, MBPP first offered its opponents a cash settlement, which was refused until it was reoffered as a trust fund to benefit the whooping crane.

2. Montague. Northeast Utilities (NU) proposed a nuclear power station for Montague, Mass. Both Montague and surrounding towns were concerned about the plant's likely environmental and socio-economic impacts. NU responded to some of these concerns by financing a study of the socio-economic impacts of the plant on Montague and by offering to finance a "town coordinator" who would help the town with the planning and administrative burdens created by

NU's power plant proposal. NU's willingness to cooperate on some issues prompted other local governments to request money for studies and for compensation for other regulatory actions necessary if the plant were to be built. In the end, the legitimacy of compensation itself became an issue in the siting process, as some of the parties used words like *bribery* and *extortion* to describe the activities of the other parties.

3. Skagit. Puget Sound Power and Light proposed a nuclear power station in Skagit County, Washington, and negotiated a Contract Rezone Agreement with local school districts and county officials. In exchange for local zoning approval, Puget Power promised compensation for fiscal impacts on schools and law enforcement, changes in project design, off-site fish breeding grounds, safety provisions, and river flow conditions. Although Puget Power sought mechanisms for satisfying all local concerns about its proposed project, it could not satisfy an anti-nuclear group which has delayed project approval.

4. Resource Recovery. From among eight communities, a regional committee chose Haverhill, Mass., for a resource recovery facility. A state statute then guaranteed any town a (non-negotiable) $.50/ton royalty for hosting such a facility, but paid no compensation to adjacent towns. The legislature later raised the royalty to $1.00/ton, an amount Haverhill at first considered satisfactory. But Haverhill later rejected host status because it believed the $1.00/ton royalty would not compensate for anticipated damages to its town image and environment. Still later, Haverhill again requested host status, since the second choice site in adjacent North Andover would have imposed the same adverse impacts on Haverhill without any compensation at all.

5. Wes-Con. Wes-Con Incorporated converted two abandoned Titan missile silos in Idaho into small hazardous waste disposal facilities, and experienced almost no public opposition. The developer voluntarily sought community concerns; he made a variety of concessions that successfully resolved those concerns over the disposal of hazardous waste and that won the community's support. His benefits "package" included, for example, free disposal services, additional fire protection, medical training, and a consent decree. His political insights and his continual efforts to monitor and respond to community concerns allowed him to successfully weather at least two potential crises.

CASE 1: THE GRAYROCKS DAM[1]
(Principal Researcher: Julia Wondolleck)

The Grayrocks Dam case has all the elements of a classic development/ environment dispute. It pitted a large power company seeking to construct a dam (for cooling water for a new power plant) against a coalition of environmentalists, farmers, and state officials. To the power company, the dam meant more electricity and jobs. To the farmers who lived downstream, it meant less water available for irrigation. And to environmentalists, it meant a threat to the habitat of the whooping crane, an endangered species. As the dispute unfolded, the battle over the dam was waged on many fronts including the courts, Congress, and in the state capitals of Nebraska and Wyoming. Ultimately, the parties got together and settled the dispute among themselves—the dam is being constructed, the farmers still have their water, and the whooping crane is still with us. This case describes how each party got what it wanted and what it took to get them all to agree to settle out of court.

THE ISSUES

In 1970, six utilities formed the Missouri Basin Power Project (MBPP) for the purpose of constructing a $1.6 billion coal-fired power plant on the Laramie River near Wheatland, Wyoming. The plant was designed to provide power for expected industrial expansion in eastern Montana, Wyoming, Colorado, North Dakota, South Dakota, Nebraska, Iowa, and Minnesota. Two million customers would be served by the plant. To supply cooling water for the plant, the consortium proposed to build a dam and reservoir on the Laramie River, a tributary of the North Platte River. The dispute over the dam was first and foremost a dispute over water rights. The project would divert 60,000 acre feet of water annually from the North Platte River. This diversion would be in addition to the 70 percent reduction in streamflow that has occurred in the last 50 years due to construction of 43 dams and numerous irrigation projects on the North Platte. Conservationists worried that the additional reduction in streamflow would be "the straw that breaks the camel's back" in its impact on North Platte River wildlife.[2]

The conservationists focused their concern on the critical habitat of the whooping crane, an endangered species.* The crane migrates annually between the Aransas Natural Wildlife Refuge in Texas and Wood Buffalo National Park in Canada. Two-hundred-and-seventy miles downstream from the dam is a sixty-mile-long stretch of sandbars that serves as a major stopover for the crane on its yearly migration. Flood waters and ice from the annual snow melt scour the sandbars and keep them free from vegetation.[3] The environmentalists worried that the additional reduction in streamflow occasioned by the dam would reduce the effectiveness of this scouring, permitting vegetation to overgrow the sandbars and thus make them unsuitable for the whooping cranes.

Farmers downstream also worried about the impact of the dam on streamflow. Water, the lifeblood of the semiarid plains states' agricultural economies, has been a source of conflict among the states for a number of years. Colorado, Wyoming, and Nebraska have feuded over the allocation of water from the Laramie River and the North Platte River. Entitlements to this water are defined by 1945 and 1956 U.S. Supreme Court decisions.[4,5] Unfortunately, the three states all interpret these decrees differently.[6] Nebraska has been able to liberally interpret its entitlement to North Platte River water because it is located farthest downstream.[7] It has taken its share of the streamflow plus whatever has been left by upstream users. Nebraska officials opposed the dam because they worried that its construction would force them to reduce the state's water usage. Wyoming officials maintained that the Supreme Court allocation formula entitled them to the additional water that would be taken from the river by the dam. Since the Supreme Court rulings were ambiguous, none of the parties could be absolutely sure who was really entitled to the water at issue.

NEGOTIATIONS BEGIN

Informal negotiations began in 1973 when MBPP formed an Environmental Advisory Committee to explore the potential impacts of the Grayrocks Dam.[8] The Committee solicited the views of concerned environmental groups and issued a report suggesting that future power needs could be met by a smaller plant with less environmental impact. MBPP apparently did not find the report persuasive. In the words of Robert Turner, Wyoming representative of the National Audubon Society, the response of officials to

---

*Conservation groups including the National Audubon Society, the National Wildlife Federation, the Nebraska Wildlife Federation, the Powder River Basin Resource Council and the Laramie River Conservation Council were also concerned about the effect of a reduction in stream-flow on other species. They concentrated on the whooping crane, however, because its status as an endangered species provided the groups with additional leverage over the dam. The effect of the Endangered Species Act is explained later in the case.

the committee's advice and recommendation was "negative in every regard."[9] The Advisory Committee was officially disbanded in 1976.

During this same period, Nebraska and MBPP officials had met more than 30 times to discuss the water rights issue.[10] These negotiations also yielded little in the way of agreement. The principals have different perceptions of what went on during these talks. William Wisdom, counsel for Basin Electric, major interest holder in MBPP, asserts that the consortium made a number of offers of specific water levels to Nebraska which were all rejected.[11] Paul Snyder, Assistant Attorney General of Nebraska, recalls that MBPP refused to concede anything during these negotiating sessions. Snyder's view is that MBPP adopted a hard line in negotiating with environmentalists and Nebraska because it thought it had the political clout needed to head off any lawsuits, especially those brought by Nebraska, part of MBPP's service area. The utilities were "used to getting away with whatever they proposed," "nobody had ever stood up to them before."[12]

LITIGATION

Frustrated in its attempts to settle the dispute through negotiation, Nebraska fired the first salvo in a complicated legal battle: in 1976 it sued the Rural Electrification Administration (REA), alleging that the REA's loans to the project were illegal. Under the National Environmental Policy Act (NEPA), major federal actions that affect the quality of the environment, including loans and permits, must be preceded by an adequate environmental impact statement (EIS). Nebraska charged that the Grayrocks Dam EIS was inadequate because it said nothing about the impact of the dam on either Nebraska water supplies or the aquatic ecosystem of the part of the North Platte River that flows through the state. Nebraska pursued the same legal strategy in a suit that sought to enjoin the Army Corps of Engineers from issuing a "404 permit," allowing MBPP to dredge and fill a U.S. waterway.

Conservationists also filed suit citing the allegedly inadequate EIS, and also charging that the REA and the Corps failed to fulfill the requirements of the Endangered Species Act (ESA). The ESA requires that federal agencies consult with the U.S. Fish and Wildlife Service to ensure that their actions do not jeopardize an endangered species. This requirement is accomplished either by not issuing the required permits or by mitigating potential impacts. In effect, the conservationists sought to stop the dam unless MBPP took steps to guarantee the habitat of the whooping crane.

The various lawsuits were consolidated into one suit. As the case progressed, the parties met a few times to discuss settlement. These efforts were futile in large part because each side felt confident of victory, hence they had little incentive to negotiate out of court.[13][14] This stalemate was broken when the court ruled against MBPP and enjoined REA from issuing the needed loan guarantee and the Corps from issuing the 404 dredge-fill permit.[15] It was at this point, in the words of Paul Snyder, Nebraska's Assistant Attorney General, that "the *real* negotiations started."

FORMAL NEGOTIATIONS

Although MBPP lost the first battle over the Grayrocks Dam, it was far from clear that they were going to lose the war. They appealed the decision and were confident that the injunction would be overturned.[16] They also had friends in Congress. In an emotional speech, retiring Representative Teno Roncalio (D-Wyo) pleaded,

> "Do you want to send me back to Wyoming, after ten years as your friend and colleague to face 2,000 unemployed people in Wheatland on account of a totally unjustified thing like this, the Endangered Species Act?"[17]

Roncalio's plea was warmly received. The House passed a bill exempting the Grayrocks Dam from virtually all federal regulatory requirements. The bill was amended in conference to limit the exemption to the Endangered Special Act *provided* that the newly created Endangered Species Committee* gave its approval.[18] Thus, MBPP had hoped that it could achieve the victory in Congress that had eluded it in the Courts. But as MBPP had learned from the District Court's decision, it could not be certain of a favorable decision. Because the Endangered Species Committee (known popularly as the "God Committee" for its power to make life-and-death decisions for both species and projects) had never decided an issue like the Grayrocks Dam, no one could be certain how it would vote.** Moreover, the longer that construction was delayed on the dam, the more expensive became the dispute for MBPP. MBPP officials estimated that they could lose close to $500 million if construction were delayed for a year. So MPBB had a clear incentive to find a quick way out of the morass.

---

*When the Endangered Species Act came up for extension in Congress in November, 1978, it was attacked as being inflexible. As a condition of extending the Act, Congress established the Endangered Species Committee. This committee will review "irreconcilable conflicts" involving endangered species that cannot be resolved through the Act's provisions. The committee will grant exemptions for projects that otherwise fall under the Endangered Species Act only if it concludes that "the public interest is best served by completing the project, that no reasonable and prudent alternatives exist, and that the project's benefits clearly outweigh the benefits of any alternative courses of action which would conserve the species or its critical habitat."[19]

**The Endangered Species Committee never ruled on the legislative exemption for the Grayrocks Dam. By the time the committee had its first meeting on January 23, 1979, an agreement between all parties in the Grayrocks conflict had been reached, so the exemption was a moot point. The committee simply ratified this agreement, thereby exempting the project from the Endangered Species Act for as long as the agreement was upheld.

Conservationists were no more enthusiastic about trusting the future of the whooping crane to the God Committee. Moreover, they did not relish the thought of an expensive court appeal.[20] Since they never intended to stop the project entirely, but merely to provide protection for the endangered crane, little was to be gained from fighting the battle to its bloody end.[21] And Nebraska also was not unalterably opposed to the project; it merely wanted to protect its water. So the dispute really was ripe for settlement.

MBPP initiated negotiations by proposing, through intermediaries, that all the parties get together to discuss a settlement. Nebraska and Wyoming quickly agreed as did the conservation groups.[22] The initial meeting was held in Lincoln, Nebraska, in October 1978. Sixty people participated with the two governors serving as co-chairmen. In the view of one of the representatives of the conservation group, the governors used the meeting primarily for "political posturing."[23] They accomplished little of substance, beyond agreeing to the date and format of the next meeting.

On November 2, 1978, a much smaller group reconvened in Cheyenne, Nebraska. At the Lincoln meeting, the parties agreed to continue discussions through six representatives: Nebraska's Attorney General, Nebraska's Director of Water Resources, Basin Electric's James Grahl, MBPP attorney Edward Weinberg, Patrick Parenteau of the National Wildlife Federation and David Pomerly of the Nebraska Wildlife Federation. Each of these parties came to the Cheyenne meeting with "bottom-line proposals" developed since the first meeting in Lincoln. Each was also accompanied by legal counsel and technical advisors. When the size of the group proved unwieldly, the lawyers and advisors were shunted to a nearby room where they remained available for consultation. The remainder of the negotiations were conducted by the principals alone.

MBPP opened the negotiations by offering the opposition group $15 million to purchase water rights to maintain whatever streamflow they thought appropriate. It was MBPP's intention that some of this money be used, if necessary, to artificially maintain the whooping crane's habitat.[24] MBPP officials arrived at the $15 million figure the same way most defendants calculate settlement offers: they estimated what they could afford to pay, how much they stood to lose if the case was not settled, and approximately what they thought it would take to satisfy the opposition.[25]

What MBPP failed to assess was how such an offer would be perceived by the plaintiffs, who rejected it for several reasons. First, Nebraska was extremely nervous about accepting any direct payment except for legal fees. Given the visibility of the negotiations and the high passions generated by the water rights issues among Nebraska farmers, it was important that Nebraska not be perceived as selling out the interests of its water users for cash.[26] Second, Nebraska was sincerely interested in maintaining the existing streamflow through the state and was not certain that the cash settlement would be adequate for this purpose.[27]

Third, the conservationists, like Nebraska, were reluctant to accept cash;[28] but they also were concerned about whether streamflow levels could be legally maintained through water rights purchases. Nebraska allocates water to users only if it will be put to "beneficial use," which includes agriculture, mining, municipal water needs, recreation, and the maintenance and propagation of fish and wildlife. Although it would seem that purchases of water rights to protect the whooping crane habitat would fall within the fish and wildlife clause, there is a catch. A "beneficial use" must also entail "physical removal of the water from the stream."[29,30,31] And since the water purchased to maintain the habitat would be left in the stream and not removed, it was not clear whether a Nebraska court would consider such a use "beneficial."

Thus, both Nebraska and the conservationists rejected the initial MBPP offer. MBPP came back with a revised offer that cut the cash settlement in half and included varying guarantees for minimum streamflow for the North Platte River for different seasons. The $7.5 million was supposed to be used to purchase additional water rights when needed and to artificially maintain the habitat.[32] While the streamflow guarantees helped assuage some of the concerns of the opposition, Nebraska and the conservationists were still reluctant to accept any cash. As a result, the parties spent much time discussing how such a settlement could be consummated and no time discussing its size.[33,34]

After much discussion, Patrick Parenteau of the National Wildlife Federation suggested using the money to create a trust fund for the preservation of the whooping crane and its habitat.[35] Nebraska agreed to the settlement on the condition that the fund be governed by an "independent" board of trustees.[36] Thirty days later, the parties affixed their names to a formal, binding agreement that included a monitoring provision to ensure implementation. The agreement established a perpetual trust fund, with the interest used for protective measures for the whooping crane and its habitat.[37,38] On January 23, 1979, the God Committee met for the first time and ratified the settlement, thus ending the Grayrocks Dam controversy.

CONCLUSIONS

The Timing of the Agreement

It took five years to resolve the environmental issues first raised by the Advisory Committee appointed in 1973. Clearly the same substantive agreement could have been negotiated earlier. Why did it take so long?

Each party to a dispute like this faces an incentive to negotiate that changes with his perceptions of the alternative. When MBPP thought it held all the cards on the Grayrocks Dam, it stood firm. In the words of one of the dam's opponents, MBPP challenged the conservationists to "go ahead and sue us."[39] Similarly, when the conservationists thought they would win their lawsuit, they were reluctant to settle. It was only after the MBPP had lost a major court decision and after the conservationists were threatened with the loss of their court victory that the parties sat down and seriously worked toward a mutual accommodation. Both sides sought to avoid letting the "God Committee" resolve the issue, much like parties avoid a strike in labor negotiations.

Frequently, power shifts back and forth in a long struggle over a development project. Each interim victory and loss leads to a reassessment of positions. For a negotiated settlement to succeed, it must offer each party something better than they think could be obtained through other dispute resolution procedures. Thus, the party that advocates a negotiated settlement must be aware of the opportunities created by the changing relative power of the actors. Furthermore, such an advocate must look for ways to convince skeptics that it's in their interest to settle. This can be accomplished through the use of carrots like MBPP's initial financial offer, or sticks like the lawsuit brought by the dam's opponents.

The Form of Compensation

People have very different perceptions of what compensation is. To MBPP, the initial offer of $15 million was a legitimate means of settling a dispute and of addressing the merits of their opponents' case. To the opposition, however, it was unacceptable because it had the appearance of a bribe. In making compensation offers, how the offer is made is sometimes as important as the substance of the offer. What one man considers a gift, another may consider a bribe. Offerors have to package their offer in a way that does not cast the recipient in an awkward light. In general, whenever people oppose a project out of concern for a third party rather than self-interest (e.g., the conservationists acting on behalf of the whooping crane), it's likely that a direct offer of compensation will offend them. The parties have to creatively structure the transaction so that it clearly benefits the interested beneficiary.

The Conduct of Negotiations

There is an old saying in the auto industry to the effect that bargaining does not become serious until it becomes private. Serious negotiation is difficult when lots of different people are involved. As the parties discovered in this case, it is often easiest to negotiate when only the principals are present. Staff tend to inhibit the give and take that is the essence of successful bargaining. Agreements often are not forthcoming until after the parties have established a reservoir of mutual respect. Usually this respect results from spending many hours together in long negotiating sessions where personal interaction is highly valued. The more people in the room, the more difficult it is to form these personal relationships.

SUMMARY

In many ways, the outcome of this case was fortuitous. Unlike some development disputes, the opponents were not unalterably opposed to the project. As it turned out, the solution that satisfied the conservationists also satisfied the interests of Nebraska. Had these parties possessed different views of what constituted an acceptable outcome, the settlement might not have been forthcoming. And the mutual uncertainty created by the God Committee is not likely to be replicated in precisely the same way in future cases. Yet the case does demonstrates that when parties really have an incentive to resolve their differences, solutions can be found that work to the advantage of all parties. In this case, compensation played a critical role in creating such a workable solution.

CASE 2: THE MONTAGUE NUCLEAR POWER PLANT[40]
(Principal Researcher: Julia Wondolleck)

In contrast to the previous case, the Montague story does not have a "happy ending." Like many proposed nuclear power plants, Montague has become the focus of often strident protest by anti-nuclear activists. It has also been opposed by neighboring cities and towns whose residents fear the plant will bring undesired growth in the demand for their municipal services. It is a story about how the power company's attempts to respond to these concerns either went awry or backfired. It illustrates some pitfalls to avoid in managing the developer/community relationship as well as many of the practical problems often encountered in negotiating compensation agreements.

THE ISSUES

In December, 1973, Northeast Utilities (NU) announced its intention to build twin 1,150 megawatt nuclear units in Montague, Massachusetts, a town of 8,600 located about 100 miles west of Boston. The individual reactors were scheduled to begin operation in 1981 and 1983 respectively. The plant offered a prospect of substantial economic benefits and high employment for Montague and, to a lesser extent, for surrounding Franklin County. According to a socio-economic study paid for by NU and commissioned by the town, operation of the plant would reduce Montague's tax rate by almost 90%. The same study predicted that the town population would grow 25–40 percent during the construction period and 600–1,000 new housing units would be built. Clearly the plant and the accompanying economic activity would create many new job opportunities for residents of Montague and neighboring communities. Thus, it is not surprising that Montague residents supported the plant three to one in a referendum held shortly after NU's initial announcement.

This support, as well as the support of the Montague Planning Board and Board of Selectmen, was important for NU. The two boards had the power to grant permits and rezone the plant site, both of which were necessary to initiate construction. The Selectmen also controlled appointments to the local Airport Commission which would have to impose restrictions on takeoff and landing patterns if the plant's two 570-foot cooling towers were to be located near the airport as planned.

NU also needed the support or acquiescence of a few other local government and regulatory bodies before it could build and operate the plant. In order to assemble a contiguous parcel of land, it needed Montague and Franklin County to legally abandon town and county roads passing through the site. (After abandonment, title to those roads would automatically revert to NU the adjacent landowner. NU also needed the support of the Massachusetts Energy Facility Siting Council (MEFSC), a state agency with legal jurisdiction to review energy projects from a statewide perspective to ensure that they are needed, cost-effective, and environmentally sound.

NU was not new to the area. Its subsidiary, Western Massachusetts Electric Company (WMECO), had serviced the region for years; Montague Selectman Willam Powers perceived it as a "friend and neighbor." NU had worked hard to earn this reputation. For one dollar it had sold the town one of its surplus buildings for use as a city hall. Moreover, because it operated a hydroelectric facility in town, NU paid more than half the town's tax revenues. In trying to secure local support for the nuclear plant, NU pursued the same strategy of community relations that had worked so well in the past. It tried to be cooperative and responsive to local concerns; and it tried to make it financially desirable for the community to go along. But as NU and Montague officials would both learn, people react differently to nuclear power plants than they do to other energy facilities.

MANAGING THE DEVELOPER-COMMUNITY RELATIONSHIP

The Socioeconomic Study

Although most Montague residents viewed NU's initial proposal favorably, they were still concerned over the impact of such a large facility on so small a town. Shortly after NU announced its plans, MEFSC staff members met with town and county officials to help develop a response to the proposal. Since neither Montague nor Franklin County had the necessary resources or expertise to evaluate the impact of such a large facility, the MEFSC staff suggested that they commission a socio-economic study. Montague, unable to afford such a study, approached NU; the utility readily agreed to underwrite the cost of a consulting report that would describe the extent of the impacts as well as what preparation or planning might be required.

The Montague Planning Board turned to Fred Muehl, a planner employed by Franklin County, for assistance in selecting the consultant. Although NU had to approve the five potential candidates Muehl suggested for Montague's consideration, Montague alone was responsible for making the final choice. To avoid any conflict of interest, NU transferred $38,000 to the town to pay for the study. Thus, Montague, not NU, was the official client for the study performed by Harbridge House, a large Boston-based planning and management consultant.

In November, 1974, Montague published *The Social and Economic Impact of a Nuclear Power Plant Upon Montague, Massachusetts and the Surrounding Area*. The report predicted that without the plant, Montague's tax rate would rise $60 by 1985, to a total tax rate of $117.* With the plant, the rate would drop to just $13. In the same period, the town population would jump between 25 and 40 percent and 600–1,000 new housing units would be built.

The report was less informative concerning the power plant's effect on neighboring communities. Notwithstanding its title, the study focused primarily on Montague where most of the benefits were located. The surrounding towns in Franklin County had a much cooler attitude toward the plant. While they too would likely experience some increase in jobs and economic activity, they were concerned that these benefits would not offset the costs they would incur from increased traffic and public service demands during construction. Unlike Montague, these communities would not receive property tax payments from NU.

---

* New England local tax rates are given in dollars per thousand dollars of assessed value. (At the time of this siting effort, assessments were often far below market value.)

Because of these concerns over development impact, the county also approached NU requesting a similar study of county-wide impacts. This time NU said "No." There are three possible explanations for NU's refusal. First, given that the Harbridge House study was intended to describe all the impacts of the plant, NU might have viewed another study as redundant, even extravagant. Second, NU might have been reluctant to fund such a study because it feared that it would reveal that the plant would be net-costly to other Franklin County towns. And third, NU might simply have concluded that it did not need to curry favor with the county because the county did not possess the same kind of regulatory leverage over the development proposal as did Montague. (Since the plant would be constructed in Montague, the town had jurisdiction over all zoning variances and local permits. Counties in Massachusetts, which are fully incorporated, have rudimentary powers.)

It makes little difference which of these theories explains NU's decision not to fund a county study, because each represents an error in judgment. Even if the Harbridge House study should have analyzed county-wide effects, it did not. As a result, the residents of surrounding communities still did not know what the impact of the plant would be on their own towns. Without this information, and given NU's reluctance to supply it, it should not be surprising that these communities chose not to support the plant. If NU were concerned that a comprehensive report would cast it in a bad light, it should have realized that this information would eventually come out when the full environmental impact statement was prepared, and efforts to delay it would only engender feelings of mistrust. Finally, NU seriously erred if it assumed that the county lacked leverage over its proposal. As noted before, the county had to abandon the roads on site if NU were to proceed. The county would use this leverage later to try to obtain additional concessions from NU.

The Town Coordinator Position

It was clear from the beginning that the additional planning and management responsibilities created by the NU proposal would sorely tax the capabilities of Montague's part-time government. To alleviate this problem, and in response to concerns expressed by Montague selectmen, NU volunteered $30,000 to fund a "town coordinator" position. In June 1974, Lucien Desbien, a local school teacher, was hired to fill this position. His responsibilities were to:

1. "Act as an administrative assistant to selectmen in the relationship between the town and NU.

2. Keep selectmen informed of the utility's action and NU of Montague's needs during construction of the plants, as well as providing a liaison among utility, citizen, and official town groups on specific utility-related needs.
3. To provide assistance to NU on its administrative responsibilities in meeting regulations and requirements of the town.
4. To act as a 'guided' spokesman for the town in relations with appropriate state, federal, and local agencies during the construction process.
5. To provide selectmen with assistance on the day-to-day operations of their office as well as providing staff assistance in gaining grants and procurement assistance at state and federal levels."

Desbien lasted less than two years in the job. When he denied Sam Lovejoy, a Montague resident and leading anti-nuclear activist,* access to written communications between NU and himself, Lovejoy charged that these letters and memoranda were public documents and that the continuing existence of the NU-funded town coordinator position constituted an illegal conflict of interest. Lovejoy filed suit in a local court and won, and Montague abolished the town coordinator position.

This incident alarmed Montague officials. They wanted the Montague plant very badly and were doing "whatever they could" to assure that it would be built. The town coordinator position had not struck any of them as illegitimate. After all, it was NU that had imposed these additional planning requirements on Montague; therefore, it seemed only fair that NU pay for them. Lovejoy's successful conflict of interest suit led Montague officials to take a very cautious attitude toward all further offers of assistance from NU. This caution colored all of their future negotiations over permits and compensation. For example, shortly after the Desbien affair, the town approached NU with an offer to purchase 64 acres of NU's surplus land located adjacent to the town's industrial park. The town meeting had already appropriated $40,000 for the purchase. NU responded by offering to return the $40,000 to the town, not as a gift, but to offset expenses incurred by the town

---

* Lovejoy was the co-founder of both the Alternative Energy Coalition and the Northeast Clamshell Alliance. He is very active in the anti-nuclear movement and—literally—violently opposed to a nuclear power plant in his home town: He singlehandedly knocked down a meteorological tower NU had erected on the Montague site for the purpose of weather monitoring. He turned himself in but was acquitted on a technicality. He has purchased stock in NU to gain access to shareholder's meetings and information. He stated his categorical opposition to the NU plant in a statement to the Congressional Subcommittee on Energy and the Environment.

"I can tell you right now that that nuclear power plant will not be built in Montague, no way, no how, unless Sam Lovejoy is dead or in jail, and it is that simple."[50]

in planning for the power plant. The selectmen refused the offer for fear that it would be popularly perceived as a bribe.

Road Abandonments

Montague had relatively little trouble deciding to abandon its road through the NU site. The roads were rarely used and meant little to the town. Moreover, abandonment would end town responsibility for their maintenance. Although Sam Lovejoy argued vigorously against abandonment at the town meeting considering this issue, the town meeting approved the abandoment precisely because it wanted the plant.

County road abandonment was another story. As noted earlier, road abandonment was the county's only leverage over NU. Fred Muehl, the county planner who assisted Montague in selecting the consultant and was an opponent of nuclear power, argued that the roads were public property and should not be abandoned for private purposes without compensation. In return for road abandonment, the county asked "NU to agree to . . . offsite monitoring, an evacuation plan, building towers lower than the 570-foot towers originally announced and a study of the social and economic impact on the rest of the county, not Montague alone." To date, NU officials have resisted the county's request for compensation because they question whether "anyone, anywhere has had to pay for a county road abandonment?" The road abandonment issue has pitted town against county. Montague Selectman Powers has charged the county commissioners with holding the roads "hostage" in the siting process. The issue has yet to be resolved.

Turner Falls Airport Restrictions

By now, confusion was mounting in Montague. Although the town selectmen still wanted the plant, public opposition was growing. The town was reluctant to accept compensation and NU, in its dealings with the county, had indicated that it was reluctant to pay compensation to just anyone who demanded it. The issue of the propriety of compensation came to a head in the discussions over the imposition of restrictions on the operation of the Turners Falls Airport.

The plans for the power plant included two 570-foot cooling towers, designed to withstand the impact of a 15,000 pound aircraft without releasing radioactivity in excess of Nuclear Regulating Commission guidelines. To ensure the integrity of the tower, NU requested two restrictions on airport operations: first, that takeoffs and landings be limited to planes weighing less than 15,000 pounds; and second, that the airport adopt a right-hand turn pattern instead of the conventional left-hand pattern. NU presented these requests to the Airport Commission in November, 1975. Before the next commission meeting in December, Alfred Lucas, Commission Chairman, initiated discussion with NU over compensation for the restrictions on air space. When the utility did not respond with an offer, the commission voted 2–1 to reject the request.

NU reapplied for the restrictions in April, 1977. Two months later, the *Greenfield Reporter* reported that NU had offered the commission $35,000 as compensation for the restriction. When the Montague selectmen learned of this offer, they were outraged. They accused the commission of "putting an arm" on NU and demanded that the utility withdraw its offer. NU's denial that it had ever made the offer lent credence to the selectmen's view that the alleged offer was really a thinly veiled demand *from* the commission. Selectman Powers charged that the commission was "blackmailing the utility." Commission Clerk George Schact responded by saying, "No. It's selling a valuable product." Clearly the commission and the selectmen had different views on the propriety of compensation.

Ultimately the impasse was broken by reappointments to the commission. Shortly after the dispute over the restrictions, two vacancies opened up on the three-member commission. The Selectmen, who controlled commission appointments, filled one of the vacancies with Warren Lemon, a supporter of the plant. Lucas, the Commission Chairman, was reappointed on the condition that he follow the lead of town officials on the restriction issue. The commission reconsidered the issue at its November meeting and voted to grant the restrictions.

CONCLUSIONS

In Chapters 5 and 6, we suggested that compensation could be useful in resolving conflict over development proposals. Clearly this was not the case in Montague. Instead of easing tensions, the offers and demands for compensation heightened tensions. At times, the propriety of compensation became the central concern in the local debate over the desirability of the plant. This happened for a number of reasons.

First, the Montague selectmen never settled on a strategy for dealing with NU. Although it is clear that they coveted the plant, they never decided whether this support was unqualified or conditioned upon subsequent actions by NU. This failure to be specific contributed to the confusion over the airport restrictions. Second, neither Montague nor NU paid enough attention to appearances. Because of the strong local opposition to the plant, both sides should have realized that all deals would be closely scrutinized. Had the parties dealt with each other on an arm's length basis, some of the characterizations of compensation as bribery might have been avoided. Finally, NU failed to fully appreciate the strategic dimensions of this dispute. The towns surrounding Montague had little to gain and something to lose if the plant were built. Thus, NU should not have been surprised when the county exercised the only leverage it possessed—road abandonments—to obtain the conditions satisfying county concerns. If the costs that a new development imposes on a group of people are much larger than their benefits, those threatened will seize upon whatever opportunity they have to avoid the costs. In such cases, developers are unlikely to make much headway by claiming, as NU did, that the people (or town or county) are acting unfairly by withholding something that had always been granted in the past.

CASE 3: THE SKAGIT COUNTY REZONE CONTRACT[41]
(Principal Researcher: Alan Weinstein)

In many ways, the Skagit County case is very similar to the Montague case. Both involve a proposal to build a nuclear power plant in a rural area. In both cases, local officials worried about the socio-economic impact of the plant on the surrounding community. In both cases, the utility offered to compensate for development impacts. What differs between the two cases is the way compensation was perceived: in Montague it was viewed with suspicion and actually complicated the siting process, while in Skagit County, the propriety of compensation never became an issue.

THE ISSUES

In January 1973, Puget Sound Power and Light announced its plans to construct a two-unit nuclear generating station near Sadro Woolley, Washington. The 1,500 acre site was zoned "forestry/recreational and residential" at the time. Before construction could begin, Puget Power had to have 260 acres of the site rezoned "industrial" by the Skagit County Board of Commissioners.

Skagit County, located about 70 miles northeast of Seattle, is lightly populated and predominantly agricultural. The low population density and agricultural orientation make it a desirable site for a nuclear plant. When Puget Power first announced its plans, there was widespread public support for the plant, although some residents expressed concern that the development might alter the rural character of the area.[42] The proposed plant also caused concern among local planning and school district officials. During the eight-year construction phase, the influx of construction workers would swell the enrollment of local schools in addition to placing additional demands on local fire and police services. While eventually the county would receive additional property tax revenues from the plant, most of these would not arrive until after completion of the construction phase. In the years when the county would need money the most, tax revenues would be the lowest.[43] Thus, the county was reluctant to approve the rezoning request until the construction impact financing problem was resolved.

Not surprisingly, the proposal to construct a nuclear power plant also touched off debate on environmental impacts. The Skagit Environmental Council, the Skagitonians Concerned About Nuclear Plants (SCANP) and three local Indian tribes all opposed the plant, citing, among other things, the impact of the plant on fish in the Skagit River, seismic issues, and radiological impacts.[44,45] In the end, Puget Power succeeded in resolving only some of these issues.

NEGOTIATING THE REZONE CONTRACT

The Washington statute governing the siting of energy facilities that was in effect when Puget Power announced its plans required energy developers to obtain the approval of local planning officials before filing for state permits. In the words of William Finnegan, Director of Conservation and Environmental Affairs for the utility, this gave Puget Power a strong incentive "to make peace with its neighbors."[46] Puget Power worked hard to achieve this goal by sending representatives to meet with almost every political, civic, and private group in the county.[47] The purpose of these meetings was not only to drum up support, but also to learn about how Puget Power could respond to local concerns over the plant.

While Puget Power was out talking, local planning officials were contacting other towns that had hosted nuclear plants to learn about likely impacts.[48] At about the same time, local officials were also considering what procedure should be employed to change the zoning status of the plant site. The county commissioners rejected an application from Puget Power for an "Unclassified Use Permit" on the advice of legal counsel that such a permit would not withstand judicial scrutiny because of its similarity to spot zoning. Instead, the county commissioner decided to develop a new comprehensive plan that permitted an industrial zone in the portion of the county that included the plant site. Also on the advice of counsel, Puget Power prepared an environmental impact report (required by state law) and on November 20, 1973, filed an application for "contract rezone."[49] A "contract rezone" is a procedure that permits local authorities to attach extensive conditions to rezoning requests. In this case, Puget Power asked that 200 acres of the 1,500 acre site be classified "industrial" with the remainder designated "forestry/recreation."[50]

Since the county was favorably inclined towards the plant, the public hearings that followed focused, in large part, on the conditions to be included in the rezone agreement. None of the participants can recall who suggested the idea of impact payments.[51,52] It did not come from the survey of other communities that had hosted nuclear plants, because the survey yielded little information. In the opinion of Robert Scofield, Director of the Skagit County Planning Commission, it was only natural to include impact payments to school districts and law enforcement agencies during the construction period because the basic problem for local communities posed by the plant was the lack of money up front to pay for the temporary increase in demand for local services. Since Puget Power acknowledged this problem and was anxious to obtain local zoning approval so that it could get on with federal and state permits, the parties were able to reach an agreement. On March 26, 1974, 15 months after Puget Power announced its plans, a rezone contract was executed.

THE AGREEMENT

The rezone contract contained ten separate articles that defined the rights and responsibilities of both Puget Power and Skagit County.[53] Articles one through three executed the rezoning of the site and included a pledge by Puget Power to leave unimproved land in a natural condition. Article four prohibited fuel reprocessing and the permanent storage of radioactive waste on site. It also established a radiological monitoring program and an evacuation plan. This article was included to try to blunt some of the criticism coming from environmental groups. Article five described in detail how Puget Power would make payments to the Skagit County treasurer to offset public service expenditures during the construction phase. All payments for education were based on the number of "construction impact students" residing in the county. The agreement defined such a student as the child of a construction worker who (1) resides in the county, (2) is working directly on the project as an employee of a contractor or subcontractor, and (3) did not reside in the county for more than 30 days during the six months immediately preceding these months in which he began work on the project. Puget Power agreed to make monthly payments for each such student enrolled in a public school in the county on the first school day of any regular school month in which at least 50 construction workers were employed on the project. The parties settled on a per pupil payment rate of 1.5 × the school district's monthly rate per student for the relevant fiscal year.* The 1.5 multiplier,

---

*The monthly rate (defined in the contract) approximates the per pupil maintenance and operating cost borne by the school district alone.

known as the secondary impact factor, was included to account for students who were children of people who moved into the county as a result of construction activities but who were not directly employed on the project. Puget Power also agreed to pay the "reasonable" costs of obtaining portable classroom space and transportation for the additional students. The agreement also provided for payments to cover the additional costs incurred by local police. All such payments under the rezone contract were considered as prepayment of taxes and credited against future property tax bills. The agreement set up an arbitration panel to resolve any disputes.

The remaining articles described measures to mitigate the land use and the environmental and transportation impacts of the plant. In one article, Puget Power agreed to alter the facility design slightly, adopting a different type of fresh water intake system that was more expensive but which would significantly reduce the probability of fish larvae entrainment. Of particular interest was article nine which addressed the problem of fish kills on the Skagit River. Puget Power agreed to construct a fish hatchery that would put to productive use warm water from the plant's cooling system. The fish would be turned over to the state for use in restocking Washington rivers. This provision represents an excellent example of a form of compensation "in kind" that is designed to replace amenity lost through other actions.

The rezone contract also spelled out enforcement provisions and stipulated that it would expire on December 31, 1979, if construction had not begun by that date.

SUBSEQUENT EVENTS

Following the signing of the agreement, the Skagit Environmental Council, a group interested in a number of environmental issues in addition to the nuclear plant, gradually faded out of the picture. In the opinion of the attorney for the other major environmental group (SCANP), the Environmental Council just did not want to commit all of its resources to opposing the plant.[54] SCANP, however, maintained its active opposition, participating in NRC hearings and challenging both the Energy Facility Site Evaluation Council and the National Pollution Discharge Elimination System permits in state court.[55] SCANP was not mollified by the concessions made by Puget Power in the rezone contract because it opposed construction of *any* nuclear facility in Skagit County. Ultimately, SCANP's legal opposition took its toll. In a history reminiscent of Seabrook, construction costs for the plant tripled and the rezone agreement expired. The county commissioners refused to renew it after voters overwhelmingly opposed the project in a referendum held in the fall of 1979.

The change in public sentiment towards the plant can be explained by a number of factors. The Three Mile Island accident radically altered the public perception of nuclear plant safety. Also, SCANP experts raised serious questions about the proximity of the plant to suspected earthquake faults. The attitude of the county commissioners toward the plant cooled when they learned of unanticipated local impacts from the construction of a nuclear plant in Grays Harbor County.[56] The commissioners feared that the existing agreement would not cover these same types of events if they occurred in Skagit County.

CONCLUSIONS

As in the Montague case, compensation failed to resolve all of the disputes that arose over the Puget Power nuclear plant. Opposition based on the fervently held belief that nuclear power is bad *per se* remained even after negotiation of the contract rezone agreement. But the fact that such opposition continued to exist should not be interpreted as a failure of the concept of compensation. In fact, compensation worked quite well in this case for both the developer and the county—the developer got the local permission needed to go forward with other regulatory procedures; the county received assurance of financial aid to cover additional public expenses if the plant should be built; and residents received assurances of additional human and environmental safeguards. What should be learned from this case is that compensation is helpful only when the parties do not hold absolute positions that leave little room for compromise; fortunately, most development disputes fall into this category. If disputants are willing to consider in-kind transfers (like the fish hatchery here to ensure the continued health of the river), then many development/environment deadlocks can be broken.

Another important lesson from this case is that it is very difficult to anticipate all the impacts of a project when it is still on the drawing board. Although Skagit County officials had the benefit of an environmental impact report to guide them in negotiating with Puget Power, they still overlooked some local impacts, and this oversight ultimately gave them pause. To avoid such a problem, drafters of compensation agreements should consider a provision that permits renegotiation of the agreement in the event of unanticipated impacts.

We now turn to the question posed at the beginning of this case study: Why was compensation itself not an issue in this controversy?

A number of factors distinguish this case from Montague and help explain why the propriety of compensation never became an issue. First, unlike Montague, all of the major impacts in this case were confined to one jurisdiction, Skagit County, which also happened to be the jurisdiction that controlled the needed local permits. In contrast, the impacts in the Montague case extended beyond the town that controlled local permits. As a result, when NU discussed compensation with Montague, it created an expectation among other towns of similar offers even though they had little to give NU in return.

Second, the payments in Skagit were clearly intended to offset costs that all sides recognized as inevitable and that were closely tied to construction of the plant. In contrast, compensation became an issue in the Montague case when the county and the airport commission demanded payment for actions that imposed no demonstrable cost on the party demanding compensation, but that restricted future airport development. For example, it was relatively easy to characterize the airport commission's request for compensation as extortion because the requested restriction would have had little effect on the airport's current operations. In contrast, Puget Power would have had a hard time denying the legitimacy of Skagit County's request to accelerate the payment of taxes to offset construction-related impacts that would immediately increase expenditures on public education.

Third, Puget Power dealt with Skagit County at arm's length; there was no appearance of coziness such as plagued the Montague-NU relationship.

Fourth, Puget Power was very open and direct in meeting with each and every group, listening to their concerns, and discussing what it would take to assuage their fears. Puget Power discovered that rather than just trying to sell the plant, in the long run it was more important to be a good listener.

Finally, the Washington State Energy Facility Site Evaluation Council had instructed them to "make peace with their neighbors" and receive all necessary local permits before requesting their state permits. Thus, a state government body had at least indirectly blessed and legitimized efforts to resolve any local concerns that surfaced through the local permitting process. Even though the facility was not built, and public support for the Contract Rezone Agreement later deteriorated, Puget Power still remains convinced that this approach to facility siting is the best way to proceed, and intends to voluntarily adopt it in any future siting efforts.[57]

CASE 4:
REGIONAL RESOURCE RECOVERY IN MASSACHUSETTS
(Principal Researcher: Stephen Hill)

In 1973, the Commonwealth of Massachusetts announced plans to implement a regional resource recovery program facilitating construction of several resource recovery facilities that would incinerate municipal solid waste and recover energy in the form of steam.* Resource recovery is an environmentally attractive alternative to landfilling and traditional incineration, the typical methods for disposing of municipal solid waste. However, because of the large capital expenditures and waste volume required for an economic resource recovery facility, regionalization is necessary in all but the largest communities.

Although less offensive than other waste disposal facilities, a resource recovery plant is not a desirable neighbor. To operate efficiently, a resource recovery plant needs to process as much as 1600 tons of waste per day, brought to the plant by trucks at a steady rate. Additional truck traffic is generated by the transport of incinerator residue to sanitary landfills, and in some cases by the transport of recovered materials to purchasers. Resource recovery plants may also produce some noise and air pollution although within legal limits. The other major adverse impacts of a resource recovery plant are psychological; few communities want the stigma associated with being a regional "dump."

Given a choice, nearly every community in a resource recovery region would rather not be the site for the regional waste disposal facility. The Commonwealth of Massachusetts tried to respond to this problem by adopting a law that required the payment of a per-ton royalty to communities hosting regional resource recovery facilities. This case describes how the prospect of such payments affected one siting process. Unlike the other cases, it illustrates a crude attempt to use compensation as a tool to help locate an otherwise noxious facility, and not merely to resolve the conflict that often arises after siting decisions have been made.

THE SITING PROCESS

In the late 1960s, the northeast region of Massachusetts faced serious solid waste disposal problems. Many community landfills and incinerators in the region did not meet state environmental standards and faced fines and closure. New landfill sites that met standards were either not available or prohibitively expensive. In 1969, several communities formed a regional committee to study regional disposal solutions—the Greater Lawrence Solid Waste Study Committee (GLSWSC), composed of elected representatives from the member communities of Andover, North Andover, Lawrence, and Methuen.[58] Despite their efforts, a 1972 proposal for a regional landfill in Methuen met with strong local opposition, and the committee disbanded soon after.[59]

_____

* Traditional incineration simply burns waste, and recovers no energy from combustion.

In early 1974, officials from the Massachusetts Bureau of Solid Waste Disposal (BSWD) met with a reconvened GLSWSC—now the Greater Lawrence Solid Waste Committee (GLSWC). The BSWD proposed a regional resource recovery facility as a solution to the region's waste disposal problems, offering technical assistance to the committee and publicizing the availability of compensation to the host community.[60] GLSWC was still interested in a regional approach, and responded favorably to the state's proposal. The BSWD suggested a site selection process, which the committee conducted during 1974. Each community was asked to nominate possible sites and provide relevant information; eight sites were eventually nominated. Communities assumed that they would receive a per-ton royalty in return for hosting the recovery facility, although the legislature had yet to require such payments. At this point, neither the recovery technology nor a specific project had been selected; the communities knew only that the facility would process between 1,800 and 3,000 tons per day (TPD) of refuse.[61]

With the assistance of BSWD, the GLSWC established site review criteria—concerning site acreage, location, accessibility, zoning, and so forth—and evaluated the nominated sites. After deliberation, GLSWC selected a site in Haverhill* "because of its excellent accessibility, relative isolation from residential users, and presumed environmental soundness."[62] The Haverhill City Council in September 1974 agreed to host the regional facility on four conditions, one of which required a per-ton royalty of $1.00 to be paid to the city.[63] Haverhill's choice of this figure apparently did not reflect any analysis of facility impacts; city officials picked the $1.00 rate because it would provide a "reasonable" return to the community.**[64,65] Because it also desired the revenue, Methuen reportedly offered to host the facility for a smaller royalty.[66] With communities starting to bid on the facility, the GLSWC decided to defer its site selection decision.

While this siting process was underway, the state legislature considered several bills to extend the per-ton royalty to resource recovery facilities. Senate Bill 707 (S. 707) in the 1974 session called for regional waste disposal facilities to make payments in lieu of taxes to the host community, based on an agreement to be negotiated by the two parties. In the 1975 session, S.1064 proposed that privately-operated resource recovery facilities pay a $1.00 per ton tax to the host community. A House bill was introduced that required a $.50 per ton tax for recovery facilities, indexed for inflation.[67] In July 1975, the legislature settled on a $1.00 per ton figure for resource recovery facilities

---

*The Haverhill site was identified by an area-wide planning agency; shortly thereafter Haverhill nominated the site and joined GLSWC.

**Based on expected facility size—1,000 to 3,000 TPD—the resource recovery plant would generate between $500,000 and $1,000,000 annually in property tax revenues, if it were taxed.

"in lieu of all taxes, fees, charges, or assessments" imposed by the host community, except for real estate taxes on the land on which the facility was located.[68] That amount was adopted since it was reportedly acceptable to Haverhill and one of its preconditions for accepting host status.

Meanwhile, serious opposition to the northeast facility developed in Haverhill. GLSWC had decided on a 3,000 TPD project and residents began to worry about the impacts of such a large facility on their town. Dr. Gene Grillo, consulting Environmental Engineer to the city, claimed the plant would adversely affect the quality of life in the town, citing the impact of increased truck traffic, noise, and air pollution.[69] Other opposition, by state Representative Francis Bevilacqua and various residents, focused on the changes in community character that the plant might cause, including growth. Residents also worried about the town's self-image; designation as a regional refuse center appeared to carry with it a definite stigma. For those opposed to the plant, compensation did not make much difference; they never sought more or better compensation.

In the face of this opposition, Haverhill's City Council withdrew its host offer in September 1975. The resource recovery facility became a focal issue in the 1975 elections, and Haverhill's voters elected a council supportive of the project. Support for the facility came from the Greater Haverhill Chamber of Commerce and various labor union locals. The region faced substantial unemployment, and these groups assumed that the project would make their area more attractive to industrial developers, thereby stimulating economic development and reducing unemployment.[70] Following the election, the City Council voted to resume host status. The approval contained some new conditions, including one requiring $1.00 per ton royalty and a minimum flow of revenue, regardless of the facility's level of utilization.[71]

But opinion was still very much divided in Haverhill. Opponents continued to cite the non-economic impacts of the plant, things like a change in community character that would not be redressed through additional revenue. Continued opposition led to a non-binding referendum in November 1976 in which voters opposed the facility by nearly a two-to-one margin.[72] The City Council subsequently voted to withdraw its host offer once again, and GLSWC decided to seek a different site.

The Northeast Solid Waste Committee (NESWC)* initiated a second site selection process in late 1976. Site selection followed the earlier procedure, but this time communities nominating sites knew more about both the proposed project and its likely impacts. Also, any uncertainty over compensation had been resolved by adoption of the state law requiring $1.00 per-ton payments. Six communities nominated seven sites, and competition was fierce due to both the compensation offer and the project's other economic

---

* The GLSWC was thus renamed in 1976 to reflect its broader "membership."

benefits.[73] In May 1977, NESWC awarded North Andover "preferred status"; this choice was influenced by North Andover's virtually unanimous approval of the project at an earlier town meeting.[74]

North Andover was enthusiastic about hosting the facility because of the economic activity the town assumed the project would spur.[75] Town officials viewed the facility as a desirable industry; it was relatively "clean" and the steam it produced would attract other industries to the area. In addition, project impacts were likely to be minimal; there were no residents near the site, and truck traffic would bypass the town almost completely. Support for the project was also more broad-based than in Haverhill. The project had been discussed at several North Andover town meetings, and in each case, residents voiced near-unanimous support.[76] The project also was desirable for its direct economic benefits; compensation just made it more attractive.

After NESWC settled on North Andover as the site, a few problems arose. A number of adjacent communities, including Haverhill, quickly realized that if the plant were built in North Andover they would still incur many of its adverse impacts but without the benefit of compensation. NESWC also encountered problems in locating a site for the regional landfill needed to receive residual material from the North Andover plant. Amesbury, NESWC's choice for the site, opposed the landfill, preferring instead a resource recovery facility that would pay a higher per-ton royalty ($1.00 versus $.50 for landfills).[77] In addition, NESWC had been unsuccessful in persuading communities to commit their solid waste to the projects. NESWC could not accurately estimate per-ton disposal costs, so local officials in its service area were understandably reluctant to commit their communities to a long-term program without first knowing its cost.*

THE ROLE OF COMPENSATION

This case provides a good illustration of both the strengths and weaknesses of using compensation as an integral component in the siting process. The state's early attempts to locate a site for a regional resource recovery facility met with little success, in part because no community wanted the adverse impacts that went hand-in-hand with the facility. When a fee of $1.00 per ton was offered to host communities, six towns came forward offering sites for the facility. Had the state been willing to allow negotiation to both the level and form of compensation (instead of fixing them by statute) it is likely that other communities would have offered to host the facility.

One consequence of allowing communities to nominate sites in response

---

* By early 1981, changes in relative prices of waste disposal and power generation plus improvements in cost calculations and contract have resulted in several communities committing their waste to the proposed plant.

to the state offer of compensation is that each community has an incentive to suggest a site that minimizes adverse impacts. This is in marked contrast to other site selection procedures for undesirable facilities. Often when the state seeks a site for something that no one wants to live near, each community invests heavily in demonstrating that no feasible site exists within its jursidiction. Because compensation made the resource recovery facility desirable, communities like North Andover looked hard for sites that did little harm to the local environment while still entitling the community to the compensation. From a societal perspective, a siting process that encourages communites to identify environmentally sound sites is preferred to one that encourages communities to oppose sites.

Finally, the case lends credence to two conclusions drawn from earlier cases. As in Montague and Skagit, offers of money compensation alone are unlikely to assuage fears based on lifestyle concerns. When people fear that a resource recovery facility will bring "rats as big as dogs,"[78] knocking a few dollars off their tax rate is unlikely to make them feel much better. And as we saw in Montague, if the offer of compensation does not extend to all people adversely affected by the project, problems are likely to result. Had the Massachusetts statute provided at least some relief for neighboring communities like Haverhill that would suffer from construction of a resource recovery facility in an adjacent town, at least one problem with implementation of the agreement could have been avoided.

CASE 5: WES–CON[79]

In 1973 and again in 1979, after Love Canal had raised national hazardous waste consciousness, Wes-Con successfully sited two small hazardous waste disposal facilities in rural Idaho. Part of its success can be attributed to its choice of technically superb sites—the newly formed company purchased sites containing abandoned Titan missile solos, and converted them into hazardous waste disposal sites. But what is most informative about this story is how Wes-Con acquired and maintained public support for its facilities. It voluntarily sought out community concerns over its proposed facilities, even though legally it needed no local approvals. It then "packaged" with its proposed facilities a variety of programs, benefits, and concessions designed both to prevent any adverse impacts being imposed on communities and to provide additional benefits. These amenities ranged from guaranteeing bills incurred by workmen in local commercial establishments, to training local doctors to handle any hazardous waste incidents, to providing free disposal service for area ranchers, to signed consent decrees. These amenities were specially tailored to respond to the communities' concerns, fears, and desires.

THE SITING STORY

1973-1976: Grand View

In 1973, a local university professor with extensive experience handling chemical waste hit upon the idea of converting the abandoned Titan missile silos into hazardous waste depositories. He formed Wes-Con, Inc., and purchased a site near Grand View, Idaho. The site itself occupies approximately 20 acres; the surrounding hydrogeology of the site is very well suited to hazardous waste disposal. In addition, Grand View (population 260), the nearest town, is 10 miles away, and the nearest rancher is two miles away. The site is otherwise surrounded by Bureau of Land Management grazing lands. The site is within Owyhee County, which has no zoning controls.

In early 1973, Wes-Con applied for its state Conditional Use Permit and completed an environmental assessment of the site. During that period of time, it also undertook several initiatives to build trust with the local communities and surrounding neighbors. Wes-Con solicited support of the Owyhee County Commissioners, even though they had no legal leverage over the proposed facility. In addition, it solicited support of the local Cattlemen's Association.

With the support of both groups and with its state permits in hand, Wes-Con undertook the necessary changes to ready the abandoned missile silos as a hazardous waste disposal site for pesticide wastes, electroplating sludges, and laboratory wastes. It hired well-known locals for a management staff, donated salvage materials to local schools, farmers, and private citizens, and invited visitors to tour the facility. In addition, Wes-Con offered to process certain local wastes (mostly pesticides) free of charge; it provided free first aid classes to neighbors, allowed area ranchers free use of Wes-Con's heavy equipment, and supported local charities, and it agreed not to accept any "political" wastes (i.e., nuclear wastes and nerve gases). Wes-Con began operations in November 1973, and received no public opposition or major complaints.

After operations began, the one and only neighbor (a woman living two miles from the facility) complained of odors and inherent dangers. A state investigation revealed no problems, but she sold her property to a ranch developer. He improved the property and resold it. The property is now being ranched, and no further complaints have been voiced.

In the fall of 1976, two events forced public attention on Wes-Con's facility. Allied Chemical approached Wes-Con to accept Kepone wastes. And about the same time, several fires at the facility led to a state investigation of the Grand View site. Wes-Con deferred the decision concerning Kepone disposal to the Governor, thereby maintaining its political support and public credibility. In early 1977, the state completed its technical re-evaluation of the Grand View site, and revised its conditional use permit. It required Wes-Con to lower barrels into the 160-foot silo (rather than dropping them) and to maintain more firefighting equipment on-site. In addition, the state required Wes-Con to sign a consent decree, agreeing to cease operations and to have its permit automatically revoked in case of another fire. Wes-Con signed the consent decree and purchased the first fire truck ever available to local ranchers and farmers.

1977-1979: Bruneau

In the spring of 1977, Wes-Con decided to repeat the Grand View siting process, again within Owyhee County. The site was similar—an abandoned missile silo occupying 20 acres surrounded by an additional 100-acre buffer zone. Bruneau (population 100), the nearest town, is 20 miles away, as is the nearest rancher.

Wes-Con went through the same procedures as before—approaching the local officials and organizations for support, and offering services and benefits to protect the community and improve its well-being. The Owyhee County Commissioners and civic leaders saw the Bruneau facility as an extension of the Grand View operation, and again gave their approval.

In July 1978, the state held a public hearing for Wes-Con's conditional use permit. Some "outsiders" (from Boise) voiced opposition. But the locals were willing to accept the site if the state and federal laws would guarantee its safety. As a result, the state again required Wes-Con to sign a consent decree and incorporated into its conditional use permit all the improved operating features adopted at the Grand View facility. The Bruneau facility began operating in 1979, with no local opposition.

THE WISDOM OF WES-CON

Many aspects of this siting story were in Wes-Con's favor, especially the choice of technically viable sites, with few neighbors, in a region demonstrating much respect for individual property rights. However, those advantages aside, Wes-Con voluntarily adopted the elements of a "sound" siting process that contributed a great deal to its success.

First of all, Wes-Con understood real power, and was not deceived by the presence or absence of "local" rights. Even though the county officials, the Governor, townspeople, and the area farmers had no legal regulatory control over the proposed facilities, Wes-Con recognized that each group maintained a great deal of power over the projects. As a result, Wes-Con informed them early on of its proposed projects and solicited their support. In both cases, Wes-Con won local support before receiving the necessary state permit.

Second, Wes-Con actively sought information concerning "social costs," those aspects of the proposed facilities that someone might perceive as damaging to his lifestyle or pocketbook. Rather than presume from a distance that they understood how people might perceive the proposed facility, Wes-Con actively solicited responses from those who might perceive themselves as being made worse off by the construction and operation of the facility.

Third, based on people's perceptions of the facility and their own social and economic needs, Wes-Con tailored the proposed facility to minimize adverse impacts on its neighbors and to maximize benefits where economically feasible. As a result, Wes-Con provided more than a dozen different types of benefits designed to reassure nearby residents that the facility would *not* adversely affect them. For example, Wes-Con publicized the type of waste to be disposed and its origin, trained local doctors on the nature of the hazardous wastes being handled and provided first aid lessons for local residents, and guaranteed the bills incurred by workmen in local commercial establishments should they skip town. Although the last example may sound inconsequential to most of us, it was a real concern to this rural community previously overwhelmed by migrant construction workers.

In addition to programs and promises designed to minimize adverse impacts, Wes-Con provided additional benefits that demonstrated its desire to support the communities in exchange for community approval. These benefits ranged from supporting the local 4-H Club to providing free disposal services.

Fourth, and perhaps most important, once Wes-Con won local trust and local support, it carefully maintained them. Wes-Con certainly had a legal right to accept Kepones, but it recognized that to do so would jeopardize public trust of the Governor (who had already promised that Kepones would not be accepted). Wes-Con could have resisted the consent decrees or the more strict fire safety measures, but doing so would have damaged the community's trust in Wes-Con's good intentions.

CONCLUSIONS

The benefits Wes-Con provided communities and ranchers probably cost very little in time or dollars, but they certainly convinced the community that Wes-Con would be a desirable neighbor. Wes-Con's approach to siting demonstrates how creative responses to community concerns and fears can prevent local opposition, build trust, and allow sound facilities to be built and operated, even after difficulties arise.

SUMMARY

These case studies describe a wide range of experiences with compensation, negotiation, and the use of information. By analyzing them in light of the theories advanced in the previous chapters, we hope to improve our understanding of how negotiated compensation agreements have been useful, and how they might be better utilized in the future. We think it is possible to draw a number of lessons from the cases.

First, people negotiate only when they perceive that they have something to gain by doing so. Northeast Utilities negotiated with the town of Montague over a number of issues because it recognized that it needed the town's acquiescence to go forward with its plans. In contrast, it refused to negotiate with Franklin County because it believed the county powerless to stop the plant, an assumption that later proved erroneous. Had Franklin County done a better job of demonstrating what it had to trade (e.g., road abandonments) it would have been more successful in bringing NU to the bargaining table. Similarly, in the Grayrocks case, the power company did not agree to negotiate with the conservation groups and the state of Nebraska until it became clear that the opponents had the power to delay construction through lengthy court battles.

Second, people reach agreement only when the cost of doing so is less than the cost of non-agreement. Getting people to the bargaining table is only half the battle. Both sides must prefer a negotiated settlement to the alternative (usually litigation) if agreement is to be reached. For example, in the Grayrocks case, the parties settled to prevent the Endangered Species Committee from deciding the issue, an outcome that was mutually distasteful to all concerned. Thus, people negotiate with their attention divided: they continually compare the prospect of a settlement with what Roger Fisher and William Urey term the "BATNA" (Best Alternative to a Negotiated Agreement).

Third, some siting issues are more easily negotiated than others. Not all impacts appear to be compensible. The cases suggest two criteria for distinguishing compensible impacts: First, impacts that are unambiguously attributable to the development are more compensible than those that are not. Thus, it was difficult to negotiate an agreement governing fiscal impacts in the Skagit case because causality could not clearly be established. The parties had difficulty agreeing on a formula which accurately assessed the fiscal impacts of the proposed power plant simply because so many other factors contributed to changes in the demand for municipal services. Second, reversible impacts are more readily compensated than irreversible impacts. In Skagit, when the parties succeeded in isolating the fiscal impacts attributable to the project, they had little difficulty in determining the appropriate compensation; Puget Power agreed to make the county whole through money payments. Similarly, agreement was possible in the Grayrocks case because the parties were capable of reversing the impact of the dam on streamflow by purchasing water rights from other sources. Had these rights not been available, it is less likely an agreement would have been forthcoming. Instead, the parties would have had to address the difficult question of what constitutes the proper compensation for the irreversible loss of a species. And in the Haverhill case, the state's offer of monetary compensation failed to assuage the concerns of citizens who feared that construction of the resource recovery facility in their town would irreversibly damage the town's image and reputation.

The fourth lesson to be drawn from the cases is that people are unwilling to negotiate compensation agreements unless they are confident that the agreements will be binding. This statement implies two questions: are the parties *capable* of promising certain benefits or future behavior, and if so, are they likely to *deliver?* In the Montague case, the town initially accepted Northeast Utilities' offer to fund a town coordinator position; later a state court judged the expenditure a conflict of interest. Subsequently, Montague did not discuss compensation with NU because the town was uncertain about NU's legal capacity to make binding commitments. In other cases, when the developers negotiated with opposition groups, they did so only with well-organized groups having a recognized leadership, well-known objectives and concerns, and an identifiable constituency. By negotiating with such groups, developers had some assurances that there would be consistency in negotiations over time, and that agreements negotiated by the leadership were not likely to be repudiated subsequently by the general membership. Also, it was "legitimate" for a developer to approach a group about issues with which the group had long been associated.

FOOTNOTES

1. Additional sources not footnoted in this case include the following: Michael Reilly, Legal Counsel, U.S. Army Corps of Engineers, Omaha, Nebraska, telephone interview March 5, 1979; David Westly, U.S. Fish and Wildlife Service, Office of Endangered Species, Arlington, Virginia, telephone interview March 16, 1979; Lonnie L. Williamson, Secretary, Wildlife Management Institute, Washington, D.C., telephone interview March 13, 1979; Bruce Hamilton, "The Whooping Crane: A Success Story," May/June 1979, vol. 64, no. 3, *Sierra, The Sierra Club Bulletin,* p. 56; Steven L. Yaffee, "Prohibitive Policies and the Endangered Species Act," unpublished Ph.D. dissertation, M.I.T., Department of Urban Studies and Planning, Cambridge, MA, May 1979; *The Washington Post:* (a) "Whooping Crane Safety Promised, Dam Fight Ends," November 28, 1978, (b) "Saving a Place for Cranes", Editorial, November 29, 1978.
2. "Rare Whooping Crane vs. Western Power Project," *The Washington Post,* November 27, 1978, pp. A1, A7.
3. Wildlife Management Institute, *Outdoor News Bulletin,* "Settlement Leaves Whoopers in Jeopardy," February 9, 1979, vol. 33, no. 3, pp. 1–3.
4. Paul W. Snyder, Assistant Attorney General, State of Nebraska, Lincoln, Nebraska, interview March 13, 1979.
5. William Wisdom, General Counsel, Basin Electric Power Cooperative, Bismarck, North Dakota, interview March 9, 1979.
6. Edward Weinberg, Attorney, Missouri Basin Power Project, Washington, D.C., interview March 8, 1979.
7. Wisdom, *op. cit.*
8. Robert Turner, Wyoming Regional Representative, National Audubon Society, Sheridan, Wyoming, interview March 13, 1979.
9. Turner, *ibid.*
10. Weinberg, *op. cit.*
11. Wisdom, *op. cit.*
12. Snyder, *op. cit.*
13. Patrick Parenteau, Attorney, National Wildlife Federation, Washington, D.C., interviews December 19, 1978 and January 26, 1979.
14. Snyder, *op. cit.*
15. Snyder, *ibid.*
16. Weinberg, *op. cit.*
17. "Rare Whooping Crane vs. Western Power Project," *op. cit.*
18. *Ibid.*
19. Robert Cahn, "Perspective—The God Committee," *Audubon Magazine,* May 1979, vol. 81, no. 3, page 10.

20. Turner, *op. cit.*
21. Parenteau, *op. cit.*
22. Snyder, *op. cit.*
23. Parenteau, *op. cit.*
24. Wisdom, *op. cit.*
25. *Ibid.*
26. Snyder, *op. cit.*
27. *Ibid.*
28. Parenteau, *op. cit.*
29. Wildlife Management Institute, *op. cit.*
30. Brant Calkin, "An Archaic Quirk of Western Water Law," *Sierra, The Sierra Club Bulletin,* February/March 1978, vol. 63, no. 2, p. 31.
31. Hank Fischer, "Montana's Yellowstone River—Who Gets the Water?" *Sierra, The Sierra Club Bulletin,* July/August 1978, volume 63, no. 5, pp. 13–15.
32. Wisdom, *op. cit.*
33. Parenteau, *op. cit.*
34. Snyder, *op. cit.*
35. Parenteau, *op. cit.*
36. Snyder, *op. cit.*
37. *Agreement of Settlement and Compromise,* Basin Electric Power Cooperative *et al.,* December 4, 1978.
38. Wildlife Management Institute, *op. cit.*
39. Wildlife Management Institute, *op. cit.*
40. Condensed from Julia Wondolleck, "The Montague Nuclear Power Plant: Negotiation, Information and Intervention," *Nuclear Energy Facilities and Public Conflict: Three Case Studies;* Laboratory of Architecture and Planning, M.I.T., Cambridge, MA. 1979.
41. Additional sources not footnoted in this case include the following: Fred Clagett, *Energy Centers in Washington State: A Socioeconomic Institutions Summary,* Washington State Office of Community Development, January 1977; Martha Curry, *et al., State and Local Planning Procedures Dealing with Social and Economic Impacts from Nuclear Power Plants,* Battelle Memorial Institute, January 1977; Elizabeth Peele, *Internalizing Social Costs in Power Plant Siting: Some Examples for Coal and Nuclear Plants in the United States,* Oak Ridge National Laboratory, November 17, 1976; Washington, Energy Facility Site Evaluation Council, *Site Certification Agreement Between the State of Washington and Puget Sound Power and Light, for Units 1 & 2,* January 5, 1977; Theodore F. Thomsen, lawyer representing Puget Sound Power and Light, telephone interview.
42. David Myrha, "One Nuke Gets a Warm Welcome," *Planning,* September 1975.
43. Robet Schofield, Director, Skagit County Planning Commission, telephone interview.
44. Michael Gendler, Associate of Roger Lead, lawyer representing SCANP, telephone interview.
45. Roger Leed, lawyer representing SCANP, telephone interview.

46. William J. Finnegan, Director, Conservation and Environmental Affairs, Puget Sound Power and Light. Telephone Interview.
47. Myrha, *op. cit.*
48. Schofield, *op. cit.*
49. Myrha, *op. cit.*
50. *Ibid.*
51. Finnegan, *op. cit.*
52. Schofield, *op. cit.*
53. *Contract Rezone Agreement,* Puget Sound Power and Light and Skagit County, March 26, 1974.
54. Leed, *op. cit.*
55. Gendler, *op. cit.*
56. Leed, *op. cit.*
57. Shelly Smolkin, "Environmental Doves," *The Weekly,* May 14–May 20, 1980, Seattle, Washington, p. 14,30.
58. Karen Higgs, *Siting Energy Facilities: Northeast Massachusetts Resource Recovery Facility Revisited,* Energy Impacts Project, M.I.T., January 1978.
59. Lawrence Susskind and Richard Newcome, *The Obstacles to Regional Resource Recovery: A Massachusetts Case Study,* Environmental Impact Assessment Project, M.I.T., December 1977.
60. *Ibid.*
61. Frank Emilio, Haverhill City Council, interview April 3, 1979.
62. Susskind, *op. cit.*
63. Susskind, *op. cit.,* page 25.
64. Emilio, *op. cit.*
65. Warren Frye, former member Haverhill City Council. Interview March 26, 1979.
66. Susskind, *op. cit.*
67. William Gaughan, Director, Massachusetts Bureau of Solid Waste Disposal. Interviews March 23, 1979 and April 5, 1979.
68. General Court of Massachusetts, Acts of 1975, Chapter 500.
69. Susskind, *op. cit.*
70. *Ibid.*
71. Emilio, *op. cit.*
72. Susskind, *op. cit.*
73. Higgs, *op. cit.*
74. *Ibid.*
75. Former Representative Charles Long, Commonwealth of Massachusetts. Interview March 26, 1979.
76. Gaughan, *op. cit.*
77. Higgs, *op. cit.*
78. Susskind, *op. cit.*
79. Summarized from United States Environmental Protection Agency, *Siting of Hazardous Waste Management Facilities and Public Opposition.* SW–809, 1979, pp. 144–156.

9
Negotiated Compensation in the Traditional Process

Our discussion to this point has been critical of the rules under which we are forced to try to site, build, or oppose major facilities. Indeed, in the next chapter we will present a complete revision of the legal facility siting process. But neither a project developer nor a potential opponent has the power to change state laws: what should they do when a siting dispute looms under the existing legal structure? The cases in the previous chapter illustrate significant opportunities to apply the insights of this study to almost any siting dispute; in the following pages we present recommendations for participants in siting problems that can be implemented in many current cases.

The first half of this chapter describes eight attributes of development disputes that, together, characterize situations where compensation is likely to be useful. In practice, all eight attributes usually won't be present, nor all absent, in any single dispute. Since most situations will fall somewhere between "hopeless" and "easily compensible," the purpose of this list is to provide a set of questions to ask in trying to decide whether to proceed with compensation as a strategy to avoid or resolve conflict. The list also should give people interested in using compensation some idea of the problems likely to be encountered along the way.

The second half of the chapter contains "how-to-do-it" advice for implementing the insights of the previous chapter within the conventional siting process. It describes common pitfalls and gives some suggestions as to how they might be avoided. Although we have divided this section into "advice to developers" and "advice to groups adversely affected by development," we encourage people in both groups to read both sections. We believe that it will be a lot easier to resolve disputes over development if each side understands the problems and concerns of the other.

CHARACTERISTICS OF THE DISPUTE

While not absolute prerequisites, the following eight characteristics of development disputes describe the ideal conditions under which compensation might be tried. If any condition is absent, those initiating compensation procedures should note the shortcomings and try to anticipate the problems that might arise. Following a description of these characteristics, we offer an example of a dispute that is tailor-made for the use of compensation and another example of a dispute that is not.

1. Few Parties to the Dispute

Compensation agreements are easiest to negotiate when there are few parties to the dispute, or when proponents and opponents communicate through only a few organizations. Multilateral negotiations tend to be complicated and time consuming for a number of reasons: (1) each new bargaining position often must be explained separately to each party; (2) each party must be given an opportunity to respond to each new proposal; (3) it is difficult for negotiators to develop the personal relationships that often lead to successful agreements; and (4) the bargaining positions taken by different groups interact, so a series of bilateral agreements will usually not suffice. In general, the fewer the parties, the easier it is to find a common ground.

2. Opponents Geographically Defined

Sometimes people oppose a project because they live nearby and will be adversely affected if the project is constructed. In other cases, opponents do not share geographic proximity but instead some common interest in the proposed facility. It is easist to negotiate compensation agreements when the opposition is geographically defined. In the first place, project opponents are easily identified. Second, to the extent that the project detracts from the local environment, compensation can be directed at enhancing the quality of the local environment in ways that are valued by the opposition. And third, geographically-defined opposition corresponds with some local governmental jurisdiction, giving developers a recognized entity with which to negotiate. This correspondence also creates the potential for other types of compensatory exchanges such as community financial assistance, property value guarantees, public services' assistance, promises to hire local workers, and so on.

In contrast, it is difficult to compensate geographically diffuse opposition because most forms of compensation involve providing tangible benefits to a specific locality or political jurisdiction. When the opposition is spread out all over the country, it is not clear who should be compensated nor how to reach them.

3. Opponents Well Organized

An opposition group that is well organized internally has an advantage in negotiating with a developer because the developer knows who speaks for the group. A strong, representative leader usually knows what bargaining positions are likely to be acceptable to the members of the group. Moreover, strong leaders typically are capable of persuading reluctant members to go along with a settlement. In general, groups that are well organized internally have an easier time persuading developers that they will abide by promises made during the course of negotiations than loosely knit coalitions that cannot speak with a single voice.

4. Mutually Acceptable Outcomes Exist

Basically, a compensation agreement is a compromise between a developer and groups affected by the development. A compromise can only occur, however, if possible outcomes exist that are mutually acceptable to all parties. If one party (or more) adopts an absolutist position (e.g., "I cannot tolerate the development under any circumstances"), then an agreement will not be forthcoming. (Notice that parties may make such *statements* for strategic reasons even in circumstances where there is some room for compromise.) To the extent that a rich set of possible outcomes exists, it will be easier to negotiate a compensation agreement than if only a few such outcomes, each very different, exist.

5. Impacts are Clearly Traceable to the Project

Sometimes the impacts of a project are obvious. For example, it is usually easy to trace noise pollution to its source. In other situations, the causal relationship between the project and the surrounding environment may be due to an upturn in the local economy which has attracted new residents, the temporary presence of workers constructing a new power plant, or the construction of new housing. It is easiest to negotiate compensation agreements when impacts are clearly traceable to the devlopment under discussion. When impacts are less direct, negotiations often become bogged down over whether the developer is actually responsible for observed changes in the local social, economic, or natural environment.

6. Recreation of the Status Quo is Possible

All impacts are not the same; only some can be prevented before a project is undertaken. For example, use of low sulfur coal will prevent some types of air pollution in coal-fired boilers. Others cannot be prevented but can be reversed: construction of new classrooms, for example, can eliminate overcrowding in schools caused by population increases attributable to new projects. Still others can be neither prevented nor reversed. In such cases, the developer has the unpleasant task of asking people to suffer the damage and accept compensation "equal to" their suffering. In general, it is much easier to negotiate compensation agreements for the first two types of impacts than for the third. When the *status quo ante* cannot be restored, then the parties affected by development must reach some consensus concerning what constitutes a fair exchange for the damage incurred. Often this type of consensus is very difficult to reach. Moreover, people often are reluctant to exchange one type of amenity for another, and thus may refuse, say, a proposal by a developer who offers to build a new park to compensate for the increase in air pollution caused by his power plant.

7. Parties Capable of Offering a Binding Commitment

When parties sit down to negotiate a compensation agreement, the substance of the bargaining usually centers on the exchange of mutual promises. The developer, for example, may promise to pay compensation in return for a promise by a community group to support or refrain from opposing the project. Compensation agreements are much easier to negotiate when the parties possess the capacity to bind themselves legally to their commitments. A party that lacks such capacity may have a hard time convincing its negotiating opponents that it will live up to its promises, or that it can be forced to.

8. Absence of Initial Hostility

Negotiating a compensation agreement is not a simple task under the best of circumstances. It is all the more difficult if the parties are hostile towards each other prior to entering into negotiations. If prior relations have resulted in resentment and animosity, then negotiations may be plagued by mistrust and suspicion. Negotiations are more likely to be successful if the parties harbor neutral feelings towards each other than if previous relations have been characterized by conflict.

EXAMPLES

An Outdoor Music Theater

A developer in the Midwest is considering constructing a large amphitheater near a residential area. Following announcement of the proposal, property owners in the immediate vicinity of the project band together to oppose the project. They fear that pop concerts will bring noise to their homes on hot summer evenings.

This dispute is tailor-made for the use of compensation. The opposing parties are few in number, geographically defined, and well organized. They are not unalterably opposed to the development; they can live with it provided that their concerns are met. The primary impact—noise—is clearly traceable to the project. Options are available for neutralizing the impact of the noise. For example, landscaping can be used to reduce noise transmission. Alternatively, the developer might offer to buy air conditioners for the affected homes so that the homeowners can keep their windows shut on hot summer nights during concerts. Each party is capable of giving a legally binding commitment—the developer can sign a contract with each owner. Finally, since the parties have had no contact with each other prior to the announcement of this project, they would not have to overcome any residual mistrust.

The Seabrook Nuclear Plant

Contrast the above example with the conflict over the construction of the Seabrook nuclear power plant in New Hampshire (as discussed in Chapter 2). There, the developer faced opposition from many scattered, loosely organized interests including local fishermen, environmentalists, groups opposed to nuclear power *per se,* and even New Hampshire electric customers who resented attempts by the utility to pass along construction costs through surcharges on local utility bills. The opposition was not geographically defined; opponents traveled from all over the country to participate in anti-Seabrook rallies on the construction site. The Clamshell Alliance that coordinated anti-Seabrook activities had no formal meetings, no elected officers, and no official spokesman. Since many of the Seabrook opponents opposed construction of any nuclear plant, or any power plant on the site, outcomes did not exist that were mutually acceptable to the developer and all the opposition.

The parties disagreed strongly over whether cooling water discharge from the plant will harm aquatic life. Furthermore, if it does, project opponents insist that the damage will be permanent and irreparable. Even if the developer and the nominal leaders of the Clamshell Alliance could reach some agreement, the Alliance cannot guarantee that its members will abide by the agreement. Finally, given the past history of mutual mistrust, it is unlikely that the parties will ever engage in meaningful negotiations. In short, compensation will probably not be helpful in resolving this type of problem.

Most disputes will fall somewhere between the amphitheater and the Seabrook case. By analyzing the characteristics of a dispute using the eight attributes described in this chapter, the parties can determine whether compensation might be helpful either as a means to resolve a dispute, or to keep a small controversy from consuming a whole project.

HOW TO DO IT

If compensation seems worth a try, what should be done next? The answer depends on whether one is a developer or someone adversely affected by development.

Advice to Developers

1. *Recognize that while your project may be good for an area as a whole, it is likely to make at least a few individuals or groups genuinely worse off.*

Pay special attention to the distribution of costs and benefits from your project. Few projects make everyone better off; inevitably someone will feel disadvantaged because of your activities. Opposition is most likely to come from these disadvantaged groups, and the success of your project may depend on how well you respond to these individuals.

2. *Find out who loses if your project is constructed and why.*

Solicit comments from all potentially interested parties as early as possible (even those not obviously capable of delaying the project). Try to understand how people view the project. Determine who dislikes aspects of your project and why. Listen to people. Don't trust your judgment of what they like and dislike. Keep reassessing public reaction to your project—perceptions often change over time.

3. *Be sensitive to people's fears.*

People often want economic benefits for themselves and their community, but worry about threats to their health and safety or to their environment, no matter how small. You will not assuage their concerns merely by asserting that the feared event is unlikely or will not occur. Your statements inevitably will be viewed as self-serving. You must find a way to respond to their fears. Be prepared to take steps to reduce the probability of the undesirable event. If you sincerely believe that the event will not occur, then you should be willing to accept responsibility for its consequences. For example, if you really believe that your new paint factory will not harm fishing on a popular lake, you should be willing to restock the lake if it does. Given the low probability that you ascribe to the event, this is a nearly costless concession.

4. *Think creatively about ways to make people whole—to leave them as well off after the facility is built and operating as they were before.*

Consider the project as a package including not only the facility but also benefits, guarantees, special conditions, and adverse impacts, and as one that is still in its design phase. First concentrate on changes to *prevent anticipated damages* from occurring—alter the design, add pollution control devices, change operating practices, change location, hire local workers, provide public services, monitor emissions and discharges, and so on. Then concentrate on methods to *correct unavoidable damages*—construct fish breeding grounds, expand over-utilized public services, build a wildlife refuge, etc. Where preventing or correcting damages is either impossible or exorbitantly expensive, concentrate on various types of compensation payments to be made now or in the future as damages occur. Whatever change is made—either preventative, corrective, or compensatory—make it correspond as closely as possible to the expected cost or damage. And finally, expect to negotiate the amount, type, and timing of compensation—only through negotiations can you fully understand the point at which compensation makes people whole in their own eyes, and this leaves them feeling at least neutral toward your project.

5. *Be sensitive to the fact that your actions to initiate negotiation of compensation agreements may offend opponents.*

Opponents may perceive an offer as an effort to "buy them off." They may also fear public accusations that they were bought off, were participants in an under-the-table deal, or that they blackmailed the developer. They may also doubt the legality of such negotiations.

Try to introduce compensation indirectly by asking leading questions. How can we respond to your concerns? How can we modify the project to eliminate this damage you expect? If this fails, try to get a trusted neutral third party to bring up the idea of compensation.

Avoid actions that might cause people to look as if they are compromising the health and safety of future generations for current economic gain, or actions that in any other way conflict with people's values. In places where compensation has never before been suc-

cessfully introduced, seek legal or political support for such procedures before doing so.

6. *Focus on bargaining rather than gift-giving.*

Focus on what each party has to offer the other. Whenever possible,
attempt to strike bargains in which each side exchanges mutual promises. Outright gifts may create resistance if opponents believe gifts
might make them beholden to you, or socially indebted, or less
capable of pressing their concerns. As long as an open market
operates, in which parties negotiate over the exchanging of benefits,
then opponents are more likely to perceive themselves as equally in
control and to perceive negotiating as a worthwhile and productive
process.

7. *Presume mistrust.*

In many cases, opponents will automatically mistrust developers and
will look for evidence that reinforces this belief. Be sensitive to this
predisposition. Evaluate your actions from your opponent's perspective, and avoid actions that might be construed as deceptive or
threatening.
   Try to build and maintain trust through your actions and demonstration of your previous record, not just through words. Be prepared
to support every claim, and to make your promises legally binding.
Readily embrace other institutions or procedures that the public
trusts, such as legal contracts, mediators, government agencies,
elected officials, etc. Opponents will not negotiate unless they know
that someone or some system can prevent you from taking advantage
of them or from failing to live up to your agreement.

8. *Be forthcoming with information.*

Withholding information from the public can be costly. Damaging information almost always finds its way into the public domain, either
through regulatory proceedings or because someone leaks it to the
press. If you divulge this information on your own, you will at least
have an opportunity to explain it. If someone else releases it, espe-

cially over your objection, the information is likely to be far more damaging to your position. Moreover, your credibility will suffer and you will appear deceptive. If the information is going to come out anyway, release it yourself and take credit for being forthright.

9. *Recognize that if opponents don't know much about your project, they are likely to assume the worst.*

People will not negotiate with you unless they understand the likely consequences of the project. Ignorance often leads to fear and extreme bargaining positions. Try to respond to your opponents' informational needs. If necessary, offer to underwrite the cost of a study which *they* commission to assess the impacts of your project.

10. *Suggest ways to resolve future disputes.*

Assume future disputes will arise, and establish mechanisms for resolving them as part of your formal agreement. Show willingness to negotiate the future disputes, especially when actual impacts are fairly uncertain. When possible, specify conditions under which agreements can be renegotiated, the procedure to be used, and the procedures for discussing and resolving future disagreements.

11. *Be "up front" with your offer.*

Opponents often expect to find the developer "in bed" with local officials, and you should try to avoid that perception. Keep your interaction with the community and the opponents as open as possible. Assume that any secret meetings will eventually become public knowledge. If offers or negotiations are clandestine, you risk reinforcing your opponents' perception of you, creating mistrust, and quite possibly destroying a cooperative working relationship.

12. *Try not to appear intransigent.*

It is remarkable how frequently developers alienate community groups by refusing to even discuss their development plans. There is a high return to soliciting comments before your plans are finalized; don't miss this opportunity.

Advice to Opposition Groups

1. *Think creatively about acceptable arrangements that satisfy your concerns and allow some type of project to go forward.*

You probably do not face an all-or-nothing choice; can you transform the proposed project into one that would satisfy your concerns? Consider the proposed project as a package including not only the facility but also additional amenities, benefits, and conditions, all subject to change within broad, economic and institutional constraints. Think creatively about facility changes, new programs, policies, and promises that the developer might accept or guarantee which would satisfy your concerns. Be willing to suggest alternatives to the developer's proposal that would allow the project to go forward but would leave you and other opponents feeling at least neutral toward it.

2. *Demonstrate to the developer that it is in his interest to negotiate with you.*

First, show the developer the advantages he gains by taking you seriously—reduced costs of delay, public support, improved public image as a cooperative and environmentally conscious developer, and so forth. Second, reinforce that evidence by displaying the strength of your bargaining position, and your preference for negotiation and compromise rather than drawn-out legal and political conflicts. Negotiations will introduce different costs and risks for the developer, and your task is to show that he has more to gain than to lose by negotiating.

3. *Don't commit yourself to a position from which it will be impossible to compromise.*

If there are any circumstances under which you could live with the development, then don't put yourself in a position where you can't accept it. Avoid taking positions that foreclose compromise.

4. *If you are a leader, demonstrate that you are firmly in control of the opposition.*

First, make sure you really *are* in control—otherwise you risk destroying your credibility, as well as that of other opposition groups in the future. Find ways of demonstrating your control, rather than expecting the developer to accept your word for it. Remember that the developer will have to justify his actions to his superiors and shareholders, and will want firm evidence that you fully understand the opposition's concerns, that you can negotiate on their behalf, and that they follow your decisions. This evidence will strengthen your bargaining position as well as let the developer know that you are capable of delivering on agreements.

5. *Build credibility with, and respect from, the developer.*

The developer probably views opposition groups with skepticism and mistrust, and may hold a stereotypical view of them as reactionary, irrational, and uncompromising. Be self-conscious of how you come across in your dealings with the developer. Through actions and words, demonstrate that you are cooperative and amenable—not strident; rational, open-minded, and reasonable—not erratic, reactionary and illogical; businesslike and professional—not emotional, naive, or inexperienced. Take care not to reinforce his likely preconception that you are too unreasonable to deal with.

Be sensitive to the political and economic constraints the developer faces, and suggest alternatives he can accept. Don't forget that the developer has to live within a budget. Don't ask him to compromise his basic objectives or take a stand that threatens his position with his superiors.

6. *Be sensitive to the developer's fear of being "blackmailed."*

Developers often fear being held-up by non-elected and presumably unrepresentative opposition groups. Rather than asking for favors or outright gifts, stress bargaining and making trades, emphasizing that you and the developer are exchanging things that one of them has and the other wants. Demonstrate what you have to offer, which is most likely public support, guaranteed end to opposition, or even assistance in managing programs or acquiring public permits.

7. *Be willing to support the developer.*

If you reach an agreement with the developer, be willing to throw him your support. Be as specific as possible about the nature and timing of that support.

10
Legislated Siting Procedures

We have argued frequently in this study that the formal procedures through which new facilities are proposed, evaluated, and licensed in the United States are ill-suited to a satisfactory process. Some of these defects can be overcome by good fortune, as when there are so few neighbors of a new facility site or they are so poorly organized or—as seems to be true of some places in the Southwest—social norms so strongly favor industrial development that the legal power conveyed by formal licensing is greater than the power of facility opponents to obstruct development. Defects of the conventional process can also be mitigated by the approaches suggested in the previous chapter. But the law that governs the siting process need not be an impediment to efficient and equitable evaluation of proposals. It can, moreover, contribute to quick development of the ones worth building.

In this chapter we describe a legal structure that responds to the insights developed elsewhere in this book, especially in Chapters 5, 6, and 7. For those readers who would like to see this structure in statute form, we have added as the Appendix at the end of this book the new Massachusetts Hazardous Waste Facility Siting Act.

The description in this chapter follows as nearly as possible the logic of the process rather than the chronological order in which events occur. Figure 10.1 diagrams the process in chronological form instead so that it may be a useful reference as the discussion proceeds.

INCENTIVES TO NEGOTIATE

Designated Parties to Negotiation

In our view, the heart of a workable siting process is explicit and formal negotiation between the neighbors a new facility will most affect and the agency or firm proposing to build it. We will call the party on one side of this table "the developer," intending the term to mean either a government agency or a private corporation. The developer's representative will be obvious for each case, but it's not clear who ought to sit across the table representing the neighbors. Our preference is for an existing general-purpose local government to have this responsibility; these negotiations are not distinguishable in theory from the negotiations that local government undertakes with public employee unions, land owners (purchasing a site for a new school, for example) or contractors providing services. For something as important as a new major facility in a small community, the chief negotiator will probably be the mayor, though his agreement should be subject to ratification by the local legislative body.

However, another view of this issue deserves mention. Many citizen group representatives and a majority of the Massachusetts state legislators feel that negotiations on behalf of the neighbors should be carried out by a special purpose commission whose members represent—and thus assure attention to—specific, identifiable interests in the community. In contrast, our preference for a general purpose government derives from the ability of such an institution to "horse trade" different kinds of benefits to different groups and from the fact that a local government, even though its representatives may change, will be a continuing presence in the future of the facility.

In any case, the statute establishing the siting process must specify representatives of local interests and either create or empower the body that will handle the negotiations.

Power to Form Contracts

One of the principal conditions for negotiations is that the parties have something to trade. Again, this condition is easily satisfied on the part of the developer; if his facility will provide any profits or net benefits to society, some share of those must be available for distribution to the community. Furthermore, he can trade many things that don't cost much, such as redesign or modification of his facility, or a change in its proposed operating procedures.

What the community has to trade is, in general terms, simply withholding its power to delay or defeat the facility. As we've argued earlier, we think the community has this power independently of the legal authority that may have been granted to it by any particular state

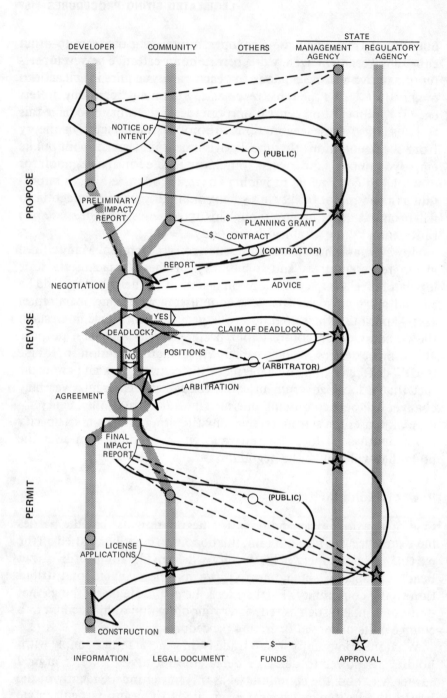

STATE

DEVELOPER   COMMUNITY   OTHERS   MANAGEMENT   REGULATORY
                                    AGENCY   AGENCY

PROPOSE

NOTICE OF
INTENT

(PUBLIC)

PRELIMINARY
IMPACT
REPORT

$ PLANNING GRANT

$ CONTRACT

(CONTRACTOR)

REPORT

NEGOTIATION   ADVICE

REVISE

YES

DEADLOCK?   CLAIM OF DEADLOCK

NO   POSITIONS

(ARBITRATOR)

AGREEMENT   ARBITRATION

FINAL
IMPACT
REPORT

PERMIT

(PUBLIC)

LICENSE
APPLICATIONS

CONSTRUCTION

INFORMATION   LEGAL DOCUMENT   ─$─→   APPROVAL
                                 FUNDS

168

law. But it is not obvious—even to members of the community—that it can really withhold its acquiescence in an effective way. Furthermore, the exercise of its power to obstruct may require illegal actions such as a sit-in, whose use cannot be threatened formally to the developer. Accordingly, it's of the essence of statutory reform of the siting process that the law be made to conform to the facts by granting the community specific formal, legal authority that corresponds to its *de facto* power to delay or obstruct. It might seem that a permit to operate could be traded to the developer through these negotiations, but serious legal problems hinder a government from contracting to use its authority in a particular way. Accordingly, our suggestion is that the specific authority to contract with the developer on all the conditions of his operation be granted to the community by statute, and that the existence of such an agreement be made a requirement for operating the facility.

The centerpiece of our proposal is, therefore, a legal prohibition against constructing or operating a new facility without what we call a "siting agreement" in the form of a contract between the developer and the community. Such an agreement becomes a vehicle for recording the conditions and the compensation exacted by the community from the developer, promises and commitments from the developer, and any promises and commitments the community government may make to the developer as well.

Requirement for a Contract

In their new book on negotiation, Roger Fisher and William Ury advance the concept of the *best alternative to a negotiated agreement*—BATNA—as a critical index of the probable success of negotiation.[1] If the developer understands the situation, he recognizes that his best alternative to negotiation in the process we are describing is probably

Figure 10.1 Facility Siting Process. Three principal phases of the proposed siting process include specific steps, most of which are supportive of the negotiations leading to a siting agreement between a developer and a host community. In the first phase, the parties are informed of the proposal and its consequences; approvals here indicate that the tep have been completed but not that the project itself is endorsed. In the third phase, state licenses are granted; this is the point at which environmental and other impacts outside the host community are formally evaluated. The second phase includes the actual negotiations.

a failure of his project. Accordingly, a negotiated siting agreement should look like a good way to proceed. However, the community's BATNA is very likely to *appear* to be successful intransigent obstruction. One reason for this is that such obstruction, at least under the old rules for siting, will probably defeat the project. A second reason is that at the beginning of the negotiation process, it's often difficult to see how the facility being proposed could possibly—no matter what is negotiated—be of benefit to the community. Accordingly, we think it is essential to reduce the community's BATNA from "the status quo with high probability" to something distinctly less attractive.

Arbitration

At this point in the analysis, many sensible people have turned to some sort of state override power, but tempting as this is, we nevertheless think it inconsistent with the real distribution of power in a typical siting dispute. Furthermore, local government has frequently shown a deep mistrust of the state agency that threatens (with or without safeguards and "ample public hearings") to "shove it down our throats." Consequently, we favor giving the developer and the state supervising agency a stick of carefully limited size: if negotiations are deadlocked, the parties should be able to call upon a state agency to throw the negotiations into binding arbitration. The arbitration should be by a representative of the developer, a representative of the community, and a party agreeable to both (or, of course, a single arbitrator agreeable to both). This arbitrator should have the power to establish the siting agreement that the parties didn't, or couldn't, reach through negotiations.

If the parties fear that the arbitrator will (inevitably) understand the issues imperfectly and will not be sensitive to either party's interest as well as the parties' representatives themselves, then the threat of arbitration should provide an incentive to negotiate. To put it another way, the parties may settle merely to avoid the "roll of the dice" that often constitutes arbitration, much as the parties in the Gray Rocks Dam case negotiated to avoid a ruling by the "God Committee."

Notice that the "status quo—no facility—arrived at by intransigent opposition" BATNA still remains for the community. As we have said repeatedly, we think the principal failure of the traditional siting process is that it does not recognize that this is an unavoidable consequence of the facts surrounding a siting dispute and something which is not subject to alteration by any power the state government can realistically bring to bear.

What the arbitrated agreement provision does is to make this BATNA much more difficult to achieve and less certain of success, and to remove one of the legal obstacles a community might otherwise put in the place of development. More importantly, a community that has refused to negotiate a siting agreement, and refuses to abide by an arbitrated settlement established without specific intervention by state government, is in a very poor position to attract the kind of sympathetic support from other pressure groups that so often make a winning coalition in siting disputes when a small group of citizens seem to be abused by an insensitive bureaucracy.

Nevertheless, we don't want to overstate our claim. While we think many siting exercises that would otherwise collapse in hopeless deadlock will advance to a satisfactory outcome by the process we are proposing, there's no guarantee that our suggestions will deal conclusively and universally with the problem of local opposition. We think this siting process is the best thing available, but we don't think it's surefire. In particular, we think its most likely mode of failure will be that neighbors of *some* proposed facilities will not believe that a negotiated settlement could ever be a more useful strategy for them than fighting tooth-and-nail; the community that fights tooth-and-nail will probably succeed in deflecting new development.

Statutory requirement of a negotiated agreement on operating conditions and compensation, coupled with a provision for arbitrating such an agreement if negotiations fail, is the engine that drives the siting process we advocate. Its other elements are either retained from the conventional process (such as state licensing), modified to better serve their original purposes (such as the environmental impact review process), or added to encourage making a deal.

INFORMATION MANAGEMENT

Even when people have something to trade and have assurance that each can be held to an agreement, it will be impossible to negotiate a settlement if one party doesn't know what the other is talking about. Community negotiators are likely to feel at a distinct disadvantage relative to the developer in discussing technical matters like potential health and safety problems that might be mitigated or avoided through negotiation. We are deeply out of sympathy with the traditional response to this lack of sophistication, which is to compel someone to provide the community with an environmental impact report. For the reasons described in Chapter 7, the impact report provides the wrong information to the wrong people in the wrong form at the wrong time. Instead, we propose to take seriously our observation that there is no such thing as a report that will be treated as objective by all parties to a controversy: rather than force the community to depend on the developer for information, we empower the community to gather its own. The best way to do this is with money, in the form of planning grants with which the community can hire professional consultants to analyze the developer's information and to collect additional information to supplement that of the developer. (Notice that when a party to negotiations is buying information to form his own position in the negotiations, he has no incentive to deceive himself or to obtain propaganda. He wants as nearly correct a reading of the situation as he can obtain.) We wouldn't do away with impact reports entirely, but we think the impact statement process should produce an impact report that is a record of debate and information exchange. Rather than expect the developer to put "the whole objective truth" into a spiral binder, the final record would reflect the informed views of the parties involved on issues of importance and from their respective viewpoints.

Someone has to start this information-gathering process, of course, and that party is logically the developer. He should be obliged to provide a draft environmental impact report, with chapters on socioeconomic impacts, within a reasonable time after announcing his intention to begin the formal siting process. The standard for acceptability for this document, however, would be much less stringent than we now impose on impact reports; it would only have to present the issues well enough so as to serve as a basis for debate and for further information gathering.

Developers are now reluctant, however, to release such a draft report because opponents interested in stopping the project rather than negotiating will use it against them. Opponents will be looking for evidence that the project will have adverse impacts on the community; thus, developers fear releasing draft information that might be interpreted as such unless they are absolutely certain of their analysis and findings. In addition, further research leading to changes in their draft information can be construed by the public as purposefully misleading. Information can also take on a life of its own, even if published with "draft" labels and conditional statements; developers perceive that they lack the *practical* ability to change the contents of draft impact reports. As a result, community negotiators wanting early information and a more open exchange of information with developers must find means of reassuring developers that the report's "draft" status is fully understood, that changes are expected, and that its contents will not be used against the developer in court proceedings. In addition, state statutes must protect developers from opponents wanting to submit information contained in draft impact reports as part of court proceedings.

At the time the draft report is published, the community should be awarded funds with which to hire consultants to provide a variety of services as the local government sees fit—criticizing the developer's impact report, gathering information not included therein, expanding the analysis on issues of special concern to the community, and so forth. We fully expect that research undertaken on behalf of the community will be used in strategic ways in negotiations, such as by partial release, or concealment from the developer of results favorable to his case. We would require only that the complete analysis—especially if paid for with state funds—be available when the siting process has been completed, both for advancement of the art of impact prediction and as a loose discipline on the negotiating process.

When negotiations are complete and a siting agreement is in place, the facility to be built is probably different in major or minor ways from the initial proposal put forth by the developer. These changes, plus information that has surfaced through negotiations, enable him to revise his draft environmental impact report into a final version subject to approval by the appropriate state agency, and usable as a basis for the state licensing process.

LICENSES AND PERMITS

Timing of Licensing

An important reform of the conventional siting process is to move the licensing and permitting processes as much as possible to the end rather than the beginning. We explained earlier that licensing is intrinsically a bad way to redesign a complicated facility or to negotiate.

One way to avoid this misuse of the process is to have these negotiations take place in the context of the siting agreement and its surrounding political activity. The proposal taken to a licensing board after a local agreement, will not be a target for attack by all manner of opponents, as it will already have taken account, as nearly as possible, of objections to the initial proposal. Another way to put this is that it's not possible to license a facility that cannot be described, and until negotiations with the neighbors are complete, what will actually be built is not known to any of the parties.

Community leaders have sometimes argued that licensing should occur before negotiations so they can simply expand upon the protections and guarantees offered by the state licensing process, rather than inventing all of the protective mechanisms themselves. However, to do so would clearly encourage the developer to posture, to "dig in his heels" with his licensed proposal and resist community changes that might make it necessary for him to go back to the licensing board for revisions. One compromise approach is to have the state agency begin reviewing the proposal simultaneously with the community, and to issue a draft license which could easily be changed after negotiations are complete. Alternatively, the licensing board could give the community a list of their likely requirements in advance of negotiations. Whatever approach is taken, it still seems clear that (1) the community deserves some guidance about likely state licensing requirements, and (2) final licensing should not occur until after negotiations between the developer and the community are complete.

Restricting Local Permits

How state laws should regard local permits for major facilities is not a simple question. Withholding such permits, especially if the enabling legislation gives broad discretionary powers to the local body that grants them, is an obvious way to stop a facility independently of any negotiations or agreements. Accordingly, we think state enabling legislation must carefully restrict the grounds on which such permits might be withheld. The Massachusetts legislation did so for the local Board of Health permit by allowing a board to withhold it only if the facility is shown to be more dangerous than other industry. This places in the statute a standard of relative risk—that new facilities shouldn't be more dangerous than things people have already shown they are willing to tolerate—and suggests a way to compare relative risks for a particular case. Quirky local permits may be the one place that a state override power for a facility siting can be exercised without injurious results.

Local zoning power is a more troublesome problem with special characteristics. On the one hand, zoning can be a daunting obstacle to the development of (at least) private facilities (presumably local zoning power does not control development by the state). Furthermore, it's extremely easy to misuse zoning in unfair or punitive ways.[2] On the other hand, it's widely recognized that local government has the legitimate power to separate land uses to prevent inappropriate adjacencies.

Consistently with our purpose to make obstruction more difficult and more costly to the community than negotiation, we would like state law to allow local zoning power for land use management but prevent its use simply to exclude unpopular facilities from a community as a whole. While the goal of such restriction is relatively easy to express in this fashion, it has so far proved impossible to embody in legislative language that would have the desired effect in practice. The fundamental problem is that no independent court test can consistently distinguish between legitimate land use purposes and intention to exclude certain facilities from a community altogether. The problem is further complicated by the fact that the developer's remedy against illegal zoning is in most jurisdictions limited to an injunction to revise the zoning ordinance rather than money damages.[3]

Without a wholesale revision of zoning practice, it seems necessary to make do with a rather crude exemption of specified types of new facilities from zoning restrictions put in place after the effective date of a siting law. The justification for this provision is that local governments have had plenty of time to identify the parts of their jurisdiction that are inappropriate for industrial development generally; for want of a better test, the novelty of restrictions on the kind of facilities with which a siting process deals will have to be used as the test for "legitimate" zoning purpose.

A weaker form of zoning restrictions would have two parts: first, facilities of the type covered by the new legislation would be permitted by right on any land zoned industrial—that is, a community could not have a zone called "industrial excluding hazardous waste processing." Second, localities would be forbidden to change the zoning of sites after the formal or informal proposal of a facility. If this weaker restriction worked as expected, communities would not engage in wholesale anti-industrial rezoning simply to exclude noxious facilities between the time of passage of the siting law and the appearance of new proposals.

On the other hand, there's some risk that such wholesale rezoning would occur, with an implicit and unspoken invitation on the part of local government to developers of desired facilities: "we are willing to entertain proposals on non-industrial zones, and to rezone specifically for those facilities not thought to be especially noxious." It's probably not possible to know whether the stronger or weaker form of zoning restriction is necessary without some experimentation; Massachusetts has chosen the second path, and while a few communities have proposed some rezoning of the kind it was intended to discourage, it has not become a statewide epidemic. An unintended consequence of the Massachusetts approach is that it tempts developers to propose facilities prematurely in an effort to block subsequent exclusionary zoning amendments, and it discourages them from informal public discussion of potential sites, since Massachusetts law only freezes zoning when a site-specific proposal has been made.

TAKING POWER

Government generally has the authority to seize land for a public purpose, paying the owner its fair market value whether he wants to sell it or not. The use of such "eminent domain" power is widely accepted for construction of such facilities as highways, where, since it's obviously necessary for the government to own every parcel of land along the right of way, a single holdout could impose enormous costs on society as a whole. In the case of land uses that are not particularly disagreeable to neighbors—even though they may be opposed by those whose land is taken for those uses—eminent domain power is an effective means of suppressing local opposition. The reason for this is that the powers associated with legal title to land—occupancy and change of use—can be effectively exerted by a government against a single landowner. When the landowner is dispossessed, he no longer has any more to lose from the construction of the facility; in many cases, he will leave the community entirely.

However, when proposed land uses are opposed by the neighbors, then eminent domain provides little defense against local opposition. Eminent domain power does not counter the opposition of neighbors whose land is *not* being taken. Indeed, eminent domain power enables government to overcome only one, and a relatively unimportant one, of the obstacles to facility development, which is having title to a piece of land. Thus, we disagree strongly with those who think that if all else fails, "the state government can just take the best site by eminent domain and proceed with the project." Take the property it can, but the use of eminent domain power is approximately worthless against the kind of opposition that defeats projects of the sort we've been discussing in this book.

Nevertheless, eminent domain power has an important role to play in the siting of many types of facilities. It makes it possible for a developer to proceed publicly and visibly with a negotiated siting process and a licensing application on land that he does not own. Without taking power, the developer at the beginning of a siting process such as we describe would correctly foresee that a landowner could hold him up for an enormous overpayment (relative to the real value of the land itself) once he had completed his negotiations and licensing for a facility on that land. A traditional defense against such opportunistic holdouts has been for private developers to secretly option the parcels comprising a facility site through straws and agents, so that the land is available for purchase at a known price before public knowledge of the facility's likelihood of construction. Unfortunately, this sort of defensive optioning by a private developer undermines the open and explicit negotiation that a workable siting process requires. Neighbors would see an investment in land acquisition made by the developer before negotiations even started, and quite reasonably assume that no demonstration of social cost associated with that site would persuade the developer to abandon a proposal in which he had invested so much money and effort already.

Since we don't want to make it necessary (or even useful) for developers to option proposed sites before announcement of their intentions, it's necessary to make taking power available to the developer of a facility that has received all of its necessary approvals and licenses and has in place a working site agreement. We must emphasize again that eminent domain in this context has nothing to do with overpowering local opposition, but serves only the narrow purpose of allowing a developer to engage in public discussion and negotiation about his proposal without having to face exorbitant land costs, and thereby discouraging him from secretly optioning a site before negotiations.

EXCLUSION FROM THE LEGISLATED PROCESS

The process we have described so far gives a facility developer whose project falls under the scope of the act a great deal of power to affect the performance of state and local government. Unfortunately, such power may tempt developers with half-baked concepts or unnecessary projects, and a great deal of time and effort could be wasted by both state and local officials in evaluating facilities for which the state really has no use. A simple way to avoid this is to empower the siting council to find a particular proposal "unworthy of investigation through the siting process" upon a demonstration that, for example:

1. the economy of the state has no use for the service that would be provided by a new facility proposal;
2. the technology proposed to be used is outside the limits of reasonable engineering judgment as to its effectiveness or safety;
3. the developer or officers of the developing company are not deserving of the state's trust as regards their technical, financial, or moral responsibility; or
4. the developer has failed to perform as required by the siting law (e.g., not filing a draft impact statement).

It bears emphasis that this opportunity to exclude a proposal from the siting process is a narrow one and should be exercised only in cases of the grossest mismatch between the nature of the facility proposed and the state's needs and intentions. It is not, for example, a licensing review, in which the appropriateness of the site for the proposal in question is evaluated; nor is it an occasion to compare alternative technologies to be sure that the one proposed is the best that might be suggested. Distinctions such as these are exactly the sort of judgment the siting process itself is designed to make; the finding of "not worth further investigation" is meant only to exclude projects that could not reasonably justify investment in the evaluation process.

Nor does exclusion from the process prohibit construction of a facility. A developer so excluded may proceed on his own to arrange a siting agreement, and to obtain necessary permits and licenses. What he cannot do is invoke the power of the state to put negotiations with the community into arbitration, nor can the site community receive state funds for technical assistance.

Experience in Massachusetts (see the Appendix) suggests that a simpler solution to the frivolous proposal problem might be even better: requiring a substantial application fee from developers. Presumably, a developer who couldn't reasonably expect success in the process would not risk a large up-front payment just to try his luck. The disadvantage of empowering the council to make a formal "worth investigation" judgment is that the finding may appear to many local citizens as a state approval or license, granted before the facts are in, and is in any case a lightning rod for obstructionist tactics.

SUMMARY

It may be useful now to review the major steps in the siting process described in the foregoing pages as they would occur in the case of a real proposal.

Before formal notice, developers (whether public agencies or private corporations) are presumably making preliminary evaluations of different sites for different facilities that they might or might not propose to build. If the developers' executives know what they are doing, they will also have made contact with the state siting agency supervising the process and familiarize themselves with the formal procedures that will take place when they announce their intentions on a specific site.

The first formal events in the process occur when a developer makes public announcement of his intention to build a certain type of facility, either at a known site or without specifying a location. In either case, he follows his proposal with a draft environmental and socio-economic impact statement describing what he can about his project at its current state of specificity, and its effects on the site at which it might be built. Simultaneously, any proposed site community is organizing its negotiating committee, or has authorized local officials responsible for negotiations to begin meeting with the developer and reviewing the draft statement.

The negotiating body can at the same time obtain, from the state, planning grants for technical review of the proposal and of the developers' draft statement. The formal negotiation process continues until a siting agreement is established. This agreement specifies the nature of the project in detail, with local concerns taken account of, and the operating rules that will govern the community and developer both. It is established either by the parties themselves or, if negotiations run aground, by an arbitration panel.

Establishment of the siting agreement is an important watershed for the facility. Once it has been established, the developer can add the costs of any compensation or mitigation measures the agreement calls for to his other costs of doing business, and determine whether the facility he proposes is a viable proposition or not. In at least some cases, we would expect developers to abandon their projects once the siting agreement made known to them how large were the social costs that they would be expected to cover out of their operating profits. Similarly, government developers might occasionally find that cost-benefit analysis of the project revealed negative benefits when compensation and mitigation measures are included as called for by the siting agreement. We assume here that an arbitration panel will *not* consider the project's profitability as a constraint in arbitrating a settlement.

Establishment of the siting agreement also allows the formal permitting process to begin. Since most of the important local issues have been resolved, licensing will not be the occasion for a broad-ranging review of alternatives, nor a forum for last-ditch opposition to the facility.

Not everyone can predict the outcome of the licensing process perfectly; we expect that a few facilities that still look workable after a siting agreement is established will fall by the wayside as they are shown to be unlicensable as proposed, or too expensive to revise to meet licensing requirements. What this would mean is that social costs imposed on a population broader than the immediate neighbors of the facility, added to the other costs established elsewhere in the process, give rise to a sum greater than the profits or benefits of the project itself.

With siting agreement and licenses in hand, the developer who still thinks his project worthwhile could proceed to acquire his land—by eminent domain, if the landowner is by this time asking for an unreasonable sum—and proceed with construction of the project. Presumably, the siting agreement will include some provisions for local monitoring and supervision both of construction and of operations so that facilities which are intrinsically hazardous or risky to their neighbors will be under the constant review of consultants responsible not only to the state licensing and supervising authority but also to local government.

This smooth progression of events suffices for explanatory purposes, but does not represent our expectations for every siting proposal, especially the first few to come under the kind of legislation we propose. Much in this process is so novel, and so unlike conventional practice, that a great deal of mistrust at both the local and developer levels will have to be overcome bit by bit. Some of this mistrust will be expressed through litigation attacking the constitutionality of various provisions of the law or the procedures followed by the agencies implementing it.

Finally, we don't expect it to work every time. As we cautioned at the beginning of this chapter, we would be quite surprised to find it the best siting process possible. We claim only that it is the best anyone has been able to describe in detail so far, and we look forward with great interest to improvements that will reveal themselves to others and that we have been unable to foresee at the present stage of analysis.

FOOTNOTES

1. R. Fisher and W. Ury, *Getting to Yes,* Boston: Houghton Mifflin, 1981.
2. R. Ellickson, "Suburban Growth Controls: An Economic and Legal Analysis," *Yale Law Review* **86** (1977) p. 385. Also see R. H. Nelson, *Zoning and Property Rights,* Cambridge: MIT Press, 1977
3. Ellickson, *op. cit.*

Appendix
The Massachusetts Hazardous Waste
Facility Siting Act

The Massachusetts Hazardous Waste Facility Siting Act (reproduced at the end of this appendix) incorporates most of the attributes of the model siting process described in Chapter 10. The act was adopted in 1980 after a series of failures to site new hazardous waste facilities through conventional processes. The legislature flirted briefly with a preemption bill prior to passage of the Act, but when legislators from three communities under active consideration for hazardous waste facilities convinced their colleagues to *statutorily* exempt their communities from further consideration, preemption was rejected. The legislature turned instead to a siting process incorporating incentives as a strategy to overcome local opposition.

AN OVERVIEW OF THE MASSACHUSETTS
HAZARDOUS WASTE FACILITY SITING ACT

There are five important elements to the Massachusetts Act. First, the Act gives a developer the right to construct a hazardous waste facility on land zoned for industrial use if the developer obtains the required permits and completes a negotiated or arbitrated siting agreement with the host community.[1] Second, the Act limits the ability of local communities to exclude hazardous waste facilities without first showing that such facilities pose special risks.[2] Third, the state provides host communities with technical assistance grants to promote local participation in the siting process and effective negotiation with developers.[3] Fourth, the Act requires an agreement between developer and community on all conditions of design and operation, with arbitration to break deadlocks.[4] Finally, the Act provides compensation to communities likely to be affected by new hazardous waste facilities in adjacent jurisdictions.[5]

The State Role in the Siting Process

The developer and host community have the primary role; state agencies oversee the process, but have no independent authority to site facilities or to override local decisions. Three state agencies share that oversight role. The Department of Environmental Management (DEM) is responsible for planning and is charged with assessing the state's requirements for hazardous waste storage, treatment, and disposal facilities, and for attracting developers to the state.[6] The Department of Environmental Quality Engineering (DEQE) oversees facilities once they become operational and grants the necessary permits, licenses, and enforces the relevant environmental and safety regulations.[7] Because of their mandates, these two agencies lack the neutrality necessary to referee negotiations between developers and communities. Consequently, the legislature created a new agency, the Hazardous Waste Facility Site Safety Council (the Council), to oversee the negotiation process.[8] The Council has 21 members and includes representatives of all parties involved in and affected by the siting of hazardous waste facilities.

Initiating the Siting Process

A prospective developer initiates the siting process by filing a Notice of Intent (NOI) with the Council.[9] The NOI describes the prior experience of the developer in the hazardous waste field, the general characteristics of the proposed facility, and how the developer intends to finance it.[10] The developer need not have a specific site in mind when he submits the NOI; he can rely upon the siting process to identify potential sites.[11] Within 15 days of receiving a complete NOI, the Council must decide whether the project is "feasible and deserving of state assistance."[12] If the Council votes affirmatively, both the host and abutting communities become eligible to receive technical assistance grants to support their participation in the siting process.[13] The "feasible and deserving" review is intended to be a rough screen used to eliminate projects that are technically unsound, projects that are unnecessary given existing in-state disposal and processing capacity, projects that are precluded by existing law, and projects proposed by developers who are either disreputable or financially insecure.[14]

Within 30 days of the filing of an NOI, a Local Assessment Committee (LAC) is formed to represent the interests of the host community in negotiations with the developer.[15] The LAC is chaired by the community's chief executive officer.[16]

The Negotiating Process

After the developer has submitted environmental and socio-economic data in the form of a Preliminary Project Impact Report,[17] negotiations begin between the developer and the LAC.[18] The negotiations are intended to result in a formal "siting agreement," which describes the measures that the developer will take to mitigate any adverse impacts associated with the facility as well as any compensation that might be paid. A facility cannot be constructed without an approved siting agreement.[19] The statute states the "terms, conditions, and provisions" that the siting agreement must include, in addition to listing some optional provisions.[20] However, because these "requirements" are general in scope and permissive in tone, they serve more to illustrate the range of potential negotiations rather than to constrain the final result.

Arbitration

If the developer and the host community fail to establish a siting agreement, the council may declare an impasse and compel the parties to submit all unresolved issues to what the statute refers to as "final and binding arbitration."[21] If the parties fail to agree on an arbitrator, the Council may appoint one.[22] The act itself contains no explicit criteria to be employed by the arbitrator in rendering a decision other than to say that the arbitrator shall "resolve the issues in dispute between the local assessment committee and the developer."[23] Arbitration procedures and judicial review of the arbitration decision are governed by the provisions of Chapter 251, the Uniform Arbitration Act for Commercial Disputes.[24]

State and Local Permit Requirements

Before constructing a hazardous waste facility in Massachusetts, a developer must obtain a license from DEQE as well as certification of his site from the local board of health. By law, DEQE cannot issue a license unless it finds that the facility "does not constitute a significant danger to public health, public safety, or the environment, does not seriously threaten injury to the inhabitants of the area or damage to their property, and does not result in the creation of noisome or unwholesome odors."[25]

Communities cannot impose new permit requirements on hazardous waste facilities after the effective date of the act.[26] As a result, in most jurisdictions the only special local permit required of a developer (other than building permits, etc.) is site assignment by the local board of health. At the same time that the legislature adopted Chapter 21D, however, it also amended Chapter 111 to limit the circumstances under which a local board of health could refuse to assign a site. The site must be certified if the proposed facility "imposes no significantly greater danger . . . then the dangers that currently exist in the conduct and operation of other industrial and commercial enterprises in the commonwealth not engaged in the treatment, processing or disposal of hazardous waste, but using processes that are comparable.[27]

The statute also limits the power of localities to exclude unwanted facilities in one other important way. It amended the zoning enabling act to permit hazardous waste facilities to be built as a matter of right on land zoned industrial at the time a developer initiates the siting process by filing a NOI.[28]

The state retains the power to seize a site through eminent domain, but it can only do so with the approval of the local city council, board of aldermen, or board of selectmen.[29]

Declaration of an Operational Siting Agreement

After completion of the siting agreement either through negotiation or arbitration, the Council reviews the agreement. Recently adopted regulations require the Council to approve the agreement if it contains all provisions mandated by the regulations and complies with the terms of the Act.[30] If the Council approves the agreement, the developer prepares a final project impact report, which is similar in form to the preliminary report but which includes comments received by the developer, responses to these comments, a copy of the siting agreement, and—most important—takes account of changes to the project resulting from negotiations. After the appropriate agencies approve the final report, the Council decides whether to declare the agreement "operative and in full force and effect." This declaration establishes the siting agreement as a "non-assignable contract binding upon the developer and the host community, and enforceable against the parties in any court of competent jurisdiction."[31]

Abutting Communities

Abutting communities are also directly involved in the siting process.[32] They are invited to all briefing sessions conducted by DEM and are eligible for technical assistance grants from the Council.[33] Moreover, abutting communities may also petition the Council for compensation to be paid by the developer for "demonstrably adverse impacts . . . imposed upon said community by the construction, maintenance, and operation of a hazardous waste facility in a host community."[34] Unlike compensation for the host community which is determined through bilateral negotiations with the developer, the Council fixes the compensation to be paid abutting communities after a public hearing. If the abutting community is unsatisfied with the Council's award, it may request that the compensation issue be submitted to impartial arbitration. (Of course, nothing prevents the developer from negotiating with abutting communities so as to present a *de facto* agreement to the Council.[35]) The developer has no comparable right of appeal.

LEGAL ISSUES

While a complete analysis of all legal issues raised by the Massachusetts Hazardous Waste Facility Siting Act is obviously beyond the scope of this appendix, a number of potential problems are worth mentioning in the hope that they might be avoided in future siting statutes.[36] We have noted in the statute below by footnote where these problems arise.

The Extent of State Preemption

As noted above, the Act severely limits the legal authority of localities to exclude unwanted facilities by zoning, special permits, or site assignment, but, unfortunately, the Act is silent on the power of a locality to exclude a hazardous waste facility by by-law, and this strategy is being pursued by the town of Warren, one of the first communities to be proposed as a site under the new statute.[37] A Massachusetts Superior Court struck down two Warren by-laws designed to frustrate the siting of a hazardous waste facility there.

The Powers of the Arbitrator

The characterization of arbitration in the Act as "final and binding" is slightly deceptive. The terms of the arbitration award are not binding on either party in the conventional sense. A developer who finds an award excessive can simply decline to construct the proposed facility. Similarly, an arbitration award is not binding upon all the host community's actions because it can subsequently attempt to withhold the site assignment permit or challenge the state's grant of a construction and operation license. Consequently, the arbitration award only defines the terms under which the proposed facility can be constructed and operated *if* the developer still finds the project economically worthwhile and can obtain the necessary state and local health permits.

A potentially troubling omission in the Act is the failure to define criteria to be employed by the arbitrator in rendering a decision. In states that cling to the non-delegation doctrine, this omission could prove fatal. A number of criteria, however, are implied in the Act. In practice, an arbitrator is likely to be called upon to make three types of judgments: (1) the mitigation measures, operating controls, and post-closure management techniques that the developer must use, (2) the services that the host community must provide to the developer, and (3) the compensation that the developer must pay to the host community.

In determining which measures the developer must employ to safeguard health and the environment, the arbitrator should be guided by the same standard that governs the local health board's issuance of the site assignment: the arbitrator should require that the facility not create risks greater than comparable industrial facilities. In assessing the reasonableness of a developer's request for services from the host community, the arbitrator should examine the need for such services, their availability from sources other than the host community, the legal and institutional capacity of the host community to provide the services, and the standard practices of other communities hosting similar industrial facilities. In deciding on compensation for social costs and costs incurred in providing services, the arbitrator should be guided by the theory embodied in the Act: that communities should be made whole, to the extent possible, for the costs associated with hosting a hazardous waste facility.

The Powers of the Siting Council

The Act is also silent on the criteria to be employed by the Council in deciding whether to declare a siting agreement "in full force and effect." For example, it does not state whether the Council may impose additional public safety requirements beyond those already embodied in the Act, the siting agreement, and the relevant regulations and permits. In our view, the Council should oversee the siting process, not superpose an additional layer of substantive review on the existing regulatory structure. Accordingly, the function of the Council's final declaration should be to signal the end of the siting process and certify its procedural validity. If, in adopting a siting statute, a legislature intends otherwise, it should describe the substantive powers of the Council more explicitly in the statute.

Judicial Review of an Arbitration Award

Judicial review of an arbitration award is governed by the judicial review provisions of the Uniform Arbitration Act for Commercial Disputes. This act provides review only under very limited circumstances: if the arbitrator has committed fraud, has shown demonstrable partiality, or has exceeded his or her powers.[38] The leading Massachusetts case interpreting this standard of review states that, absent this finding, courts will not overturn an arbitrator's award even if it contains gross errors of law or fact.[39] Courts have generally upheld such limits to review of commercial arbitration awards because the parties voluntarily agreed to submit their dispute to arbitration.[40] Under the Massachusetts Act, however, at least one of the parties has not specifically agreed to submit differences to an arbitrator; arbitration is compulsory once the Council finds that negotiations are deadlocked. Courts have generally required a fuller review of compulsory than of voluntary arbitration.[41] For example, in upholding the Massachusetts compulsory labor arbitration statute, the Supreme Judicial Court emphasized availability of judicial review as an important safeguard against arbitrary action.[42] Under closer scrutiny, however, the analogy between the Massachusetts Siting Act and other compulsory arbiration statutes proves false. For example, the compulsory labor arbitration statute examined by the Massachusetts court binds both the municipality and the union.[43] An egregious award could bankrupt a municipality or, conversely, threaten the integrity of the union. The court was justifiably reluctant to sustain this substantial grant of power to a private arbitrator without the safety mechanism afforded by judicial review.[44] By contrast, the siting process does not impose affirmative obligations on the host community;[45] the community is deprived of property only to the extent that the social costs of the facility are not fully covered by the compensation agreement. And since the Act does not give host communities an entitlement to full compensation for all social costs, more extensive review would not be available on a due process theory.

THE MASSACHUSETTS STATUTE IN PRACTICE

The "Feasible and Deserving" Decision

As of the beginning of 1983, three Notices of Intent have been filed with the Council. The project that has advanced the furthest is a proposal to build a solvent recovery facility on the banks of the Merrimac River in Haverhill. The Preliminary Project Impact Report was completed in January and negotiations were expected to begin sometime in the spring. A local assessment committee has been formed for the Haverhill site, and so far has received almost $125,000 in technical assistance grants from the Council. Local residents opposed the facility from the beginning, ostensibly because of the company's past management practices and the riverside location of its Haverhill site. The company had an explosion at its New Jersey facility, and the community requested that the Council revoke the company's "feasible and deserving" status; the Council reviewed the requested, re-evaluated its decision, and denied the request. In July, 1982, the company had an accident at its Connecticut facility, and again people requested that the Council revoke its earlier "feasible and deserving" decision for SRS, Inc. However, before the Council could complete action on that request, SRS, Inc. and the Haverhill LAC negotiated and signed an agreement in which SRS agreed to drop the Haverhill site, to amend its NOI to be non-site-specific, and to not build a hazardous waste facility for at least one year; in exchange, Haverhill agreed to support requests that the Council revoke its decision to reconsider its previous "feasible and deserving" decision concerning SRS, Inc. The Council agreed to this request: the project is dead in Haverhill, and SRS is no longer actively pursuing sites in Massachusetts.

A second NOI has been filed for a multi-purpose waste processing facility in Warren. Two sites, one of which is on stateowned land, are being considered. Like the Haverhill proposal, the Warren proposal has inspired intense local opposition; however, the Warren LAC and several local officials have not strongly opposed the facility, but have instead adopted a "wait and see" posture.

In each of these two cases, both the merits of the developers' proposals and the siting act itself have come under public attack. In Haverhill, the city turned to the courts to try to overturn the Council's affirmative "feasible and deserving" vote. Its efforts proved unsuccessful, and the Court upheld the Council's action.[46] In Warren, the town has tried to defeat the proposal by adopting a by-law that prohibits hazardous waste facilities within its boundaries,[47] and by seeking a court decision that the Siting Act violated the Massachusetts Constitution—but the town has also formed its LAC, has outlined its priorities for negotiations, and has begun meeting with the developer, who looks with favor on the Massachusetts process.[48] Although the communities lost both of their court cases, these first two proposals have underscored one of the major shortcomings of the Act: the "feasible and deserving" decision.

As noted earlier, the legislature intended the "feasible and deserving" decision to be a crude sieve for screening out only grossly inappropriate proposals. Thus, a detailed substantive review of the merits of any proposal was not to occur early in the process, but instead during the environmental impact assessment process, the DEQE licensing process, the local permitting process, and in the course of negotiations. Accordingly, the legislature gave the Council only 15 days in which to rule on whether a proposal is feasible and deserving of state assistance, and the consequence of an affirmative decision is simply to make the LAC eligible for technical assistance grants and to allow the proposal to proceed into the next stage of the siting process.

However, it has proven extremely difficult for the Council to convey to the public the limited nature of the feasible and deserving review. In both Haverhill and Warren, local residents with legitimate questions concerning the merits of the proposals have urged the Council to resolve these issues before voting on "feasible and deserving." In each case, the Council has declined to do so, citing the substantive review that the Act provides in later stages of the siting process. And in each case, the Council has come under heavy criticism for giving its "approval" to a proposal while "ignoring" the concerns raised by the interested public.

The problem just described is general and not specific to the Massachusetts statute. Given the publicity attending hazardous waste disasters like Love Canal, local residents are understandably skeptical about proposals to build new facilities. They tend to form judgments about the merits of proposals quickly, and once formed, these judgments are not easily swayed. Further exacerbating the problem is the fact that it is easier to raise questions about the merits of a proposal than it is to answer them. Consequently, criticism of preliminary screening devices like the "feasible and deserving" decision is inevitable. Perhaps a better approach would be to require the developer to pay a filing fee at the time of his initial submission; in Massachusetts, this would occur at the time of the filing of the NOI. The purpose of the fee would be to screen out frivolous proposals. By delaying the first administrative review of the merits of a proposal until later in the process, the fee might have the salutary effect of discouraging the staking out of positions.

Size of the Council

Another problematic aspect of the law is the size of the Council. A 21-member council has proven to be unwieldy. Meetings are difficult to schedule and even harder to conduct. Because individual members exercise relatively little influence on the actions of the Council as a whole, each member has only a modest incentive to master all of the issues that confront the Council. A much smaller Council, on the order of three or five people, would operate much more efficiently. Arguably, it would also be more accountable as each member could (1) more easily be held responsible for his or her actions; and (2) have the freedom to balance issues since no member of a small council would represent a narrow constituency (see Chapter 10).

Perceptions of the Council

A common criticism leveled at the Siting Council throughout its brief history is that it has been biased in its actions in favor of developers. In many respects this criticism is inevitable given the administrative structure created by the Siting Act. The law gives the Council three major administrative responsibilities: (1) it must decide whether a notice of intent is feasible and deserving of state assistance; (2) it must decide whether to award technical assistance grants to communities; and (3) it must decide whether to declare an impasse in negotiations and refer unresolved issues to arbitration.

Because the statute obliges the Council to decide the "feasible and deserving" issue within fifteen days, before the legitimate questions of the community can be answered, it is inevitable that the Council will appear callous to these concerns and "in bed" with the developer. Similarly, requests for technical assistance grants have created an uncomfortable relationship between communities and the Council; since the Council administers a limited budget for these grants, it has occasionally had to inquire into the propriety of individual requests. Not surprisingly, when the Council has denied requests for technical assistance, it has been perceived by communities as indifferent to their informational needs and partial to the developer. And although the Council has yet to exercise its power to declare an impasse, it is clear to us that when it does so it will be seen as operating on behalf of the developer's interests; since the costs of nonagreement fall most heavily on the developer, anything that expedites the process such as arbitration is likely to be perceived as done for the developer and at the community's expense.

We think that some of these problems might be overcome through more careful structuring of the Council's responsibilities. For example, substituting a non-discretionary screening mechanism (such as the filing fee described earlier) for the feasible and deserving review would help. Similarly, incorporating the schedule of technical assistance grants into the legislation would relieve the Council from having to pass judgment on the propriety of individual grant requests. The statute also might provide for arbitration after a statutorily defined period has elapsed, subject to waiver by mutual assent of the parties. Alternatively, the governor or some other state official might be given the power to declare an impasse. At this stage, these suggestions are more conjecture than carefully crafted reforms. We are more confident of our diagnoses of the act's problems than with our prescriptions for solutions. Drafters of future statutes need be sensitive to these issues.

An overall evaluation of Massachusetts' approach is premature. To date, no project has been killed by "end-runs" like legislative exclusion or political power plays, and the prescribed events are occurring as the statute provides.

THE MASSACHUSETTS HAZARDOUS WASTE
FACILITY SITING ACT

Chap. 508. AN ACT FURTHER REGULATING THE DISPOSAL
OF HAZARDOUS WASTE MATERIALS.

Whereas, The deferred operation of this act would tend to defeat its purpose which is, in part, to immediately encourage and expedite the process of
development of hazardous waste treatment and disposal facilities which provide adequate safeguards to protect the public health, safety, and environment of the commonwealth, therefore it is hereby declared to be an emer-
gency law necessary for the immediate preservation of the public health,
safety, and convenience. _____

Be it enacted, etc., as follows:

[*Sections 1–3, omitted here, are not relevant to facility siting.*]

SECTION 4.   Chapter 111 of the General Laws is hereby amended by
inserting after section 150A the following section:—
Section 150B.   The definition of "facility" in section one of chapter
twenty-one D shall apply to this section. Any such facility shall be subject to
this section and not subject to section one hundred and fifty A.

No place in any city or town shall be established or maintained or operated
by any person, including any political subdivision or agency of the commonwealth, as a site for a facility, unless such place has either been assigned by
the board of health of such city or town as a site for a facility after a public
hearing, subject to the provisions of any ordinance or by-law adopted
therein under chapter forty A or corresponding provisions of earlier laws,
or, in the case of an agency of the commonwealth, has been assigned by the
department of environmental quality engineering, in this section called the
department after a public hearing and unless public notice of such assignment has been given by the board of health.

The assignment of a place as a site for a facility shall be subject to such
limitation with respect to the extent, character and nature of operation
thereof as will insure that the facility imposes no significantly greater danger
to the public health or public safety from fire, explosion, pollution,
discharge of hazardous substances, or other construction or operational factors than the dangers that currently exist in the conduct and operation of
other industrial and commercial enterprises in the commonwealth not engaged in the treatment, processing or disposal of hazardous waste, but utiliz-
ing processes that are comparable. In assessing the significance and degree of
danger, the board shall consider and evaluate such evidence as all interested
persons may submit to it including, but not limited to, evidence comparing

the procedures and practices proposed for the conduct and operation of a facility with the procedures and practices existing in the conduct and operation of other industrial and commercial enterprises in the commonwealth not engaged in the treatment, processing or disposal of hazardous waste which are conducted and operated in accordance with law and sound principles of modern engineering practice. The board of health shall notify the department upon receipt of an application to assign a place as a site for a facility. The department shall, upon request by the board of health, provide advice, guidance and technical assistance in reviewing the application. The department and a board of health may enter into such other cooperative arrangements in addition to those herein specified for the purpose of achieving a more effective and expeditious review of the application.

Every decision of the board of health in assigning or refusing to assign a place as a site for a facility shall be in writing and shall include a statement of reasons and the facts relied upon by the board in reaching its decision.

Any person aggrieved by the action of a board of health in refusing to assign a place as a site for a facility may, within thirty days of the publication of notice of said decision, appeal to the superior court, which may affirm said decision of the board of health, remand the matter for further proceedings before the board of health, set aside or modify said decision, or order the board of health to take any action unlawfully withheld or unreasonably delayed if the court determines that the substantial rights of any party may have been violated because said decision violated constitutional provisions or was in excess of the statutory authority and jurisdiction of the board of health or was based upon an error of law or was made upon unlawful procedure or was unsupported by substantial evidence, or was arbitrary, capricious, or an abuse of discretion, or otherwise not in accordance with law.

Any person aggrieved by the action of a board of health in assigning a place as a site for a facility may, within thirty days of the publication of notice of such assignment, appeal to the department from the assignment of the board of health. Upon such appeal or upon the department's own initiative, the department may, after due notice and public hearing, rescind or suspend such assignment or modify the same by the imposition or amendment of terms, restrictions, conditions and requirements.

Upon determination that the maintenance and operation of a facility has resulted in a significant danger to public health or is not in compliance with the terms, restrictions, conditions and requirements established for its maintenance and operation in an assignment made pursuant to the provisions of this section, said assignment may be rescinded or suspended or may be modified through the imposition or amendment of terms, restrictions, conditions and requirements at any time after due notice and a public hearing by the board of health where such facility is located, upon its own initiative or upon complaint by any person aggrieved by such assignment, or by the department upon its own initiative or upon complaint by any person aggrieved by said assignment. Every such rescission, suspension or modification shall be in writing and shall include a statement of reasons and the facts relied upon by the board of health or the department in taking such action.

Any person aggrieved by the action of the board of health or the department in rescinding, suspending or modifying an assignment may, within thirty days of publication of notice or such rescission, suspension or modification of said assignment, appeal to the superior court, which may affirm said rescission, suspension or modification, remand the matter for further proceedings, set aside or modify said rescission, suspension or modification, order any action unlawfully held or unreasonably delayed if the court determines that the substantial rights of any party may have been violated because said rescission, suspension or modification violated constitutional provisions or was in excess of statutory authority and jurisdiction or was based upon an error of law or was made upon unlawful procedure or was unsupported by substantial evidence or was arbitrary, capricious or an abuse of discretion, or otherwise not in accordance with law.

The department shall adopt, and may from time to time amend rules and regulations, and the commissioner may issue orders, to enforce the provisions of this section. Any person, including any political subdivision of the commonwealth, who fails to operate and maintain a facility in accordance with the provisions of this section or in accordance with any rules, regulations, or orders hereunder promulgated shall be punished by a fine of not less than one hundred dollars nor more than five hundred dollars. Each day's failure to comply with said provisions, rules, regulations or orders shall constitute a separate violation.

The superior court shall have jurisdiction in equity to enforce the provisions of this section upon petition of the department or any aggrieved person.

SECTION 5. Section 9 of chapter 40A of the General Laws is hereby amended by adding the following paaragraph:—

A hazardous waste facility as defined in section two of chapter twenty-one D shall be permitted to be constructed as of right on any locus presently zoned for industrial use pursuant to the ordinances and by-laws of any city or town provided that all permits and licenses required by law have been issued to the developer and a siting agreement has been established pursuant to sections twelve and thirteen of chapter twenty-one D, provided however, that following the submission of a notice of intent, pursuant to section seven of chapter twenty-one D, a city or town may not adopt any zoning change which would exclude the facility from the locus specified in said notice of intent. This section shall not prevent any city or town from adopting a zoning change relative to the proposed locus for the facility following the final disapproval and exhaustion of appeals for permits and licenses required by law and by chapter twenty-one D.

SECTION 6.   Section 19 of chapter 16 of the General Laws is hereby amended by adding the following paragraph:—

The department of environmental management shall not exercise its eminent domain authority as authorized herein for the acquisition of sites for hazardous waste treatment, processing or disposal until all permits, licenses and approvals of the city or town wherein the site lies have been granted, a siting agreement has been established pursuant to the provisions of sections twelve and thirteen of chapter twenty-one D, and the approval of said exercise of eminent domain authority has been obtained by a majority vote of the city council, board of aldermen, or board of selectmen of said city or town.

[*Section 7, omitted here, is not relevant to facility siting*]

SECTION 8.   The General Laws are hereby amended by inserting after chapter 21C the following chapter:—

CHAPTER 21D
MASSACHUSETTS HAZARDOUS WASTE
FACILITY SITING ACT.

Section 1.   This chapter shall be known and may be cited as the "Massachusetts Hazardous Waste Facility Siting Act".

Section 2.   Unless the context clearly indicates otherwise, when used in this chapter, the following words and phrases shall have the following meanings:

"Abutting community", a city or town contiguous to or touching upon any land of the host community.

"Chief Executive Officer", the city manager in any city having a city manager, the mayor in any other city; the town manager in any town having a town manager, the chairman of the board of selectmen in any other town.

"Commissioner", the commissioner of the department of environmental management.

"Committee", the local assessment committee.

"Council", the hazardous waste facility site safety council.

"Compensation", any money, thing of value or economic benefit conferred by the developer on any city, town, or person under the terms and conditions specified in the siting agreement established by sections twelve and thirteen of chapter twenty-one D.

"Department", the department of environmental management.

"Developer", any person proposing to construct, maintain, or operate a hazardous waste facility in any city or town of the commonwealth.

"Disposal", the discharge, deposit, injection, dumping, spilling, leaking, incineration or placing of any hazardous waste into or on any land or water so that such hazardous waste or any constituent thereof may enter the environment or be emitted into the air or discharged into any waters, including ground waters.

"Facility", a site or works for the storage, treatment, dewatering, refining, incinerating, reclamation, stabilization, solidification, disposal or other processes where hazardous wastes can be stored, treated or disposed of; however, not including a municipal or industrial waste water treatment facility if permitted under section forty-three of chapter twenty-one.

"Generator", a person who produces hazardous waste.

"Hazardous waste", a waste, or combination of wastes, which because of its quantity, concentration, or physical, chemical or infectious characteristics may cause, or significantly contribute to an increase in mortality or an increase in serious irreversible, or incapacitating reversible illness or pose a substantial present or potential hazard to human health, safety or welfare or to the environment when improperly treated, stored, transported, used or disposed of, or otherwise managed, however not to include solid or dissolved material in domestic sewage, or solid or dissolved materials in irrigation return flows or industrial discharges which are point sources subject to permits under section 402 of the Federal Water Pollution Control Act of 1967 as amended, or source, special nuclear, or by-product material as defined by the Atomic Energy Acts of 1954.

"Hazardous waste management", the systematic control of the collection, source separation, storage, transportation, processing, treatment, recovery and disposal of hazardous wastes.

"Host community", the city or town in which a developer proposes to construct, maintain and operate a hazardous waste facility.

"Person", any agency or political subdivision of the federal government or the commonwealth, any state, public or private corporation or authority, individual, trust, firm, joint stock company, partnership, association, or other entity, and any officer, employee or agent of said person, and any group of said persons.

"Secretary", the secretary of the executive office of environmental affairs.

"Storage", the actual or intended containment of hazardous waste on a temporary basis or for a period not exceeding nine months or another period set by regulation or the department of environmental quality engineering, in a manner which does not constitute disposal.

"Treatment", any method, technique or process, including neutralization, incineration, stabilization or solidification, designed to change the physical, chemical or biological character or composition of any hazardous waste so as to neutralize such waste or so as to render such waste less hazardous, non-hazardous, safer to transport, amenable to storage, or reduced in volume, except such method or technique as may be included as an integral part of a manufacturing process at the point of generation.

Section 3. The department of environmental management shall have the following powers and duties:

(1) to prepare and issue annually a statewide environmental impact report, after first providing the council an adequate opportunity to review and comment on the contents of said report prior to its final adoption by the department. Said statewide environmental impact report shall describe and evaluate the hazardous waste management situation existing in the commonwealth, together with such feasible alternative solutions as may be available for the treatment, processing and disposal of hazardous waste, which report shall include, but not be limited to information concerning:

(*a*) the existing sources of hazardous waste;

(*b*) the types of technologies available for the treatment, processing and disposal of hazardous waste;

(*c*) the impacts, both favorable and adverse, resulting from the use of each type of technology;

(*d*) actions which might be taken to avoid dangers, minimize risks, or remedy unavoidable consequences;

(*e*) the kinds of benefits and protective mechanisms which may be made available to host and abutting communities; and

(*f*) the existing rules, regulations, procedures and standards which have been established to protect the public health, the public safety, and the environment; and

(*g*) the sources and types of hazardous waste generated in the commonwealth, the adequacy of existing facilities for the treatment processing and disposal of said hazardous waste, and the additional facility capacity needed in order to eliminate the shortfall in capacity if any, that may exist;

(2) to give due notice to the public, and to conduct briefing sessions pursuant to the provisions of section eight of this chapter;

(3) to solicit proposals for the construction, maintenance and operation of a hazardous waste facility designed to treat, process, or dispose of such hazardous waste shortfalls in capacity as have been indicated in the statewide environmental impact report, to consider if said proposals are environmentally safe and technologically sound, and to report the results of its activities to the council semi-annually;

(4) to disseminate information widely throughout the commonwealth, in cooperation with other state departments, boards, agencies and commis-

sions, on the treatment, processing and disposal of hazardous waste, its impact on the economy of the commonwealth, the types of technology available, and the social and economic benefits and potential dangers resulting from the use of each type of technology;

(5) to publicize throughout the commonwealth all proposals for the construction, maintenance and operation of hazardous waste facilities in order to inform the public and to encourage the development of suggestions for sites; and

(6) to accept any gifts or grants of money or property, whether real or personal, from any source, private or public, including, but not limited to, the United States of America of its agencies, in order to promote the purposes of this chapter.

In preparing the statewide environmental impact report required by this section, the department may revise and update said report to comply with the provisions of this section.

The department shall adopt such rules, regulations, procedures and standards as may be necessary to carry out its powers and to perform its duties pursuant to chapter thirty A of the General Laws. Said rules, regulations, procedures and standards shall be developed by the department after appropriate consultation and review by interested and affected persons and agencies as determined by the department including, but not limited to, the hazardous waste facility site safety council, the department of environmental quality engineering, the department of public health, and city and town officials, including city and town public health officers.

The department shall cooperate with the department of environmental quality engineering and exchange information where possible to avoid duplication of activities.

Section 4. There is hereby established the hazardous waste facility site safety council whose powers and duties shall be:

(1) to observe the conduct and operation of the hazardous waste facility siting process established by this chapter and to advise all participants in the said process as to methods and actions designed to provide for the more effective, efficient and successful implementation of said process;

(2) to review the rules, regulations, procedures, and standards proposed to be adopted by the department as they relate to the hazardous waste facility siting process prior to their adoption and to recommend to the department whatever changes in said rules, regulations, procedures or standards the council determines shall serve to carry out the purposes and implement the provisions of this chapter;

(3) to review and comment upon the statewide environmental impact report prior to its final adoption by the department including, but not

limited to, the capacity shortfall portion of said report, and to review and comment upon all other documents, reports or forms prepared by the department for public distribution prior to distribution to the public of said documents, reports or forms;

(4) to administer, manage and coordinate the social and economic impact appendix of the preliminary project impact report in cooperation with the secretary who is at the same time administering, managing and coordinating the environmental impact report portion of the said preliminary project impact report;

(5) to award technical assistance grants to cities and towns upon criteria established by the council, including, but not limited to, contracts, consultants, financial experts and other assistants in the opinion of the council is necessary; provided, however, that the said grant shall not exceed fifteen thousand dollars; and further provided, that the community may petition the council for an additional grant as the need arises;

(6) may consult with the executive office of communities and development in the awarding of said grants;

(7) in carrying out its functions, the council shall cooperate with, and may obtain information and recommendations from every agency of the state government and of local government which may be concerned with any matter under the purview of the council. Each said state or local government agency is directed to provide such information and recommendations as may be requested, the council shall cooperate with other states and with the federal government or any agency thereof;

(8) to review all proposals for the construction and operation of hazardous waste facilities on proposed or suggested sites and after appropriate consultation with the department of environmental quality engineering, to reject proposals which the council finds to be unacceptable for the hazardous waste facility siting process established by this chapter;

(9) to establish the compensation to be paid by the developer to abutting communities pursuant to the provisions of section fourteen;

(10) to undertake measures and actions designed to encourage and facilitate negotiations among the developer, the host community, abutting communities, and any persons interested in proposals for the construction, maintenance and operation of hazardous waste facilities on particular proposed or suggested sites;

(11) to determine if an impasse exists between the developer and the host community in negotiations over a siting agreement which requires submission of the matter to arbitration pursuant to the provisions of section fifteen;

(12) to encourage cooperation between a host community and abutting communities in negotiations with the developer over compensation; and

(13) to adopt such rules, regulations, procedures and standards as may be necessary for carrying out its powers and performing its duties pursuant to the provisions of this chapter.

The council, which shall consist of twenty-one members, shall be comprised of the following members: the secretary of environmental affairs or his designee; the secretary of economic affairs or his designee; the secretary of public safety or his designee; the secretary of communities and development or his designee; the commissioner of environmental quality engineering or his designee; the commissioner of environmental management, or his designee; the commissioner of public health or his designee; the chairman of the public utilities commission or his designee, and thirteen members appointed by the governor one of whom shall be a representative of the Massachusetts Municipal Association; one of whom shall be a representative of the Massachusetts Health Officers Association; one of whom shall be a representative of local boards of health; one of whom shall be a representative of the Associated Industries of Massachusetts; one of whom shall be a professional hydrogeologist; one of whom shall be a professional chemical engineer; one of whom shall be a representative of the public knowledgeable in environmental affairs; and six of whom shall be a representative of the public.

The council shall meet at such time and place as determined by the chairman. Eleven members shall constitute a quorum. A quorum must be present to conclude a site agreement.

The committee may appoint two residents of the host community for the purpose of participating in and voting upon matters relative to the site selection in said community. Said residents shall serve without compensation.

No member shall have a financial interest in any of the decisions, actions or reports of the council. Such financial interest shall include, but not be limited to, service as a consultant to any person specializing in the treatment, processing or disposal of hazardous waste, or as an attorney of a party with a direct financial interest in the treatment, processing or disposal of hazardous waste.

The members of the council appointed by the governor shall be appointed for a term of five years, except that the representatives of the Massachusetts Municipal Association, the Associated Industries of Massachusetts, and two representatives of the public initially appointed shall be appointed for terms of three years; the representative of the Massachusetts Health Officers Association, the professional hydrogeologist, the representative of the public knowledgeable in environmental affairs, and two representatives of the public initially appointed shall be appointed for terms of four years; and the representative of the local boards of health, the professional chemical engineer, and two representatives of the public initially appointed shall be appointed for terms of five years. No member appointed by the governor shall be eligible to serve for more than two terms. Persons appointed by the governor to fill vacancies shall serve for the unexpired term of said vacancy.

Each member of the council appointed by the governor shall receive, (subject to appropriation,) fifty dollars for each day or part thereof for his services and shall also receive all reasonable expenses actually and necessarily incurred in the performance of his official duties.

The governor shall appoint, from among the members he has appointed to the council, a chairman.

In addition to the powers and duties of the council established by this section, the council shall appoint a full-time executive secretary to serve at its pleasure. The appointment and removal of said executive secretary shall not be subject to the provisions of chapter thirty-one or section nine A of chapter thirty. The executive secretary shall receive such salary, subject to appropriation, as may be determined by the council subject to the approval of the commissioner of administration.

The council may receive and expend such funds as are appropriated or as may be made available to it from the funds of other agencies. The executive secretary may employ such staff and consultants as are required to assist the council in the performance of its functions and duties, upon approval of a majority of the council, (subject to appropriation.)

The estimate of the amount required for the maintenance of the council required to be filed under section three of chapter twenty-nine shall be submitted by the executive secretary with the advice and consent of the council.

The council shall develop and submit to the commissioner of administration, after notice and a public hearing, a schedule of reasonable fees to be imposed upon a developer in the implementation of the provisions of this chapter by said commissioner. In developing said schedule of reasonable fees, the council shall consider the actual costs incurred by the commonwealth in the conduct and operation of the hazardous waste facility siting process established by this chapter.

Section 5. Not more than thirty days after the receipt of a notice of intent to construct, maintain and operate a hazardous waste facility on a site in a city or town, or notification by the department that this community is a host community in the final list of suggested sites established by the council pursuant to section seven, the chief executive officer of said city or town shall take appropriate action to establish a local assessment committee. Said committee shall be comprised of (1) the chief executive officer, who shall serve as its chairman, (2) the chairman of the local board of health or his designee, (3) the chairman of the local conservation commission or his designee, (4) the chairman of the local planning board or his designee, (5) the chief of the fire department or his designee, (6) four residents of said city or town appointed by a majority vote of the aforementioned city or town officials or their designees, three of whom shall be residents of the area of the city or town most immediately affected by the proposed facility; and (7) not more than four members nominated by the chief executive officer and approved by a majority vote of the city council, board of aldermen, or board of selectmen of said city or town. Said four members nominated by the chief executive officer may include representatives of abutting communities; each representative of an abutting community shall be approved by a majority vote of the city council, board of aldermen, or board of selectmen of said abutting community. A majority of the members shall constitute a quorum for the purpose of conducting all business. The chairman shall preside over meetings of the committee. All actions and decisions of the committee pursuant to this chapter shall be made by majority vote. Not more than thirty days after the receipt of a notice of intent to construct, maintain and operate a hazardous waste facility on a site in said city or town, or notification by the department that this community is a host community on the final list of suggested sites established by the council pursuant to section seven, the chief executive officer of said city or town shall submit to the council the names and addresses of all the members of the local assessment committee.

If the chief executive officer of said city or town fails to take appropriate action to establish a local assessment committee and to submit the names and addresses of its membership to the council not later than thirty days after the receipt of said notice of intent, or notification by the department that this community is a host community on the final list of suggested sites established by the council pursuant to section seven of this chapter, the council shall establish and appoint the membership of said committee.

The chief executive officer shall promptly report to the council any changes that may occur in the members of the local assessment committee.

A local assessment committee shall have the following powers and duties:

(1) to represent generally the best interests of the host community in all negotiations with the developers of proposed facilities in said community;

(2) to negotiate with the developer the detailed terms, provisions, and conditions of a siting agreement to protect the public health, the public safety, and the environment of the host community, as well as to promote the fiscal welfare of said community through special benefits and compensation;

(3) to receive and expend such technical assistance and planning grants as may be made available pursuant to section eleven of this chapter and such other funds as may become available for such purposes from any other source, public or private;

(4) to enter into a nonassignable contract binding upon the host community, and enforceable against said host community in any court of compe-

tent jurisdiction, by the decision to sign a siting agreement pursuant to section thirteen of this chapter;

(5) to cooperate wherever possible with abutting communities in negotiations with the developer over compensation for said abutting communities; and

(6) to adopt such rules, regulations, procedures and standards as may be necessary to carry out it functions and perform its duties under this chapter.

The provisions of sections twenty-three A and twenty-three B of chapter thirty-nine shall apply to all meetings of a local assessment committee except that, in addition to the purposes for which executive sessions may be held pursuant to section twenty-three B of chapter thirty-nine, an executive session of a local assessment committee may also be held to discuss strategy with respect to the negotiation of a siting agreement or to consider the terms, conditions and provisions of said siting agreement if such discussion or consideration in an open meeting may have a detrimental effect upon the negotiating position of the local assessment committee or the establishment of the terms, conditions and provisions of said siting agreement.

Section 6. Notwithstanding the provisions of any law to the contrary, any information, record, or particular part thereof, obtained by the department pursuant to the provisions of this chapter, shall, upon request, be kept confidential and not be considered to be a public record when it is deemed by the commissioner that such information, record or report relates to secret processes, methods of manufacture or production, or that such information, record or report, if made public, would divulge a trade secret. Nothing in this section shall be construed to limit or to deny the power of the department to use such information, record or report as part of aggregated statistics and computations in its statewide environmental impact report including, but not limited to, the capacity shortfall of hazardous waste facilities.

Section 7. Every developer proposing to construct, maintain and operate a hazardous waste facility shall submit a notice of intent to the council, the department, the department of environmental quality engineering, the chief executive officer of the host community, if any, any regional planning agency of which the host community, if any, is a member or in which it otherwise participates, the chief executive officer of all abutting communities, if any, and those persons owning or otherwise exercising control over the real property of any site on which the developer proposes to construct, maintain and operate a hazardous waste facility. A separate notice of intent shall be submitted by the developer for each site proposed by the developer for a facility.

The notice of intent shall include:

(1) a description of the type of hazardous wastes the developer proposes to accept for treatment, processing and disposal at the facility;

(2) a description of the technology and procedures the developer proposes to use to treat, process, and dispose of hazardous waste at the facility;

(3) the site, if any, proposed by the developer as a possible location for the construction and operation of the facility;

(4) a description of the present suitability of the site, and of what additional measures, if any, will be required to make the site suitable for the purpose of constructing, maintaining and operating a facility; or in the event such developer is not proposing a site, the requirements and characteristics of a site that would be appropriate for said facility;

(5) preliminary specifications and architectural drawings of the proposed facility;

(6) a copy of the most recently published statewide environmental impact report issued by the department pursuant to section three; and

(7) any other information required to be submitted in accordance with the rules, regulations, procedures and standards of the department or the council.

In submitting a notice of intent, the developer shall attach thereto such documents prepared or approved by the department which describe and explain the hazardous waste facility siting process as established by the provisions of this chapter, which describe and explain the types of planning and other technical assistance available to the host community and to abutting communities from any source, including, but not limited to, state agencies and the developer, and which describe and explain the types of special benefits that may be included in a negotiated facility siting agreement between a local assessment committee in a host community and a developer including, but not limited to, direct compensation payments to the host community, safety operation and monitoring programs, and future monetary incentives to the host community.

The council shall, within fifteen days of the receipt of a completed notice of intent, and upon consultation with the department of environmental quality engineering, review the proposed project to determine if the proposed project is feasible and deserving of state assistance. The department shall publish and disseminate any determination by the council that a proposed project is feasible and deserving of state assistance by notifying all those who previously received the notice of intent pursuant to this section and the chief executive officer of every city and town in the commonwealth. The department shall include its schedule of briefing sessions pursuant to section eight of this chapter in such notification.

Section 8. The department shall conduct briefing sessions for the purposes of insuring the participation of interested persons in the hazardous waste facility siting process pursuant to this chapter and of informing the public about every proposal which the hazardous waste facility siting council has determined to be feasible and deserving of state assistance. The department shall establish whatever schedule of briefing sessions it deems appropriate to achieve these purposes, holding said sessions in such a manner, place, and at such times as in its sole discretion are best calculated to achieve these purposes. The department shall conduct its first briefing session on a proposal within thirty days after it has completed its dissemination of the determination of the council that the proposed project is feasible and deserving of state support pursuant to section seven of this chapter. The department shall given a reasonable opportunity to persons attending the hearing to discuss, comment upon, or criticize all or any part of the proposal and may ask questions of the developer, the department, or any other agencies represented at said briefing session.

Section 9. If the developer suggests a site in his notice of intent and indicates therein his unwillingness to accept suggestions for alternative sites, the council shall proceed to review the proposal pursuant to section ten. If the developer indicates in his notice of intent a willingness to accept suggestions for a site, whether as alternative sites to a site already proposed or as initially suggested sites if none has been proposed in his notice of intent, the department shall for a period of fifty days after the conclusion of the briefing sessions pursuant to section eight accept suggestions for sites proposed and submitted by any of the following persons:

(1) private individuals who own, or have a substantial financial interest in, the suggested site;

(2) the chief executive officer or the local assessment committee of a host community suggesting a site within said host community which is publicly owned and probably available for lease or sale to the developer, or which is privately owned, where reasonable grounds exist for the belief that said site might be readily available for use as a site for a facility;

(3) the developer suggesting a site either as an alternative to, or in addition to the site originally proposed in his notice of intent or as an initial suggestion for a site if none was proposed in his notice of intent;

(4) any agency of the commonwealth suggesting a site which is publicly owned and probably available for lease or sale to the developer, or which is privately owned, where reasonable grounds exist for the belief that said site might be readily available for use as a site for a facility; and

(5) the chief executive officer of any city or town in the commonwealth suggesting a site in his city or town which is publicly owned and probably available for lease or sale to the developer, or which is privately owned, where reasonable grounds exist for the belief that said site might be readily available for use as a site for a facility.

Any person or agency so suggesting a site shall prior to such suggestions notify in writing the owner or owners of record of the site and the chief executive officer of the host community.

Any suggestion of a site may be withdrawn by the person or agency making said suggestion within the fifty day period permitted for the making of suggestions. If upon the conclusion of the fifty day period, no sites have been suggested by any person or agency, the council may extend the period within which suggestions may be made for an additional thirty days and the department may suggest a reasonable number of sites in the host community which are publicly owned and probably available for lease or sale to the developer or which are privately owned, where reasonable grounds exist for the belief that said sites might be readily available for use as sites for a facility.

If, upon the conclusion of the period or any extension permitted for suggestions, more than three suggested sites have been proposed, the council shall, upon consultation with the department of environmental quality engineering, reduce the number of suggested sites to three, including the developer's suggested site, if any. The council shall determine, prior to establishing its final list of suggested sites, whether or not the owner of record desires to withdraw his real property from consideration as a suggested site. If the owner of record so desires, the suggested site shall be withdrawn and the council shall endeavor to replace said suggested site on its final list.

Within ten days after the end of the suggestion period, the department shall notify the chief executive officers of each host community and all abutting communities, the members of the local assessment committee of each host community, the owner or owners of record of suggested sites, and newspapers, radio stations, and television stations serving seach host community of the final list of suggested sites by distributing said list to them.

Section 10.   The developer shall prepare a preliminary project impact report to be submitted to the secretary and to the council for each site under consideration. Said preliminary project impact report shall consist of two parts: (1) the environmental impact report required by sections sixty-two to sixty-two H, inclusive of chapter thirty and (2) a social economic appendix as prescribed by the rules, regulations, procedures and standards adopted by the council. The secretary shall continue to administer and manage the environmental impact report as part of the preliminary project impact report pursuant to the procedures and time requirements of sections sixty-two to sixty-two H, inclusive, of chapter thirty in order to determine whether or not said environmental impact report complies with the provisions of said sections. Insofar as possible, the council shall administer and manage the social and economic appendix as part of the preliminary project impact report in accordance with the procedures and time requirements established for an environmental impact report pursuant to sections sixty-two to sixty-two H, inclusive, of chapter thirty in order to determine whether or not the social and economic appendix is in its judgment in compliance with the rules, regulations, procedures and standards which it has prescribed for said appendix. The secretary and the council shall cooperate in the administration and management of the preliminary project impact report, shall from time to time during the review process exchange reports, comments and information developed and received, and shall to the maximum feasible extent endeavor to have both parts of the preliminary project impact report proceed through the review process at the same time pursuant to the procedures and timing requirements of section sixty-two to sixty-two H, inclusive, of chapter thirty.

The developer shall file a project notification form with the secretary and the council. The council shall issue public notice of the availability of such report. The project notification form shall consist of an environmental notification form pursuant to section sixty-two A of chapter thirty and such other social and economic information as the council shall prescribe by its rules, regulations, procedures and standards.

The council shall limit the scope of the social and economic appendix as part of the preliminary project impact report. Notwithstanding the provisions of section sixty-two A of chapter thirty, the council may establish a specific procedure for the evaluation and review of the social and economic impacts of the proposed project, whether or not the secretary has designated said project as a major and complicated project. The secretary shall have the authority to determine in his sole discretion that a proposal to construct, maintain and operate a hazardous waste facility should be designated as a major and complicated project requiring the establishment of a specific procedure for evaluation and review of the environmental impact of said project pursuant to section sixty-two A of chapter thirty.

Upon the establishment of a siting agreement pursuant to sections twelve and thirteen, the developer shall prepare a final project impact report which shall be in accordance with the provisions of the siting agreement and which shall contain information, comments, and facility redesign data resulting from the negotiations preceding the establishment of said agreement. The council shall declare that an established siting agreement is operative and is to be given full force and effect only when a final project impact report has been found by the secretary and the council to be in compliance with all applicable provisions of law.

Section 11.   The local assessment committee of a host community and the chief executive officers of abutting communities may request technical assistance grants from the council. If a local assessment committee of a host community or the chief executive officer of an abutting community requests a technical assistance grant on or before the date that the secretary has defined the scope of the environmental impact report part of the preliminary project impact report, the council shall act on said request within thirty days after the secretary has so defined the scope and shall award, subject to funds appropriated therefor, such amounts as in its discretion shall be appropriate, upon consultation with the executive office of communities and development. All technical assistance grants awarded to the chief executive officers of abutting communities and to the local assessment committee of a host community which has requested such a grant after the secretary has defined the scope of the environmental impact report part of the preliminary project impact report shall be awarded in such amounts and form, subject to funds appropriated therefor, as the council in its discretion shall deem to be appropriate.

The local assessment committee of a host community and the chief executive officers of abutting communities may expend these funds, and such other funds as a city or town may appropriate therefor, to pay the costs incurred by said communities for participation in the hazardous waste facility site process established by this chapter.

Section 12. No facility shall be constructed, maintained or operated unless a siting agreement shall have been established by the developer and the local assessment committee of a host community pursuant to sections twelve and thirteen and said agreement has been declared to be operative and in full force and effect by the council. After said declaration by the council, a siting agreement shall be a nonassignable contract binding upon the developer and the host community, and enforceable against the parties in any court of competent jurisdiction.

The siting agreement shall specify the terms, conditions and provisions under which the facility shall be constructed, maintained and operated if the developer chooses to construct, maintain and operate a facility on said site, including, but not limited to the following terms, conditions and provisions:

(1) facility construction and maintenance procedures;

(2) operating procedures and practices, the design of the facility and its associated activities;

(3) monitoring procedures, practices and standards necessary to assure and continue to demonstrate that the facility will be operated safely;

(4) the services to be provided the developer by the host community;

(5) the compensation, services, and special benefits that will be provided to the host community by the developer, and the timing and conditions of their provision;

(6) the services and benefits to be provided to the host community by agencies of state government, and the timing and condition of their provision;

(7) any provisions for tax prepayments or accelerated payments, or for payments in lieu of taxes;

(8) provisions for renegotiation of any of the term, conditions of provisions of the siting agreement, or of the entire agreement;

(9) provisions for resolving any disagreements in the construction and interpretation of the siting agreement that may arise between the parties; and

(10) appendices of the compensation to be paid abutting communities established pursuant to the provisions of section fourteen.

The siting agreement may also include, but shall not be limited to, the following:

(1) provisions for direct monetary payments from the developer to the host community in addition to payments for taxes and special services and compensation for demonstrable adverse impacts;

(2) provisions to assure the health, safety, comfort, convenience, and social and economic security of the host community and its citizens;

(3) provisions to assure the continuing economic viability of the project; and

(4) provisions to assure the protection of the environment and natural resources.

Any financial benefits received by host communities or abutting communities, other than taxes on real or personal property, shall not be deducted from any amounts of state assistance, reimbursements or distributions provided by general and special laws or under the local aid fund established by section two D of chapter twenty-nine.

Section 13. A siting agreement may be established by the signature of the chief executive officer of a host community who has been directed by a majority vote of the local assessment committee of said host community to sign and the signature of any officer of the developer expressly authorized by the developer to sign said agreement, or by arbitration pursuant to section fifteen.

All state agencies shall endeavor to assist in facilitating negotiations between local assessment committees, the chief executive officer of abutting communities, and the developer. The council shall be available during such negotiations to assist in the exchange of information and to encourage and facilitate access to opinions, reports, documents and other materials relevant to the siting agreement including, but not limited to, all public records produced as part of the hazardous waste facility siting process established by this chapter.

Section 14. The chief executive officer of any abutting community may, within sixty days of the determination by the secretary and the council that a preliminary project impact report is in their judgment in compliance with applicable law, petition the council for the establishment of compensation to be paid by the developer to the abutting community for the demonstrably adverse impacts to be imposed upon said community by the construction, maintenance and operation of a hazardous waste facility in a host community. As a condition precedent to the filing of said petition, the chief executive officer shall agree in writing on a form prescribed by the council, and he is herewith given the authority to bind his city or town to such an agreement, that his city or town shall either accept the compensation to be determined by the council or the compensation established by arbitration pursuant to the procedures established in this section in full settlement of any claims for demonstrably adverse impacts imposed by the current proposed project. The chief executive officer shall also agree, as an essential part of said condition precedent, that he will sign an agreement with the developer accepting the amount established by the council or by arbitration pursuant to this section, which agreement shall be a nonassignable contract binding on the abutting community and the developer, and enforceable as such in any court of competent jurisdiction.

The council, after due notice to the developer, the local assessment committee, and the chief executive officer of the abutting community which has petitioned shall conduct a public hearing to determine and establish the compensation to be given to the abutting community by the developer. If the chief executive officer of the abutting community or the developer is aggrieved by the amount of compensation established by the council, either party may appeal to the council to establish an arbitration panel, which shall be comprised of three arbitrators, to resolve the dispute. The council, upon such appeal, shall establish said arbitration panel by appointing one arbitrator selected by the chief executive officer of the abutting community, one arbitrator selected by the developer, and the third an impartial arbitrator, who shall be selected by the chief executive officer of the abutting community and by the developer and who shall act as chairman of the panel or, if the chief executive officer of the abutting community and the developer agree, a single impartial arbitrator acceptable to the chief executive officer of the abutting community and the developer.

If an arbitration panel or single arbitrator has not been selected within thirty days after an appeal for arbitration has been filed, the council shall appoint the arbitrator or arbitrators necessary to complete the three person panel, which shall act with the same force and effect as if the panel had been selected without the intervention of the council.

The arbitration panel by a majority vote or single arbitrator shall within forty-five days after establishment determine the amount of compensation to be paid by the developer to the abutting community. The council, upon request of the arbitration panel or the single arbitrator, may extend the time for the conduct of arbitration.

The arbitrators or arbitrator, subject to appropriation, shall receive from the council such compensation for each day or part thereof for his services as a majority of the council shall establish. He shall also receive, subject to appropriation, all reasonable expenses actually and necessarily incurred in the performance of his official duties.

The developer shall agree in writing on a form prescribed by the council that, as a condition precedent to the establishment of a siting agreement, he shall accept the amount established by the council or by arbitration pursuant to this section as the amount of compensation he shall pay to the abutting community. The developer shall also agree, as an essential part of said condition precedent, that he will expressly authorize one of his officers to sign an agreement with the chief executive officer of the abutting community, which agreement shall be a nonassignable contract binding on the developer and the abutting community, and enforceable as such in any court of competent jurisdiction.

The provisions of chapter two hundred and fifty-one shall govern the conduct of arbitration proceedings pursuant to this section, including the provisions of said chapter for judicial review of an arbitration award.

Section 15. If sixty days after the secretary and the council determine that the preliminary project impact report is in compliance with applicable law, the department, the developer or the local assessment committee of the host community informs the council that an impasse in the negotiations of a siting agreement exists, the council, upon investigation, may determine that such an impasse exists and may proceed to frame the issues in dispute between the local assessment committee and the developer for submission to final and binding arbitration. Upon request of both the developer and the host community, the council may postpone the making of its determination that an impasse exists and that the issues in dispute should be resolved by final and binding arbitration for such a reasonable period of time as the council in its sole discretion shall determine to be appropriate. Upon the making of the determination that an impasse in the negotiation of a siting agreement exists, the council shall establish either an arbitration panel which shall be comprised of three arbitrators, one selected by the developer, one selected by the local assessment committee of the host community, and a third, an impartial arbitrator who shall act as chairman of the panel, who shall be selected by the developer and the local assessment committee of the host community, or, if the developer and the local assessment committee of the host community can agree, a single impartial arbitrator acceptable to the developer and local assessment committee of the host community.

If an arbitration panel or single impartial arbitrator has not been selected within thirty days after the council's determination that an impasse exists, the council shall appoint the arbitrator or arbitrators necessary to complete the three-person panel, which shall act with the same force and effect as if the panel had been selected without intervention of the council.

An arbitrator shall receive from the council such compensation for each day or part thereof for his services as a majority of the council shall establish. He shall also receive reimbursement for all reasonable expenses actually and necessarily incurred in the performance of his official duties.

The arbitration panel or the single arbitrator shall within forty-five days after establishment resolve the issues in dispute between the local assessment committee and the developer. The council, upon request of the arbitration panel or single arbitrator, may extend the time permitted for the conduct of arbitration.

In the event that the parties mutually resolve each of the issues in dispute and agree to be bound, they may at any time prior to the final decisions of the panel or single arbitrator request that the arbitration proceedings be terminated, the panel acting through its chairman, or the single arbitrator, shall terminate the proceedings.

The provisions of chapter two hundred and fifty-one shall govern the conduct of arbitration proceedings pursuant to this section, including the provisions of said chapter for judicial review of an arbitration decision.

Section 16.   No license or permit granted by a city or town shall be required for a hazardous waste facility which was not required on or before the effective date of this chapter by said city or town. All permits and licenses required for a hazardous waste facility in a city or town shall be granted or denied within sixty days after application for said permits and licenses by the developer, or twenty-one days after the establishment of a siting agreement pursuant to sections twelve and thirteen, whichever is the later.

Section 17.   If all permits and licenses required by law have been issued to the developer and a siting agreement has been established pursuant to sections twelve and thirteen, the developer may petition the department to exercise its eminent domain authority pursuant to the provisions of chapter seventy-nine as authorized by section nineteen of chapter sixteen. Upon a showing by the developer, after due notice and a hearing thereon, that he has been unsuccessful in a good faith attempt to acquire all or a portion of the site by purchase or lease, the department shall exercise its eminent domain authority to make said acquisition, subject to approval by a majority vote of the city council, board of aldermen, or board of selectmen pursuant to the provisions of section nineteen of chapter sixteen. The department shall lease any land acquired under this section for a hazardous waste facility for the treatment, processing or disposal of hazardous waste to the developer for the purpose of construction, maintaining, and operating a privately owned hazardous waste facility. Any land acquired under this section may be disposed of by the department upon termination of a hazardous waste facility or completion of use of a site, with the concurrence of the department of environmental quality engineering, in the best interest of the commonwealth and for a use compatible with local zoning by-laws or ordinances; provided, however, that in no event shall such land be so disposed of unless said department, with the concurrence of the department of environmental quality engineering, first offers, in writing, to convey it to the city or town wherein such land lies for an amount of money not less than the fair market value of the land as determined by an independent appraisal which the department has caused to be made, and such offer is not accepted within two months after being made or is refused by the chief executive officer of the city or town wherein such land lies.

Section 18.   This chapter shall not apply to any hazardous waste facility exempt from the licensing requirements of chapter twenty-one C which was lawfully organized and in existence on May first, nineteen hundred and eighty, or to any hazardous waste facility which was licensed as such by any division of the department of environmental quality engineering as of May first, nineteen hundred and eighty. If any facility has its license revoked and reapplies for a license after May first, nineteen hundred and eighty, the provisions of this chapter shall apply to said reapplication; provided, however, that the provisions of this chapter shall not apply to any facility, or the operation of any facility under receivership by a federal or state agency or by a judicially appointed and supervised receiver of any court of competent jurisdiction where the license of the facility has been suspended or revoked and said receivership has been imposed.

Chapter twenty-one D shall not apply to any generator who stores, treats, processes or disposes of hazardous waste produced exclusively on-site; provided, however, that chapter twenty-one D shall apply to any such generator who disposes of hazardous waste into or on the land. For purposes of this section, "on-site" shall be defined to mean the same or geographically contiguous property which may be divided by public or private right-of-way, provided that the entrance and exit between the properties is at a crossroads intersection, and access is by crossing as opposed to going along the right-of-way; as well as non-contiguous properties owned by the same person but connected by a right-of-way which he controls and to which the public does not have access.

Section 19.   Notwithstanding the first paragraph of section eighteen, chapter twenty-one D shall apply to the increase of capacity to store, treat, or dispose of any particular type of hazardous waste, unless an existing siting agreement established pursuant to the requirements of chapter twenty-one D provides for the conditions under which such increase of capacity shall be permitted.

[Sections 9–11, omitted here, are not relevant to facility siting]

SECTION 12.   It is hereby declared that the provisions of this act are severable, and if any provision of this act shall be declared unconstitutional by the valid judgment or decree of any court of competent jurisdiction, such unconstitutionality shall not affect any of the remaining provisions of this act.

FOOTNOTES

1. See ch. 40A, sec. 9. All references unless otherwise noted are to Mass. Gen. Laws Ann. with citations to the appropriate chapter. The relevant sections of the Siting Act are reproduced in their entirety at the end of this appendix.
2. ch. 111, sec. 150B.
3. ch. 21D, sec. 11.
4. *Id.* sec. 12, 15.
5. *Id.* sec. 14.
6. *Id.* sec. 3.
7. ch. 21C.
8. ch. 21D, sec. 4.
9. Id., sec. 7.
10. Regulations of the Hazardous Waste Facility Site Safety Council, 990 CMR (4.02)
11. ch. 21D, sec. 9.
12. Id., sec. 7.
13. Id., sec. 11.
14. Regulations of the Hazardous Waste Facility Site Safety Council, 990 CMR (5.00)
15. ch. 21D, sec. 5.
16. *Id.*
17. ch. 21D, sec. 10.
18. Massachusetts Special Commission on Hazardous Waste, Report (Aug. 8, 1980), p. 4.
19. ch. 21D, sec. 12.
20. *Id.*
21. Id., sec. 15.
22. *Id.*
23. *Id.*
24. *Id.*
25. ch. 21C, sec. 7.

26. ch. 21D, sec. 16
27. ch. 111, sec. 150B.
28. ch. 40A, sec. 9.
29. ch. 16, sec. 17.
30. Regulations of the Hazardous Waste Facility Site Safety Council, 990 CMR (14.03).
31. ch. 21D, sec. 12.
32. Id., sec. 8, 11, 14.
33. *Id.*, sec. 8.
34. Id., sec. 14.
35. *Id.*
36. Readers interested in a more complete legal analysis of the Massachusetts Hazardous Waste Facility Siting Act are referred to L. Bacow and J. Milkey, "Overcoming Local Opposition to Hazardous Waste Facilities: The Massachusetts Approach," *Harvard Environmental Law Review* (Spring 1982).
37. See *Town of Warren* v. *Hazardous Waste Facility Site Safety Council,* Mass. Sup. Court No. 82–21740 (divided Jan. 5, 1983.).
38. ch. 251, sec. 12(a).
39. *Trustees of the Boston and Maine Corp.* v. *Massachusetts Bay Transportation Authority,* 363 Mass. 386, 390, 294 N.E.2d 340, 343 (1973).
40. *Id.* The court stated that the rationale for the limited scope of review in commercial arbitration is that the parties "received what they agreed to take, the honest judgment of the arbitrator as to a matter referred to him." 363 Mass. at 390–391, 294 N.E.2d at 344 (citation omitted).
41. See *Division 540, Amalgamated Transit Union* v. *Mercer County Improvement Auth.,* 76 N.J. 245, 386 A.2d 1290 (1978); *Mount St. Mary's Hosp.* v. *Catherwood,* 26 N.Y.2d 493, 260 N.E.2d 508, 311 N.Y.S. 2d 863 (1970).
42. *Town of Arlington* v. *Board of Conciliation & Arbitration,* 370 Mass. 769, 352 N.E.2d 914 (1976).
43. *Id.*
44. Similarly, a New Jersey court found that, because a compulsory arbitration statute required the municipality to fund the award, the constitution required judicial review to assure that the statutory scheme did not deprive the municipality of property without due process of law. *Division 540, Amalgamated Transit Union* v. *Mercer County Improvement Auth.,* 76 N.J. 245, 386 A.2d 1290 (1978).
45. The affirmative obligations of mandated services to the developer are not relevant to this discussion because: (1) they are subject to broad judicial review in a contractual action brought by the developer to enforce the arbitrator's award, and (2) Massachusetts law requires that any services mandated by the state also be funded by the state.
46. *City of Haverhill* v. *Hazardous Waste Facility Site Safety Council,* Civ. Action No. 82–683 (Mass. Dist. Ct. filed Feb. 9, 1982).
47. *Town of Warren* v. *Hazardous Waste Facility Site Safety Council,* Civ. Action No. 82–21740 (Mass. Dist. Ct. filed Jan. 17, 1982).
48. *Boston Globe,* August 2, 1982.

Index

INDEX